RESTORING
SPRITES & MIDGETS
an enthusiast's guide

by

GRAHAME BRISTOW

Restoring Sprites & Midgets: An Enthusiasts Guide

Published by Brooklands Books Limited

Brooklands Books Ltd.
P.O. Box 146, Cobham,
Surrey, KT11 1LG. UK
sales@brooklands-books.com

ISBN 1 85520 598X

A-MGSMR

© 2002 Grahame Bristow and Brooklands Books Limited

Printed and bound in China

CONTENTS

Foreword

Whenever I see a rebuild guide I am impressed by how easy everything looks - every job seems to be so straightforward. Not surprisingly, since they have been written by seasoned professionals who have all the tools, own large workshops and have worked on the same cars for years.

What they all have in common is that seasoned professionals are not the same as many of us. It's time that these guys started to think about real people. No, we don't own workshops, probably not even a double door garage - rarely even a single door garage. Many of us work on our cars outside on the road or a driveway, where a level surface is a dream. We are often tackling restoration problems for the first time.

For example, a few years back, over the course of seven or eight months, I watched the slow building of a Peugeot 205 rally car. It was certainly an interesting and time consuming project; which included painting the bare shell inside and out. In fact I noticed that almost every day a bit more work had been done - as did many others amongst thousands of motorists who use the A316 Chertsey Road (one of the great London arteries) every single working day. The owner stripped and built the car on the rough grass verge outside his flat much to the admiration and enlightenment of many a humble commuter.

Just like the rest of us, here was an enthusiast getting on with the job, without a workshop or garage, he just worked on the roadside. No power tools, no Blackhawk jig, nothing more than simple tools, four axle stands and his wits.

Not only is working space at a premium, but so are specialist tools - even a trolley jack is a luxury for many. Also, surprisingly, many of us cannot weld or wish to learn that black art. Even if we could, where would we do it - on the grass verge outside our house, in a cramped garage, or in the yard? I didn't buy my MG with the intention of rebuilding it, I just wanted to drive it. The painful truth dawned later, and boy did I learn the hard way.

I couldn't lay claim to being a great mechanic or being very knowledgeable about Midgets or Sprites. As you'll see, I made some fundamental errors building my own Midget, but I got there in the end, without much help and without being too adept in the spanner department. I simply intended to get it right, and if I got things wrong, well I just started again.

Hopefully this guide, in conjunction with a little of your own research, will lead to a successful rebuild of your own. I've tried to cover as much as I can within these pages, but my knowledge is pretty shaky in some areas, especially with regard to the 1500 engine. If your car proves to be at variance with what has been written here, its not necessarily wrong, just that you will need to do some detective work of your own.

Have fun. And when you've finished building the car, drive it - that's what they made it for...

Thucydides boat

There is a question that has been asked countless times. One could ask the same question again and again, using the same arguments, yet always come up with a different answer. It is the eternal question, the question of originality. One might imagine the very question being at least as old as the first ever concours d'elegance. The question, and the philosophy (oh yes, there is a philosophy), is at least as old as the Greek empire - perhaps as far back as the time of Thucydides.

HISTORY AND GENERAL DATA

Of course, the Greeks weren't too interested in cars, but they were a great maritime nation, and as such pub talk consisted largely of girls, boys and boats; what could be finer than a good day's cruising and boat polishing followed by the bar.

Even in those days the question of originality was not ignored. Rumour has it that Thucydides' boat was in for repair. Some timbers required replacement and it was an old boat, a classic. Thucydides wanted the boat restored to "original" condition.

When the boat was completed Thucydides went to view the work, but was faced by a dilemma. Was it, technically speaking, the same boat. It looked the same. It felt the same, but it wasn't really the boat that it once was. It wasn't the boat that had been built by his father. It had many new timbers and a new sail. So in essence, though it looked like the old boat, it wasn't quite the old boat. In fact so many timbers had been replaced it might almost be called a new boat but using some old scrap timbers from a wrecker.

The boat builder listened to Thucydides conundrum with great interest and, being a keen philosopher himself, helped Thucydides extricate himself from the dilemma by convincing him that it was indeed the same boat in essence. It looked the same, it felt the same, it sailed as well as ever and therefore it was the same boat.

Greatly relieved, Thucydides thanked the boat builder profusely and declared his undying gratitude for the man's good sense. There was however one final sticking point. Technically speaking, old boat or new, it wasn't Thucydides boat until he paid the bill...

Sometimes, philosophy is no help at all...

Notes on the MG Car Company, Important Characters and Great Cars

1910   William R Morris opened the Morris Garage (vehicle sales).

1913   Morris Garage became Morris Garages.

Morris Garages developed into half dozen showrooms selling both cars and motorcycles. New cars included a wide range of Ford, Morris, Humber, Singer and Wolseley cars among others.

In the same year Morris set up WRM Motors Ltd. (vehicle manufacture).

1919   WRM Motors Ltd. became Morris Motors Ltd.

1921   Cecil Kimber was appointed Sales Manager of Morris Garages.

1922   Aged only 34, Kimber was appointed General Manager.

Kimber began to design special bodies for Morris Cars, which were then fitted to existing Morris chassis at the Morris Garages workshops. One particular design, with an all-over Chummy hood and revised rear springs, became known as the "Morris Garages Chummy". Displaying its own Morris Garages badge, it sold well.

1923   Production moved to Alfred Lane

A full time production team of two were employed. Bodies for the cars were supplied by Carbodies of Coventry. Chassis arrived from Morris Motors.

The introduction of bodies from Charles Raworth of Oxford allowed the "Raworth Two-Seater" to be developed, also with a Morris Garages badge.

1923   Morris purchased the Hotchkiss factory.

Hotchkiss moved to Britain during the first world war. Following the purchase, the factory became Morris' Engine Branch. Here's the interesting bit. The MG T Series engines used metric and imperial threads because the tooling dated back to when Hotchkiss imported metric machinery into the UK. Morris never converted tooling for imperial applications but carried on using metric threads.

1924   The famous MG badge appeared for the first time in an advertisement.

Old Number One
Old number One wasn't (despite popular belief), the first MG. It began production as late as 1924 with Longwall staff modifying an existing Morris Cowley chassis. Fitted with a Hotchkiss engine, it was dumped at the back of the workshop for months before completion.

The body was actually the 48th supplied to Morris Garages for conversion, registered on 27th March 1925 - just in time for Cecil Kimber and Wilfred Mathews to compete in the Lands End Trial - qualifying for a gold.

1925   Morris Garages outgrew the Alfred Lane site so Morris allowed Kimber's crew to move into the old radiator plant at Bainton Road. Morris Garages now had 50 staff producing cars.

1927   Funded by Morris Motors, Kimber built a £10,000 factory at Edmund Road, Cowley in Oxford.

Wolseley Motors and SU Carburetter Company were purchased by Morris.

The MG Badge
It seems likely that no MGs produced before late 1927 had an MG badge. It was at that time that a Morris Garages 14/40 incorporated a German Silver MG logo on its honeycomb grill. At the same time a few cars had a small MG octagon badge placed over the centre of the Morris Garages badge.

1927   July: Morris Garages was registered as a limited company.

November: Morris Garages legally accepted responsibility for all MG guarantees - formally with Morris Motors.

From that date each new car carried a brass plate with an MG car number instead of a Morris chassis number.

The first car was a 14/40 - number 2251
The first 18/80 Six was number 6251
The first Midget - M0251
The first 18/80 Mk II - A0251.

The new 18/80 MG Six was the first to be fully designed by MG. It incorporated a Morris (not Wolseley) 6 cylinder ohc engine. Known as the "Quick Six", many part numbers specific to the car were prefixed QS.

The 251 number became quite a feature of MG sportscars - as mentioned later.

1928   MG Car Company was registered as a subsidiary of Morris Garages

Two famous motoring names first appeared. The Morris Minor and the MG Midget. The Minor incorporated the Wolseley 8hp 4-cylinder ohc engine, which in March the following year, was used to power Kimber's new Midget.

MG Assembly
The MG Car Company didn't really manufacture cars. Components may have been modified on site but generally they arrived as parts and assemblies, to be put together on site. Even the chassis and bodies were produced elsewhere and supplied to the factory complete.

1929   Cecil Kimber resigned from Morris Garages to work at the MG Car Company full time.

MG had outgrown Edmund Road in Cowley. The company moved again to Abingdon where by accident or design (nobody knows for sure) the telephone number was Abingdon 251.

The MG Car Company moved into what had been an extension of the Pavlova Leather Company premises.

Syd Enever joined MG at Abingdon, moving across from Morris Garages.

1930   "Safety Fast" adopted as the company slogan

The MG Car Club was formed and allocated office space in the Abingdon factory.

1931   John Thornley joins MG becoming honourary secretary of the MG Car Club.

1933   Rationalisation begins in earnest within the Morris organisation.

The MG Car Company was increasingly being pressured to buy stock from Morris Motors and help reduce Morris overheads by consolidating the business empire that was growing. Towards the end of the year body orders switched from Carbodies to Morris Bodies branch

1935   Rationalisation gets worse.

MG's terrific success in sporting events didn't stop its forced withdrawal from racing. At the same time, the design office, experimental office and racing departments were all closed by the newly appointed Leonard Lord.

Morris was intent on limiting the specialisation of MG and increasing its compatibility with stock components to reduce overheads. A feud with Kimber over racing also boiled over following accidents at recent race meetings and events.

The design office moved to Cowley, but even there Kimber worked hard to influence design so that the characteristics of MG still showed. Syd Enever remained at Abingdon.

1936   TA Midget appeared.

1939   WW II began.

Kimber put the factory on a war footing. He gained contracts to produce light pressings, tank parts and assembling army trucks - even winning a contract to repair armoured cars.

Repaired vehicles were 'road tested' on the nearby Berkshire Downs. The local RAF squadron based at Abingdon Aerodrome, always on the lookout for some light relief, took to the skies and bombed the vehicles with bags of flour whenever the hapless test drivers were spotted.

1941   Kimber resigned from the MG Car Company following a dispute over gaining the contract to build Albermarle aircraft parts.

Many companies had applied for the contract but could not deal with the complexity involved. MG engineers designed new tools and test rigs specifically for the job. The company built 600 units and completed another 300.

H.A Ryder and S.V. Smith followed as General Managers.

1945   4th February: Cecil Kimber died in a railway accident at Kings Cross.

Following the War the MG Car Company became a forgotten part of the Nuffield group, left without a vision for the future and lacking any investment capital.

With no budget money available, the old TB Midget was revamped hastily to produce the TC. It was this car that made the MG name popular in the US.

Over 2000 were exported to North America and also great numbers were purchased by US Air Force crews who, at their government's expense, took the cars home.

1947   The Y Type saloon was introduced.

The Y Type was an important step forward for MG, utilising rack and pinion steering and independent front suspension with coil springs. The design found its way onto later MGs including the MGA, MGB and Midget.

1949   May: Nuffield transferred production of Riley models into Abingdon.

Jack Tatlow of Riley took over as General Manager at Abingdon - moving in when Riley production began at the site.

Once again, MG was given no money to develop a replacement for the ageing TC. So, in the space of two weeks and with the use of a number of hammers, the workshop produced the prototype MG TD model.

1952   John Thornley become General Manager

The British Motor Corporation (1952)
Nuffield Group amalgamated with the Austin Motor Company, becoming the third largest motor manufacturer in the world. Lord Nuffield relinquished all control, leaving Sir Leonard Lord in sole charge.

A few things worth remembering at this point are:- Herbert Austin and William Morris had openly entered into a legal mud slinging match over the purchase of Wolseley - a battle won by Morris. Leonard Lord, who had acted as Morris's aide, had resigned after a furious row over profit sharing and bonuses, and had gone to work for Austin, Morris's major competitor in the U.K.

1952   MG wanted to develop its TD engined EX175 into a replacement for the existing TD, but BMC management refused to allow any investment, turning their attention instead to the new Healey 100 which was being shown at the Earls Court Motor Show.

Lord saw the car at the show, striking a deal with Healey there and then to produce the car at Longbridge. Overnight the car became known as the Austin Healey 100.

Lord, pleased with his decision, saw no reason for a second sportscar, and this was why BMC refused to allocate MG any funds to move forward with a replacement for the TD.

BMC's decision proved calamitous, TD export sales plunged against more modern opposition. In an effort to halt the decline BMC management offered sufficient funding for a face lift - leading to the rapid development of the TF, the latest in a line of cars stretching back to before the war.

The face lift took all of two months to develop, since BMC's funding was strictly limited, but MG designers and engineers did the best they could under such obviously hostile circumstances.

1953   The TF appeared at the 1953 Motor Show to the derision of the press.

Also at the show was the new TRX sportscar of Standard Triumph, soon to become the TR2. The Wolseley 4/44 designed by Gerald Palmer also appeared. This car had originally been intended as a new MG sports saloon. Shortly after the show the car was badge engineered, given an MG grille to become the ZA Magnette.

Attitudes towards MG worsened, being reduced now to petty nit-picking. The traditional 251 chassis number given to every new model of the production line was replaced by 501- a needless action thought out by an apparently anti-MG management, clearly determined to stamp out any individuality and self-determination MG may formerly have enjoyed.

1955   BMC established a competitions department at Abingdon under Marcus Chambers.

Throughout the late fifties and sixties the Competitions Department proved enormously successful, especially with the Big Healeys.

August: Production began on the MGA.

1957   The new Austin Healey 100/6 was produced at Abingdon

BMC transferred production of the Austin Healey 100-6 to the MG factory, replacing the Riley which had just ceased production. When the Sprite was being developed the phrase "The Big Healey" came into being, used purely as a workshop reference at Abingdon.

1958   May: Austin Healey Sprite went into production.

In the same year BMC discontinued the popular ZB Magnette and badge engineered the 1½ litre saloon as the Magnette Mk III. In fact it was not built at Abingdon, and was the first MG not to be built on-site for 30 years.

1960   The factory began building Morris Minor vans and estate cars.

1961 May: Sprite Mk II announced
June: Midget announced

The Sprite front end had been redesigned by Healey, the rear was designed by Syd Enever.

1962 100,000 MGAs had been produced.

July: MGB production began at Abingdon.
October: Sprite II / Midget received 1098cc engine.

1964 March: Sprite III / Midget II announced

1965 October: MGB GT production began.

1966 October: Sprite IV / Midget III announced

1967 BMC merged with Jaguar to form British Motor Holdings.

The MG Car Company was renamed MG Division.

1968 May: British Motor Holdings merged with Leyland, who owned Triumph, to form British Leyland Motor Corporation.

Under Donald Stokes all BMC magazines, including Safety Fast, *were stopped. Support was withdrawn from all clubs, again including the MG Car Club. Soon after support was withdrawn from the MGCC.*

The BLMC empire was divided into three and, instead of being grouped with the Specialist Car Division, MG was lumped in with the Austin Morris Division.

1969 July: John Thornley retired as GM. Following in his footsteps many older staff also took early retirement

October: the "Leylandised" Sprite and Midget were introduced.

1970 August: the Competitions Department closed

1971 January: The rights to the Healey name were lost and the last Austin Healey Sprite was produced.

From now on the car became simply the Austin Sprite and, indeed, even that variant died out in June of that year.

1974 October: Midget 1500 introduced

1977 Michael Edwards took control of British Leyland at the request of the Government.

Edwards took control of a terrible mess. His first job was to pay the staff some wages, but the company had no funds to pay them - so he had to borrow more money from an incredulous Labour government. Jim Callaghan loaned the money but not without taking a snipe at the Triumph TR7, its awful reputation and its production difficulties. Since its inception, the cars built at Speke had proved themselves to be of very poor quality, while the site itself was riddled with industrial unrest. The Speke strike, in progress at the time of Callaghan's comments, led to its ultimate closure.

While the rest of BL was pulling itself to pieces and stamping on anything related to Lord Nuffield's side of the business, MG staff quietly developed the 'O' Series engine for the ageing MGB. The engine never made it into the MGB but got dropped into the Princess II and other cars, such as the early Rover 216.

1979 9th September: Abingdon staff celebrated 50 years of MG with a festival.

10th September: An impeccably timed press announcement by thoughtless BL press office staff broadcast to the world that the MG factory would be closed in July 1980.

October: A consortium led by Aston Martin tried to purchase MG. Eventually the attempt failed, but not without considerable press coverage.

November: the last MG Midget was produced.

1980 August: It was formally announced that the MG factory was to be shut down.

Statistical fact: In 1980 Longbridge staff built seven cars per man. At Abingdon, 50 cars were built per man employed!

23rd October: the last MGB rolled off the production line.

Production of "real" MG cars ended.

RV8 The MGRV8, a model based on the MGB, was built using Heritage built bodyshells, themselves manufactured using original MGB jigs.

MGF Built at Longbridge (there's one in the eye for Herbert). The MG name, so persistently trod into the dirt by the anti-Morris faction, is virtually all that is left of BMC and BL.

Interestingly enough, the first MGF off the production line bore the numbers 251 as part of its VIN number!

Some Record Breaking MGs

If you don't know much about MG or Austin Healey, beyond the fact that you have enjoyed the fun of owning your own MG Midget or Austin Healey Sprite, you may not realise how impressive a history MG has on the track. Donald Healey, himself a great enthusiast for sporting events, regularly took part in trials such as the Lands End Trial and other rallies. Healey worked for Triumph before building his own business and worked with Nash in the US before designing the Healey 100.

Cecil Kimber was equally experienced behind the wheel, more than likely competing against Healey in the trials. MG however, unlike Healey, had a long time in which to build up an impressive array of "firsts" - in fact, they broke so many records, so consistently, and won so many events, that its difficult to see why people do not consider MGs to be thoroughbreds.

The record breaking history of MG is seriously impressive - the first 750cc car to reach 100mph, the first 750cc car to reach 140 miles per hour - how about the first 1250cc car to cover ten miles at 170mph and then cover 140 miles every hour for twelve hours. MG did all these things and more - in cars designed by MG staff and built in the workshops at Abingdon. These cars were the experimental cars and all of them shared one thing in common - the EX mark!

EX120

Designed along the lines of a French sports car called the Rally, EX120 incorporated the Rally's unusual chassis and axle arrangement. Fitted with a heavily modified M type engine it was famous as the first 750cc car to reach 100mph.

At Montlhery on 30th December 1930, the car, driven by George Eyston, covered 100km at 87.3mph before the engine failed. Several Austin records were broken during that run.

On the 16th February 1931, Eyston and EX120 again went to Montlhery. Determined to get ahead of Austin and Malcolm Campbell, Eyston made an attempt to take the 100mph record. At first the attempt it fell short, but by hammering out an old oil drum, the front of the car was streamlined and the record was broken. Speeds up to 103.13mph were achieved and the record was taken.

Later that same year Eyston returned to Montlhery where the car covered 101.1 miles in the hour before being engulfed by flames. Eyston, injured during the incident, was hospitalised.

EX127 "The Magic Midget"

Even as EX120 lay burning in a foreign field, EX127 was being developed. Again a 750cc engine was used to power what became known as the Magic Midget. Eyston was still in hospital when Ernest Eldridge drove the car at 110.28mph over a 5km stretch.

You would have thought that a spell in hospital would have put him off but, on the 22nd December 1931, Eyston reached 114.77mph in the Magic Midget.

In 1933 The Magic Midget went to Montlhery; achieving 110.87 miles in the hour and 128.63 mph over the flying mile.

In May 1935 Bobbie Kohlrausch, having acquired the Magic Midget, reached 130.41mph over the flying mile.

In 1936 he got the Magic Midget to reach 140.6mph - still using the 750cc engine.

EX135

EX135 was a converted K3.

1934: George Eyston's new EX135 managed 128.69mph in the flying mile and 120.88 miles in the hour.

In 1938 EX135 was fitted with a new Reid Railton designed body. Goldie Gardner (another keen speed freak working closely with MG), developed an 1100cc engine and fitted it into EX135 with a supercharger.

November 1938: EX135 covered the flying mile at 187.62mph.

In 1939 the car returned to Germany covering the flying mile at 203.5mph.

WWII then stopped play

After the war, Gardner once again turned his attention to record breaking - despite disappointing support from MG's new boss H.A. Ryder, later replaced by S.V. Smith. A string of record breaking assaults followed with EX135 taking records in five out of ten classes.

In 1949 EX135 was fitted with a supercharged 1250cc TD engine built by Syd Enever and his team. The engine gave 213bhp at 7000rpm.

In 1951, at the Bonneville Salt Flats, Utah, the car achieved a speed of 202.14mph. During the second attempt the car spun out of control injuring Gardner. The injury proved worse than expected and he never made another record attempt again.

EX175

In 1950 Syd Enever began working on a replacement for EX135. EX175 appeared in 1952 with a body of similar shape to the George Phillips Le Mans TD. A design bearing a striking resemblance to the later MGA. This was the design MG hoped to use as a replacement for the TD.

EX179

George Eyston persuaded Leonard Lord to back another record attempt at the Bonneville Salt Flats in Utah. EX175 proved unsuitable for the assault and so a new body was produced for the spare chassis and this car became EX179.

EX179 incorporated the new XPEG engine of 1416cc, unsupercharged. The XPEG engine was a development of the older 1250cc XPAG unit fitted to the TD and early TF. This was the the unit later used in the TF 1500 model.

Eyston and Miles achieved 153.69mph and also ran the car at over 120mph for a 12 hour period.

In 1956 EX179 broke 16 international 1500cc records including 10 miles at 170.15mph and 141mph for 12 hours.

In 1957 EX179, now fitted with a 948cc engine, went back to Utah to cover 118.13mph for 12 hours (at over 49mpg).

In supercharged form (that same year) EX179 reached 143.47mph over the flying mile.

EX181

Syd Enever went on to design EX181. In 1957, the car, fitted with a 290bhp 1500cc engine and driven by Stirling Moss took five international records. The average top speed was 245.64mph.

In 1959 EX181 returned to Utah. Driven by Phil Hill it reached 254.91mph.

EX182

EX182 was based on the chassis of EX179 with a body seen as early as 1951 in the Le Mans car.

EX182 was the experimental number given to the special parts produced for the prototype MGAs that ran at Le Mans. Three cars were entered and two finished. Following the launch of the MGA one car went to Montlhery as part of a five-car BMC team and covered 102.54mph in an hour. A race-prepared MGA, driven by John Gott, recorded 112.36mph.

Just A Few More Things

Racing Colours

Until the 1950s countries raced in particular colours. Germany used silver (in fact early BMW motorbikes were not even painted, just polished to save weight). Italy raced in red and Britain, of course, used green - which is why Racing Green was such a popular colour for British sportscars. So why did the Competitions Department break with tradition and paint cars red and white during the late 1950s and 1960s?

During one of the famous Italian Mille Miglia races one of the MGA drivers, Peter Scott Russell, noticed that railway crossings stayed open long enough to let red cars through. He reported back to the Competitions Department at Abingdon.

The following year, all the team cars sent out to Italy were painted red (with white hardtops to reflect the heat and keep the interiors cool). The subterfuge caught the crossing patrols off guard resulting in great success during the rally.

Water Proofed

At Sebring in 1965 Timo Makinen was driving one of two open topped Midgets when a tropical storm struck. The track was awash and Timo's car quickly filled with water, to the extent that when he accelerated, the water covered his shoulders. He cured the problem by opening the driver's door during rapid cornering to let the water out!

A Quick Guide To Recognising Model Type

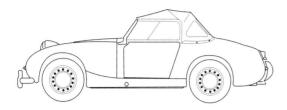

Austin-Healey Sprite Mark I (HAN 5)
Announced May 20, 1958.

948-cc, 1/4-elliptic rear springs, all-in-one bonnet and wings. Known as the "frog-eye" Sprite. Price included hood, sidescreens, rear overriders and spare wheel.

Dimensions: Height (hood up)   4' 1 3/4" (1.25m)
            Length   11' 5 1/4" (3.49m)
            Wheelbase   6' 8" (2.03m)
            Ground clearance   5" (12.7cm)
            Width   4' 5" (1.35m)

Options: Front bumper & overriders
          Heater   Radio
          Tachometer   Screenwash
          6-ply tyres   Laminated windscreen
          Fresh-air unit   Tonneau cover
          Hardtop**   Locking petrol cap**

          ** available 1959-60

UK Prices: 1958:   £678.17.0
             1959-60:   £631.10.10

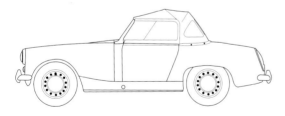

Austin-Healey Sprite Mark II (HAN 6)
MG Midget (GAN 1)
Announced May 1961 (Sprite Mark II)
Announced June 1961 (MG Midget)

Restyled front with fixed wings and separate bonnet. Rear end now followed MGB styling with boot lid. Engine power was increased, while the close-ratio gearbox became standard fitment.
    The MG version had a vertically slatted grille with centre plinth, chrome side and bonnet strips, superior seats and flecked rubber floor trim. The Austin Healey was given an Austin house-style crinkly chrome grille and retained a more spartan interior.
Price included windscreen washer, front & rear bumpers, overriders, tachometer, and adjustable passenger seat.

Dimensions: Height (hood up)   4' 1 3/4" (1.25m)
            Length   11' 5 7/8" (3.5m)
            Wheelbase   6' 8" (2.03m)
            Ground clearance   5" (12.7cm)
            Width   4' 5" (1.35m)

Options: Hardtop
          Hardtop with sliding sidescreens
          Heater   Radio
          Heavy-duty tyres   Whitewall tyres
          Fresh-air unit   Laminated windscreen
          Cigar lighter   Tonneau cover and rail
          Twin horns   Locking petrol cap
          Rear seat cushion   Ace wheel discs
          Luggage carrier and wing mirror
          Wing mirror only

UK Prices: AH Sprite: June 1961: £641.9.2
                               July 1961: £660.9.6

             MG Midget: June 1961: £669.15.10
                               July 1961: £689.11.5

AH Sprite Mark II 1100 (HAN 7)

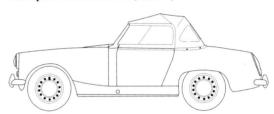

MG Midget 1100 (GAN 2)
Announced October 1962

Larger 1,098-cc engine fitted to make the car go faster and disc brakes were added to help it stop. The synchro-mesh gearbox was revised and carpets replaced the cheaper rubber mats. Generally, the trim was improved and a padded roll was added to the facia. The drilled wheels were replaced with plain ones part way through production.

Dimensions: Height (hood up)   4' 1 3/4" (1.25m)
            Length   11' 5 5/8" (3.5m)
            Wheelbase   6' 8" (2.03m)
            Ground clearance   5" (12.7cm)
            Width   4' 5" (1.35m)

Options: Radio   Heater
          Tonneau cover   Laminated windscreen
          Hardtop   Cigar lighter
          Heavy-duty tyres   Twin horns
          Luggage carrier   Rear seat cushion

UK Prices   1962-63:   Sprite: £586.12.0
                               Midget: £598.13.9

Austin-Healey Sprite Mark III (HAN 8)
MG Midget Mark II (GAN 3)
Announced March 1964.

A new windscreen and winding windows were fitted, necessitating the loss of the door pockets. Interior door locks were moved to an impossible location toward the rear of the now lockable doors. A wrinkle finished fascia was added to improved trim. An MG designed cylinder head was fitted, giving more power and semi-elliptic rear springs made the car a little less twitchy.

Dimensions: Height (hood up) 4' 1 3/4" (1.25m)
            Length   11' 5 5/8" (3.5m)
            Wheelbase   6' 8" (2.03m)
            Ground clearance 5" (12.7cm)
            Width   4' 5" (1.35m)

Options: Radio   Heater
            Hardtop   Luggage carrier
            Twin horns   Heavy-duty tyres
            Wheel discs   Tonneau cover
            Wire wheels

Prices: U K 1964-66:   Sprite: £610.15.5
                              Midget: £622.17.1

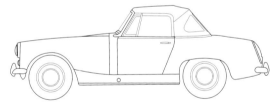

Austin-Healey Sprite Mark IV (HAN 9)
MG Midget Mark III (GAN 4)
Announced October 1966

1275 engine. A longer cockpit gave room to stow a new folding hood. A half tonneau was supplied to cover the hood. The cars otherwise looked the same as before.

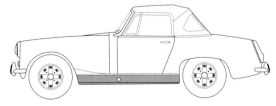

Revised October 1969
Sprite HAN 10 and Midget GAN5
Austin Sprite AAN 10 (announced January 1971)

Black grille and sills marked the most obvious changes, fitting in with the new British Leyland house style. Quarter bumpers fitted to rear. Overriders finished with black rubber facings. Rostyle wheels were supplied.

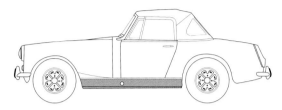

Revised October 1971
Round rear wheel arches were introduced. Rostyle wheels revised. Rocker switches fitted.

Dimensions: Height (hood up) 4' 1 3/4" (1.25m)
            Length   11' 5 1/2" (3.5m)
            Wheelbase   6' 8" (2.03m)
            Ground clearance 5" (12.7cm)
            Width   4' 5" (1.35m)

Options: Heater   Radio
            Seat belts   Tonneau cover
            Hardtop   Wire wheels

Prices: UK 1966-67:   Sprite: £672.00.00
                              Midget: £684.00.00

MG Midget 1500
Announced October 1974.

Triumph Spitfire engine and gearbox fitted, along with all Spitfire engine ancillaries; black rubber bumpers fitted and ride height raised due to stringent US legislation. Safety crash testing led to the re-introduction of squared-off rear wheel arches.

Dimensions: Height (hood up) 4' 1 1/4" (1.25m);
            Length   11' 9" (3.58m)
            Wheelbase   6' 8" (2.03m)
            Ground clearance 6" (12.7cm)
            Width   4' 5 5/8" (1.36m)

Options: Wire wheels   Hardtop

Prices: UK 1975: £1,559.61

Engine Numbers

Model	Engine No. Commences	Engine No. Finishes
AH Sprite	9C/U/H101	9C/U/H49201
AH Sprite Mk II (948)	9CG/Da/H (or Da/L)101	9CG/Da/H (or Da/L) 36711
AH Sprite Mk II (1098)	10CG/Da/H (or Da/L) 101	10CG/Da/H (or Da/L) 21048
AH Sprite Mk III	10CC/Da/H101	10CC/Da/H16300
AH Sprite Mk IV	12CC/Da/H101	12CC/Da/H16300
AH Sprite Mk IV	12CE/Da/H101	not known
AH Sprite Mk IV	12CD/Da/H101 (USA)	not known
AH Sprite Mk IV	12CG/Da/H101 (USA)	not known
Midget (948)	9CG/Da/H (or Da/L)101	9CG/Da/H (or Da/L) 36711
Midget (1098)	10CG/Da/H (or Da/L) 101	10CG/Da/H (or Da/L) 21048
Midget Mk II	10CC/Da/H101	10CC/Da/H16300
Midget Mk III	12CC/Da/H101	12CC/Da/H16300
Midget Mk III	12CE/Da/H101	not known
Midget Mk III	12V/586F/101	not known
Midget Mk III	12V/671Z/101	not known
Midget Mk III	12V/588F/101	not known
Midget Mk III	12V/778F/101	not known
Midget Mk III	12CD/Da/H101 (USA)	not known
Midget Mk III	12CF/Da/H101 (USA)	not known
Midget Mk III	12CG/Da/H101 (USA)	not known
Midget Mk III	12CH/Da/H101 (USA)	not known
Midget Mk III	12CJ/Da/H21201 (USA)	not known
Midget Mk III	12CK/Da/H101 (USA)	not known
Midget Mk III	12V/587Z/101 (USA)	not known
Midget 1500	FP001-E (UK)	not known
Midget 1500	FP300-UE (USA)	not known
Midget 1500	FP400-UCE (California)	not known

Chassis Numbers

Model	Chassis No. Commences	Chassis No. Finishes
AH Sprite	H-AN5-501	H-AN5-50116
AH Sprite Mk II (948)	H-AN6-101	H-AN6-24731
AH Sprite Mk II (1098)	H-AN7-24732	H-AN7-38828
AH Sprite Mk III	H-AN8-38829	H-AN8-64734
AH Sprite Mk IV	H-AN9-64735	H-AN9-85286
AH Sprite Mk IV (Leyland)	H-AN10-85287	H-AN10-86403
Austin Sprite Mk IV	A-AN10-86804	A-AN10-87824
Midget (948)	G-AN1-101	G-AN1-16183
Midget (1098)	G-AN2-16184	G-AN2-25787
Midget Mk II	G-AN3-25788	G-AN3-52389
Midget Mk III	G-AN4-52390	G-AN4-74885
Midget Mk III (Leyland)	G-AN5-74886	G-AN5-154100
Midget 1500	G-AN6-154101	To end of production

Torque Wrench Settings

Engine: 'A' Series

	lbf/ft	kgf/m
Connecting rod bolts, 948	35	4.8
Connecting rod nuts		
1098 - 1275 (plain)	45	6.2
1098 - 1275 (nyloc)	32 to 34	4.4 to 4.7
Crankshaft (main) bearing bolts	60	8.7
Crankshaft pulley bolt	70	9.6
Cylinder head nuts		
948	40	5.5
1098 - 1275 (plain studs)	42	5.8
1098 - 1275 (studs marked 22		
or with small drill point)	50	6.9
Cylinder side covers, 948 - 1098	2	0.3
Distributor clamp bolt (fixed bolt)	3	0.4
Distributor clamp bolt (fixed nut)	4	0.6
Flywheel bolts	40	5.5
Manifold nuts (brass)	15	2.1
Oil filter, 1275	10 to 15	1.4 to 2.0
Oil filter retaining nut		
(cartridge filter), 948 - 1098	16	2.2
Oil pipe union adaptor		
(oil filter head), 1275	19 to 21	2.6 to 2.9
Oil pump		
948 - 1098	9	1.2
1275	12	1.7
Rocker cover, 948 - 1098	4	0.6
Rocker pedestal nuts, 948 - 1098	25	3.4
Spark plug	20	2.8
Sump to crankcase, 948 - 1098	6	0.8
Timing cover bolt		
(1/4" UNF)	6	0.8
(5/16" UNF)	14	1.9

Engine: Triumph 1500

	lbf/ft	kgf/m
Chainwheel to camshaft	24	3.3
Clutch to flywheel	22	3
Con rod bolt		
colour dyed (1975 - 1976)	50	6.9
phosphated (1975 - 1976)	46	6.4
phosphated (USA 1977 on)	46	6.4
Crankshaft pulley nut	150	20.7
Crankshaft rear seal housing	20	2.8
Cylinder head nuts		
UK, USA to 1976)	50	6.9
USA 1977 on	40 to 45	5.5 to 6.2
Distributor to pedestal	20	2.8
Flywheel to crankshaft		
cadmium plated	40	5.5
parkerised	45	6.2
Gearbox and rear engine plate to block	14	1.9
Main bearing cap bolts	65	9
Manifold to cylinder head	25	3.5
Manifold, inlet to exhaust	14	1.9
Oil pressure switch to cylinder head	14	1.9
Oil seal block attachment	14	1.9
Oil sump drain plug	25	3.5
Oil sump to block	20	2.8
Rear engine mounting platform on frame	20	2.8
Rocker cover to head	2	0.3
Rocker pedestal to cylinder head	32	4.4
Sealing block to engine plate	20	2.8
Spark plug	20	2.8
Starter motor attachment	34	4.7
Timing cover to front engine plate		
large bolt	20	2.8
small bolt	10	1.4

Cooling System: 'A' Series engine

Fan securing bolts (plastic fan), 1275	10	1.2
Thermostat housing	8	1.1
Water pump	17	2.3

Cooling System: Triumph 1500 engine

Alternator to adjusting link	20	2.8
Alternator to mounting bracket and engine plate	22	3
Cylinder block drain plug	35	4.8
Fan securing bolts	9	1.2
Water elbow to water pump	20	2.8
Water pump bearing housing to pump	14	1.9
Water pump to cylinder head	20	2.8

Gearbox: Triumph 1500 engine

Drive flange nut	90 to 100	12.4 to 13.8
Flywheel housing retaining bolts	28 to 30	3.9 to 4.1
Rear extension to gearbox bolts	18 to 20	2.4 to 2.7

Rear Axle

Bearing cap to gear carrier bolts	65	8.99
Crown wheel to gear carrier bolts	60	8.3
Drive flange nut	140	19.4
Pinion bearing pre-load	8 to 10	0.09 to 0.12

Brakes

Bleed screw	4 to 6	0.5 to 0.8
Brake disc to hub	40 to 45	5.5 to 6.2
Caliper to stub axle	45 to 50	6.2 to 7.0
Master cylinder port adaptors (USA),		
1500	15 to 19	1.7 to 2.1
Plastic reservoir fixing bolts (USA),		
1500	5	0.69
Pressure failure switch, nylon (USA),		
1500	15	0.17
Pressure failure switch assembly end plug		
1975 to 1976 (USA), 1500	200	2.3
1977 on (USA), 1500	400	4.6

Steering & Suspension

Column upper fixing bolts	12 to 17	1.7 to 2.4
Hub nut, front stub axle		
disc brakes	46	6.9
drum brake	55 to 65	7.6 to 9.0
Rack mounting bracket retaining bolts	17 to 18	2.3 to 2.4
Rack to clamp bolts	20 to 22	2.8 to 3.1
Road wheel nuts		
disc wheels	60 to 63.5	8.3 to 8.7
rostyle wheels	45	6.2
Shock absorber bolts	25 to 30	3.4 to 4.1
Steering column pinch bolt	9 to 11	1.2 to 1.5
Steering lever bolts		
disc brake models	39	5.4
drum brake models	30 to 35	4.1 to 4.8
Steering lock shear bolts, where fitted	70	0.8
Steering wheel nut		
non-collapsible column	42	5.8
collapsible column	37	5.2
Tie rod end ball joint nut		
948 - early 1275	32.3 to 34.3	4.4 to 4.7
late 1275 - 1500	28 to 32	3.9 to 4.5
Tie rod inner ball joint assembly locknut		
late 1275 - 1500	80	11.1
Trunnion retaining nut	40	5.5

Electrical

Alternator pulley nut	25	3.5
Starter motor retaining nuts	34	4.7
Wiper motor yoke fixing bolts	20	0.23

Fuel System

Fuel pump (mechanical type) mounting		
948 - 1098	14	1.9
1500	14	1.9
Fuel pump top cover bolt, 1500	10 to 14*	0.1 to 0.16*
Fuel tank drain plug, 1275	9	1.2

* lbf.in / kgf. cm

Useless Tip

If you don't have a torque wrench, there is a method you can use to determine whether you have correctly torqued down any item.

1. If, after tightening, oil pours out or the part falls off, then insufficient tightening has taken place.
2. If the nut splits, the bolt breaks, thread shreds, component cracks or spanner snaps, too much torque has been applied.

In many ways this is similar to the perennial carpentry question "how do I know when I should use a nail or a screw?" The answer is to always use a nail unless the wood splits, then you know that you should have used a screw...

Keeping Cool Under Pressure...

An engineer friend and I spent a quiet few minutes ruminating the advantages of mechanical "things" over electrical "things". Electrical "things" we decided were all well and good. Press a button and they start, push another button and they stop, but there is nothing as reliable as a mechanical "thing". You turn a handle and a lever twists or a bar moves. If something gets stiff you can oil it. If something goes wrong you can take a spanner to it. But an electrical "thing" - now that's a horse of a different colour. When an electrical "thing" goes wrong, you've got a problem!

The Cooling System and Heater

It's a question of visibility really. When you break down at the side of the road because something mechanical has happened you do at least have the chance of fixing it. You can see, for example, a wheel laying in a ditch - and you can fix it, assuming you can find the wheel nuts. But an electrical "thing"... better call the tow truck now!

The Midget mentioned throughout this book came to me with an electric fan. These were the "in-things" at the time, faster warmer up time, less stress on the engine, more fuel efficient and so on. It was noisy, it worked, I got used to it. Then one summer, while Kath and I were undergoing the long drawn out process of moving from London to Worcester, the car started running hot. The fan cut in, just like it always did, but the engine began to overheat wildly. There began a slow process of solving the problem. I fitted a new radiator cap. The thermostat seemed to work but I bought a new one anyway. I took the radiator out, back flushed it and refitted it with new hoses. Still the car overheated like mad, though the radiator was universally hot from top to bottom, leaving no suggestion that it was clogged. So what was it?

By now it was mid summer and I had to run the heater fan to help keep the car cool, and boy, was it a hot summer. I even took the head off for skimming, but there was nothing wrong with it. I'd checked the timing and the carburation as well but still found nothing wrong. I gave up in despair and sent it into the garage for Krypton Tuning. I explained what was happening and what I'd done. "Surely" I said "I must have missed something obvious".

It took them five minutes to suss the problem. "It's the fan" said the mechanic, "you'll get more wind from a gnat!"

And there was the problem, the fan was dying as the brushes wore down. Its decline was so gradual as to be unnoticeable - though it was as noisy as ever. The previous winter had been so bad that the fan was scarcely needed and its deterioration had gone unnoticed. Although I saw and heard it switching on, I had no way of measuring its effectiveness.

A mechanical fan, attached to a fan belt, can only fail if it comes undone, or the fan belt slips or snaps. These faults are clearly visible and can be rectified in minutes, probably without any damage to the engine so long as sensible attention is paid during servicing. Unless an electrical fan fails completely, how do you know it is faulty?

I gave up and went back to a traditional mechanical fan and have never had a problem since. Electrical things - pah!

Some History:
Cooling & the Heater System

The H frame of the early Sprites included two uprights onto which the radiator was bolted. Even following the re-design of the front end, this system of attachment remained. The original vertical flow radiator included an integral expansion tank which allowed easy topping -up directly into the top of the radiator. The radiator was modified lightly at HAN5-6888 and again at HAN5-50116, with both later styles able to be retro-fitted if required.

During its 1275cc incarnation (HAN9 72034 / GAN4 60441, USA and HAN9 77591/GAN4 66226 else-where) the cars were fitted with a cross-flow radiator mounted into a shroud which was, in turn, attached to the H frame uprights. The radiator system incorporated a separate expansion tank, made from black painted brass, mounted to the left-hand splash plate and wheel arch. Initial filling was via a brass plug mounted on top of the radiator. Topping-up was via the expansion tank.

The introduction of the 1500 Midget with its Triumph Spitfire engine, saw a new radiator - again cross-flow - being fitted. The expansion tank, now plastic, was mounted on the opposite side of the car. Filling was via a plug located on top of the thermostat housing as per the Triumph Dolomite.

The water pump, originally in cast iron, could be completely dismantled for restoration. Onto the pump was mounted a twin-bladed, yellow, steel fan. This style of pump was fitted up to engine 12CD/Da/H1745, at which point the pump was modified to enhance the pumping capacity.

With the introduction of the 12CC engines a six-bladed steel fan was fitted, only to be replaced on the 12CD engines with a yellow, six-bladed fan manufactured from plastic.

The 1500 engines utilised a new pump design with a seven-bladed, green or orange fan fitted - though in hot climates a natural coloured fan was utilised.

Only in a country like Britain could a heater be considered an option. However, the Sprite was a budget car. The heater unit consisted of a black box, behind which sat the battery, and a heater blower - looking for all the world like an oversized hair drier. Fresh air reached the blower by virtue of a long air hose which ran down the right hand side of the engine bay to an inlet hidden behind the grille. Flow was controlled by a push/pull lever which, by twisting, also turned the fan on and off. Hot water was allowed into the heater via a stop cock mounted to the rear of the A series engine.

For countries where a heater was not required a fresh air unit was offered as an option. Basically this consisted of the heater box without the heater.

At HAN9 71121 and GAN4 58854 the trunking carrying freshly polluted air into the heater became more sophisticated. The central portion attached to the wheel arch was no longer concertina shaped, but smooth - and held in position with two clamps, not one, as shown in the parts books.

From HAN10 86378 / GAN5 91408 the heater unit was modified, and combined the heater element and blower in one single unit. Whereas formerly the fresh air was cut off via a door at the grille, this new assembly had the air shut off door mounted in the heater unit itself.

With the introduction of the 1500 model, the engine bay was so cramped that the whole heater system was fitted in reverse. The new heater box was a mirror image of the earlier style and the fresh air hose ran down the left hand side of the car. The fresh air tube had a concertina form running its entire length. Furthermore the hot water, in common with the Triumph Spitfire, ran through the inlet manifolds (an aid to rapid warm up) prior to going into the heater element. A new hot water valve allowed water to flow into the heater element, almost as inefficiently as on the earlier cars.

Vertical Flow Radiator System; early models

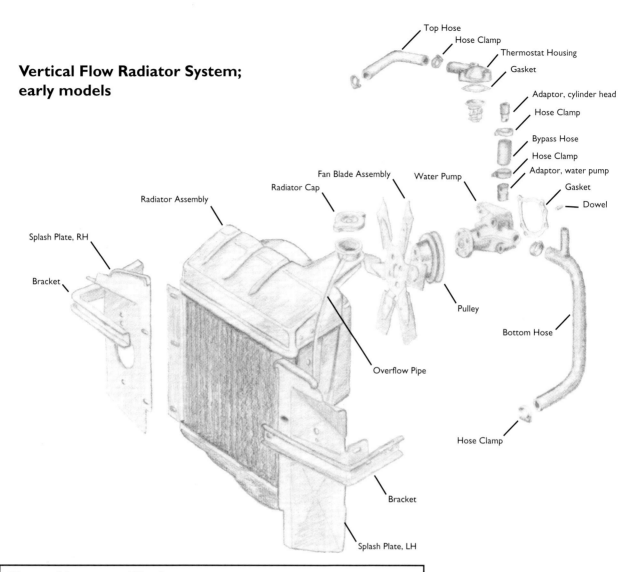

Top Hose
Hose Clamp
Thermostat Housing
Gasket
Adaptor, cylinder head
Hose Clamp
Bypass Hose
Hose Clamp
Adaptor, water pump
Gasket
Dowel
Fan Blade Assembly
Radiator Cap
Water Pump
Radiator Assembly
Splash Plate, RH
Bracket
Pulley
Bottom Hose
Overflow Pipe
Hose Clamp
Bracket
Splash Plate, LH

Green Hoses vs. Black

Sadly unavailable (well, sad for the garage trade that is) the classic green water hoses that were found under the bonnet of old cars have been replaced by black hoses. The older reader will remember the frequency with which these green hoses had to be replaced while younger readers may have never experienced the laborious job of replacing split hoses - "Ah, when I was young, blah, blah, blah...". Every garage stocked radiator hoses, because after two years of use the items in question would perish, blow up like balloons and explode sending steam everywhere. For many, hose replacement was a garage forecourt job while on holiday in Devon, with bored wives gazing out of grimy windows and kids whiningly asking "How much longer Dad?"

Garages and parts shops stocked hoses by the thousand. Whatever car you owned could be catered for with new hoses at a moment's notice, wherever you happened to be. Stocks were replenished by the box load as recalled by a colleague of mine who vividly remembers his astonishment at seeing his first ever black hose. The black hose was a great innovation, though not billed as such during its introduction. He just carried on ordering them by the ton though - not having been told of the superior (or long lasting) quality of the new "space-age" material.

Within a short time most of the United Kingdom's motor cars green hoses had perished, blown up like balloons and exploded, sending steam everywhere in the appropriate manner. In next to no time all the green hoses had been sold, to be replaced by shelves of these new black hoses - and there they've stayed for years and years.

Even now, if you should chance upon an old country garage, look in through the window, where you will see walls full of dusty black hoses with grubby labels saying "Top Hose - A30", "Heater Hose - Morris Cowley", "Water Pump to radiator - Ford Anglia" etc, etc, etc.

Crossflow Radiator System; late 1275 models

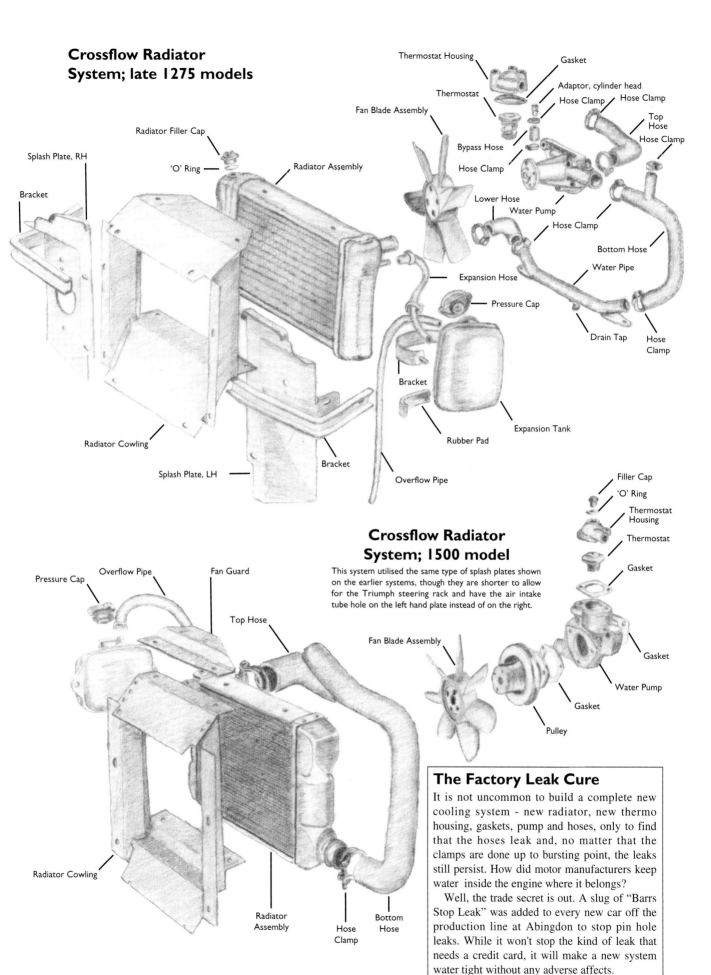

Thermostat Housing

Gasket

Thermostat

Adaptor, cylinder head

Fan Blade Assembly

Hose Clamp

Hose Clamp

Top Hose

Bypass Hose

Hose Clamp

Radiator Filler Cap

'O' Ring

Radiator Assembly

Splash Plate, RH

Bracket

Hose Clamp

Lower Hose

Water Pump

Hose Clamp

Bottom Hose

Water Pipe

Expansion Hose

Pressure Cap

Drain Tap

Hose Clamp

Bracket

Radiator Cowling

Splash Plate, LH

Bracket

Rubber Pad

Expansion Tank

Overflow Pipe

Crossflow Radiator System; 1500 model

This system utilised the same type of splash plates shown on the earlier systems, though they are shorter to allow for the Triumph steering rack and have the air intake tube hole on the left hand plate instead of on the right.

Pressure Cap

Overflow Pipe

Fan Guard

Top Hose

Fan Blade Assembly

Filler Cap

'O' Ring

Thermostat Housing

Thermostat

Gasket

Gasket

Water Pump

Gasket

Pulley

Radiator Cowling

Radiator Assembly

Hose Clamp

Bottom Hose

The Factory Leak Cure

It is not uncommon to build a complete new cooling system - new radiator, new thermo housing, gaskets, pump and hoses, only to find that the hoses leak and, no matter that the clamps are done up to bursting point, the leaks still persist. How did motor manufacturers keep water inside the engine where it belongs?

Well, the trade secret is out. A slug of "Barrs Stop Leak" was added to every new car off the production line at Abingdon to stop pin hole leaks. While it won't stop the kind of leak that needs a credit card, it will make a new system water tight without any adverse affects.

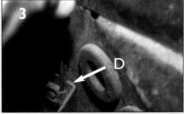

Case Study:
Cross-Flow Cooling System

Early cross flow radiator systems offered no easy means to drain out the water. After the earlier type of system, with both a drain tap in the block and at the radiator, this was a step backwards. All you can do is undo a clamp, pull off a hose and get wet feet.

1 Drain the system either by removing one of the bottom hoses, or (in the case of later cross flow cars) by removing the drain plug located at the bottom of the steel cross pipe which sits beneath the radiator. (You can just reach it from beneath the car).

2 Disconnect and remove the thermostat to radiator hose (1A), radiator to expansion tank hose (1B) and the radiator lower hoses (2C).

3 The radiator is mounted in an archaic and stupidly designed cowling. Secured with captive nuts (3D) - which are usually no longer captive - and sundry ill fitting items of hardware, old cowlings are very difficult to remove.

If the captive nuts refuse to stay still, try wedging a small screwdriver blade in there to grip them while undoing the bolt from the front of the grille area.

4 The cowling and radiator will come out as an assembly (4). Four bolts fix the radiator into the cowling (5 & 6). Examine the radiator for damage to the fins and signs of corrosion.

5 The expansion tank is held in place by a steel strap, under which are two rubber anti-vibration strips. The strap incorporates studs which fit through the left hand wheel arch to be secured by nuts and lock washers.

Prior to removal, make a note of how the overflow hose is fed down through the engine bay. The overflow hose should be a flexible black rubber tube (7) - not clear plastic!

Take care undoing the nuts of the restraining strap which, if severely rusted could cause the strap to twist and warp out of shape.

Cooling System Tips

Radiator Specialists

Radiator specialists will repair your damaged radiators and heater elements - they also pressure test them for you as well. Easy to locate; just hunt around any seedy industrial estate for a broken door from which a slimy green slush will have erupted onto a heavily soiled forecourt area. This is the natural habitat of the elusive radiator specialist.

Similar to a cobbler, you drop the item in for repair and arrange a time to collect it again. When you do return at the mutually agreed, pre-arranged time, you'll hear him say "Be ready next Thursday Sir". See, just like a shoe repair shop!

Radiator Cowling

Where fitted these are often difficult to remove. The captive nuts aren't very clever. You can buy new cowlings if the original is in too much of a mess. They are well made although the holes don't always line up like they should. They should be painted gloss black. Always use a thick grease on the captive nuts and bolts to ensure easy removal next time round.

Don't forget to fit new warning labels to the top of the cowling to warn against scalding or finger chopping!

The expansion tank and metal pipes

The 1275 cc expansion tank is made of brass - as is the heater pipe which runs along the top of the inlet manifold. To disperse the heat more readily, these components are painted black. Brass polish should be used on door knockers, horse brasses and Romany kettles. Concours entrants should lose points for polishing instead of painting the offending items, but I guess it gives them something to do.

Pressure Cap & Thermostat

Always fit a new pressure cap once the cooling system has been restored.

Thermostats vary according to the conditions in which they will be used. The opening temperature should be stamped on your existing thermostat. When fully warmed up, the temperature gauge should register just over the half way mark. If the temperature remains too cool or too hot consider fitting a different grade thermostat.

Hoses & Water Pipes

The cylinder head to water pump hose is short and often neglected. It can leak unseen and is difficult to reach. Replace it while the fan blades and radiator are out of the way.

Use the solid rubber type, not the concertina variety shown which, though easier to fit, is often not as durable.

Replace all of the rubber hoses, along with their clamps as a matter of course. Petroleum Jelly or water-proof grease on the threads of new clamps will be a bonus for the future as well.

If the lower pipe is corroded (cross-flow cars), replace it while the radiator is out of the way. This pipe incorporates a useful drain plug. It can be retro-fitted and is worth the minimal extra expense involved.

Water Pump & Fan

If the water pump shows signs of leakage , replace it - seals are simply not available individually. Check that the impeller blades rotate freely and, when refitting, ensure that a new gasket is used.

Pay close attention to the fan assembly. Damaged blades should be replaced. Plastic fans are prone to damage caused by the pressure of air. The blades flex and eventually start to weaken at the point where they meet the main body. Discoloured markings are a sure sign of damage.

Stop Cock

A stop cock, mounted to the rear of the cylinder head, allows hot water to flow into the heater matrix. After a few years, the seals tend to wear allowing water to escape. These are not restorable, but new replacements are available.

Anti-Freeze

Sprites and Midgets should always have anti-freeze in the cooling system. It also acts as a summer coolant. If you have a leak then fix it, if you can't fix it or haven't worked out where its leaking from then always top it up with an anti-freeze/water mix.

Commonly owners notice a drop in water level and fill the car up with plain water. It drops again. More water is added. It drops again and so on. Eventually all of the anti-freeze is lost to the system via some piffling leaky hose which might cost a few pounds to correct. With the arrival of a sharp frost the water freezes, expands and damages the radiator or heater element, blows all of the core plugs and generally renders a sound car inoperable.

Aluminium Corrosion

The combination of aluminium, iron and ionised water causes corrosion through electrolysis. Anti-freeze limits the effect considerably but note that the alloy water pumps and thermostat housings are prone to severe corrosion over time. Of course you won't spot this until it's too late because the corrosion happens from the inside out. Keep some water/anti-freeze mixture handy.

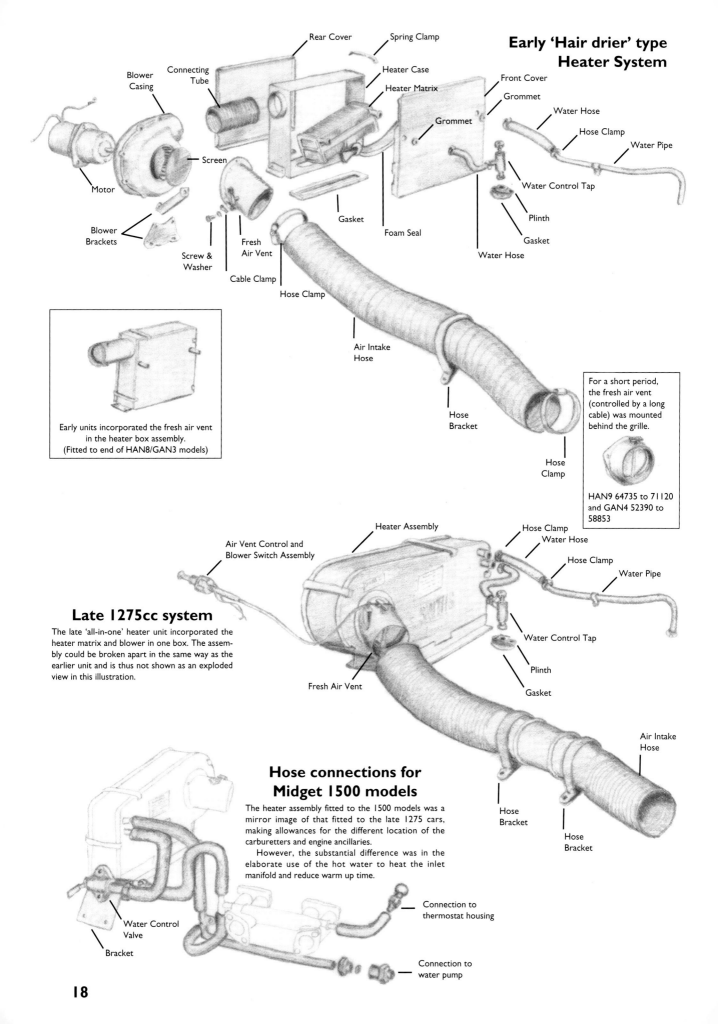

Early 'Hair drier' type Heater System

Rear Cover

Spring Clamp

Connecting Tube

Blower Casing

Heater Case

Heater Matrix

Front Cover

Grommet

Grommet

Water Hose

Hose Clamp

Water Pipe

Motor

Water Control Tap

Blower Brackets

Screen

Plinth

Screw & Washer

Gasket

Gasket

Fresh Air Vent

Foam Seal

Water Hose

Cable Clamp

Hose Clamp

Air Intake Hose

Hose Bracket

Hose Clamp

Early units incorporated the fresh air vent in the heater box assembly.
(Fitted to end of HAN8/GAN3 models)

For a short period, the fresh air vent (controlled by a long cable) was mounted behind the grille.

HAN9 64735 to 71120 and GAN4 52390 to 58853

Air Vent Control and Blower Switch Assembly

Heater Assembly

Hose Clamp

Water Hose

Hose Clamp

Water Pipe

Late 1275cc system

The late 'all-in-one' heater unit incorporated the heater matrix and blower in one box. The assembly could be broken apart in the same way as the earlier unit and is thus not shown as an exploded view in this illustration.

Fresh Air Vent

Water Control Tap

Plinth

Gasket

Air Intake Hose

Hose connections for Midget 1500 models

The heater assembly fitted to the 1500 models was a mirror image of that fitted to the late 1275 cars, making allowances for the different location of the carburetters and engine ancillaries.

However, the substantial difference was in the elaborate use of the hot water to heat the inlet manifold and reduce warm up time.

Hose Bracket

Hose Bracket

Water Control Valve

Connection to thermostat housing

Bracket

Connection to water pump

Case Study:
Heater Unit Restoration

1 Remove the six self tapers and flat washers (1) securing the heater to the battery shelf.

2 Disconnect heater motor wires (2), the vent cable if fitted (3) and remove the fresh air inlet tube.

3 Disconnect and remove the rubber water hoses - noting position of each since they are shaped differently (4).

4 Release the choke cable (attached to one of the heater case spring clips) by undoing the "fir tree" cable tie (5).

5 Lift the complete heater assembly from the battery shelf. Note the gasket assembly which sits beneath the heater. Do not throw the old gasket away (6) but retain it for later use.

6 Lever off the spring clips and gently prise off the rear face of the heater unit to gain access to the heater matrix.

7 The matrix is insulated against vibration by a foam rubber seal (7), which is simply wrapped around the unit.

The seal stops air from bypassing the heater and forces it through the element. If your heater is not working efficiently it may be that the seal has disintegrated and cold air is whistling through the gaps between the element and the heater box walls. You'll know if the heater is not working efficiently, because it will take more than five minutes to toast your legs completely and cook any passenger in the seat next to you...

8 Examine the heater matrix for leaks (8) - deposits of blue/grey minerals are a tell tale sign of a problem. If leaks are found replacement elements are available or alternatively they can be repaired by specialists.

If in any doubt about its condition then replace the unit. After all, it can be a bit of a job to get the unit out again (as you probably know by now). And, if it is leaking, or about to leak, you won't know about it until water has been leaking for a while or, worse still, when chronic overheating occurs.

9 The heater motor and fan is not restorable. Either it works, or it doesn't. If it works, leave it alone. Do not attempt to remove the fan from the motor. Due to its "force fit" design (9), any attempt to remove it normally will end disastrously, and leads to the need for corrective therapy involving a happy parts man and your wallet.

I had many Saturday morning customers asking for heater fan blades. I have no objection to these people wrecking their heaters, I just wish they wouldn't curse me because Lucas only choose to sell the motor and fan as an expensive assembly.... "Yes sir, a very nice wallet sir, now if you'll just give me all of the cash thank you, and the credit card Sir, THANK YOU !!!"

Heater Reassembly

10 Flush out the heater matrix using a hose pipe. A radiator specialist will be able to pressure test the matrix - again I must emphasise the importance of repair or replacement if there is any hint of corrosion.

11 Clean the inlet and outlet pipes with wire wool (10). When the old rubber hoses perish, deposits tend to be left on the tubes where water seeps out leaving corrosion and mineral deposits. Otherwise, although new hoses have been fitted, water may seep out due to the uneven surface of the pipes.

12 The heater casing should be stripped and repainted black (11). The fresh air vent needs to be repainted and the fittings polished (12).

13 The fresh air valve can be dismantled, cleaned and reassembled. Take careful note of the rubber seal which is not replaceable (13). Try not to lose or damage it. If you need to clean it, use a proprietary rubber cleaner.

14 Fit new grommets into the casing. Heat from the matrix usually causes the old rubber to harden and crack.

15 If you haven't done it already, wrap a new foam sealing strip around the heater element (14) and then fit it into the casing, with the tubes going through the grommets (15).

The pipes are a tight fit into the grommets - but persevere. Apply some rubber grease to the grommet and pipe walls. You'll find that the element slides into position very easily.

Should the grommets start to push out of the holes, then simply push them back in position using a suitable drift.

16 Fit the back plate and spring clips.

17 Fit the heater motor, securing the cables to one of the three screws with a P clip (16). Spin the unit by hand to ensure that it does not foul the casing anywhere (17).

If the motor does foul the casing, it is likely to be caused by deformation of the rear cover, into which the fan sits. Some manhandling may be required.

18 Temporarily secure the fir tree clip to the appropriate spring clip (18) - try not to lose it if you have a genuine article, some specialists will sell you a tie wrap ("well it fits dunnit!")

19 Finish the job off nicely by fitting new heater labels.

20 Unless the genuine heater box to battery shelf seal is now available I would recommend making your own - or refitting the original. The only alternative appears to be a long strip of draught excluder (cut to fit) which doesn't seem that clever!

Heater Vents and Demister
The vents are secured by four screws (19) and consist of a frame and door with hinges manufactured from rivets. The door is sprung loaded. The spring is easy to remove, but should you be restoring the units, note that the rivets should be drilled out carefully. The metal fabrications are very light gauge and prone to damage - so don't be heavy handed.

The demisters fit into position with two chrome screws. The heater tubes simply push fit into these and need not be secured. Rubber elbows at the heater box end push into the footwells and allow the tubes to be attached (again without security).

Fresh Air Inlet Tube
This is held in position by two clamps on the 1275 models and consists of two concertina ends with a rigid centre section (20). Genuine replacements are not currently available - so try keeping the original if possible.

Note that an earth lead is secured to the wheel arch (arrowed) with the lower clamp (21).

Adjusting the nut behind the wheel

I try to avoid being a lazy driver. I take my seat belt off when reversing, always look over my shoulder when moving off and take care to ensure that nobody is behind me before reversing. How it was that I managed to reverse square into a post box one day is a complete mystery to me.

While taking driving lessons I worked really hard on my three point turn - the dreaded "completing-a-turn-in-the-road-using-forward-and-reverse-gears". I had my technique honed down, being able to turn a car around in what I believed to be an admirably competent manner.

There was not a road, no matter how narrow, that defeated me until the day of my driving test, during which I turned right onto a road the size of an airport runway. The examiner asked me to stop the car at the side of the road and then told me to "turn in the road using forward and reverse gears". At last, my time had come, but the road was so wide I almost couldn't see the other kerb. I wasn't prepared for a road of such magnitude and it took me seven sad and sorry turns to get the car facing the other way. Humility, they say, is a wonderful thing!

A friend failed his first car test while driving his mother's aged Mini. It was one of those early ones with the sliding windows and I think the examiner must have been somewhat sadistic in his request for my friend to give hand signals when turning right. Now the seat in this Mini was broken and slid both forwards and aft without restraint. As my friend approached the junction he stuck his arm out of the window and pressed on the foot brake to slow the car down.

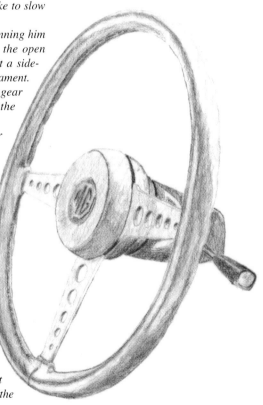

Steering Gear

At this wholly inappropriate moment the seat slid forward, pinning him against the steering wheel while trapping his flailing arm in the open window. He battled on but, realising his arm was trapped, shot a sideways glance at the examiner apparently oblivious of the predicament. Quick as a flash, my friend let go of the wheel to try changing gear whereupon the examiner spun his head round and stared at the offending hand.

It proved to be the last right turn of the test, with the examiner leaving him at the roadside holding a failure notice.

My wife Kathryn only ever took two lessons before passing her test in our MGB GT. Most of her training was done by driving our Midget in the lanes of mid Wales, around Lampeter and up on Tregaron Moor. Actually she got off to a bad start when, for her first ever attempt behind the wheel of the Midget (and only her second time behind the wheel of a car) she suffered an unfortunate mishap.

I drove her up to Tregaron, a journey of about twenty miles and we stopped at the top of the empty moor, from where, by simply releasing the handbrake we would be able to get a rolling start. We swapped seats, the handbrake was released and the car rolled forward. We hadn't gone twenty yards when a flock of sheep started to amble across the road.

Kath stopped and waited for them to cross. When they were all safe on the other side she started to roll the car forward at which point a tiny lamb ran straight back under the wheel of the car injuring itself badly. There were a lot of tears that night...

My final steering story, of which there are sadly too many to admit to, happened when I was still at school. During the summer holidays I used to do morning paper deliveries and on one bright sunny day I had just delivered The Times to a house on a quiet side road, thereby lightening my load by a factor of ten. I was cycling back towards the main road, directly into the sun which was dazzlingly bright.

It was absolutely quiet except for someone singing opera from an open window. It sounded awful, and turning to try and pinpoint the offending vocalist I cycled straight into a parked car, bouncing over the bonnet and ending up sprawling spread-eagled on the ground...

Some History: Steering

The original steering rack (so I keep being told) is from the Morris Minor - but fitted upside down. I mention this because, as with many of these things, parts get used on a number of different models!

The racks were revised for the USA (HAN9 72034 / GAN4 60441), and everywhere else, shortly after (HAN9 72529 / GAN4 61166), being replaced from GAN5 114487 (USA) and GAN5 114643 (the rest of the world). In fact these later style racks (shown below), taken from the Triumph Spitfire, were intermittently fitted to some earlier cars.

The steering column came in for a number of safety changes over the years due to horrific injuries caused either directly or indirectly during collisions. The outer column was revised first at HAN5 48627.

With the introduction of Sprite II / Midget I models optional steering locks were fitted, resulting in the requirement of a revision to the columns. The lock was revised at HAN7 34274 / GAN2 22617, and the lock / switch revised again at an unspecified point during Sprite III / Midget II production.

From HAN8 38829 / GAN3 25788 both inner and outer columns were again updated. At this point, the lock or lock and ignition switch assembly were still being supplied as optional extras. Any of three lock mechanisms may have been fitted, depending upon the market into which the cars were being sold. No clear records exist, but, the lock / switch assemblies were finally rationalised from HAN9 77534 / GAN4 64751, making the car thief's life easier.

In America, where they care about their internal organs, a collapsible column was fitted from HAN9 72034 / GAN4 61685. Canada got these new columns as well during HAN9 production; nobody knows when, but the MG chassis number was GAN4 64756. A revised switch with replaceable lock and barrel was fitted at the same time. The lock was revised at GAN5 74886 and again at GAN6 154101.

In the UK and elsewhere the column, lock and switch were revised again from HAN10 85287 and GAN5 74886. From HAN10 86766 / GAN5 96273 the lock and switch finally became standard fitment - after all we're only talking about the the 1970s.

An energy absorbing column was fitted to UK and European cars from GAN5 105501, the left hand version continuing until production ceased, the right hand variant being revised at GAN6 170990. The switch was revised for old time's sake at GAN5 115926.

The original two spoke bakelite wheel (with Sprite "Lightning" device or MG logo on the horn push) was replaced with a three-spoked, twin-wire wheel from HAN8 38829 / GAN3 25788. It stopped the bakelite from crumbling if nothing else. An Austin Coat of Arms or MG logo was then set in a clear plastic boss.

The horn push was moved to the column switch gear (USA) HAN9 72034 / GAN4 60441 (64756 Canada).

As far as I can make out, but I could be wrong, the wheel was revised again at HAN9 78731 / GAN4 66224 with revised centre bosses. Then a three-spoked, three-wire wheel was fitted from HAN9 78825 and GAN4 67476, complete with rubber centre boss and jewelled insert.

A modern alloy spoked design with round holes was fitted from HAN10 85287 / GAN5 74886 with a tacky plastic horn push (yeah, thanks Longbridge). The MG boss had an Octagon centre piece, the Sprite boss was left blank. The MG boss was revised again at GAN5 105501 to incorporate a red MG logo.

Slotted spokes were used from GAN5 123731 to stop people jamming their fingers in the holes. Obviously this didn't work too well and the slots were filled in, the spokes having a debossed impression from GAN5 135882. At GAN6 157173, the boys at Longbridge incorporated a gold MG logo on the centre boss. Wow! Abingdon staff must have been really impressed.

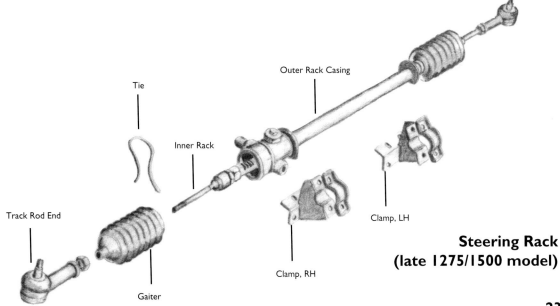

Tie

Outer Rack Casing

Inner Rack

Track Rod End

Clamp, LH

Clamp, RH

Gaiter

**Steering Rack
(late 1275/1500 model)**

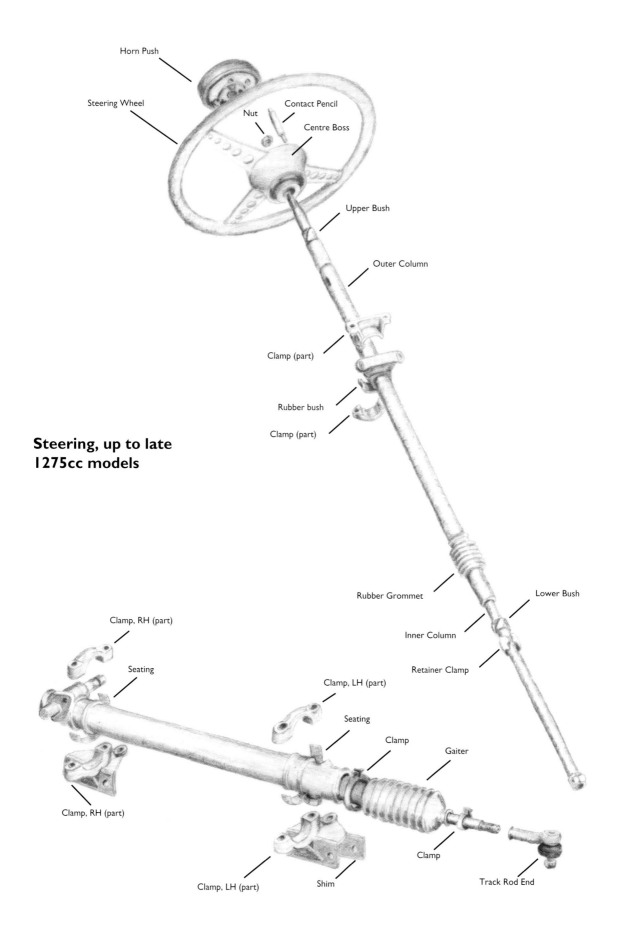

Horn Push

Steering Wheel

Nut

Contact Pencil

Centre Boss

Upper Bush

Outer Column

Clamp (part)

Rubber bush

Clamp (part)

**Steering, up to late
1275cc models**

Rubber Grommet

Lower Bush

Inner Column

Retainer Clamp

Clamp, RH (part)

Seating

Clamp, LH (part)

Seating

Clamp

Gaiter

Clamp, RH (part)

Clamp

Clamp, LH (part)

Shim

Track Rod End

Case Study:
Steering Column and Rack
Removal of the column

1 Undo the column pinch bolt and nut where the column joins the rack (1).

The column is pinched closed sometimes "trapping" the bolt. Prise apart the cut-out, visible at the base of the column, to allow removal of the bolt.

2 From inside the car remove the steering wheel and cowling. Unplug the wiring.

3 Undo the clamp assembly from inside the footwell (2).

4 Note the twisting path of the steering lock wiring looms, prior to pulling them free.

5 Withdraw the column and wheel. Note the rubber gaiter which stops the cold wind blowing through the bulkhead (3).

6 The wheel and boss is attached to the column by a single nut. The wheel is attached to the boss with six screws.

*A circular locking tab secures the six screws. Be warned, the lock tab is currently not available (at least at the time of writing). Once the tabs are broken you'll need to find another way of securing the screws. **Don't lose the tag itself though** - because it also secures the horn push / centre piece (4).*

7 Upon trying to separate the steering wheel boss from the column you'll realise why the boss often gets damaged. The steel insert in the alloy boss often rusts to the column. Some heavy blows using a wooden drift should help to release the two parts once the cowling has been undone. Its better to get the column on the bench to do this - since damage to the alloy boss so easily occurs.

8 The steering lock is held in place with shear bolts (5). These "bolts-with-a-waist" should be done up tight enough for the waist to snap, thereby stopping unauthorised removal. As we all know, the car thief's favoured tool is a sliding hammer and crow bar (fits all cars - imperial or metric) so the special bolts probably don't make that much difference. They are removed by drilling out the remains of the head though mine, like others I've seen, were still intact.

9 Remove the cowling, indicator assembly and horn brush. The indicators operate by knocking against a clip. Mark its position with tape prior to removal to enable accurate realignment (6).

10 The cowling can be cleaned and polished using a light rubbing compound such as "T Cut Metallic".

11 The horn ring (7) is secured by two screws and should be replaced if worn (I mean the ring, not the screws). Coat the brass ring lightly with Vaseline to limit wear.

12 Having removed the centre boss the inner column can be separated from the outer.

Note that the lower bush is secured by a steel clip (8) which needs to be released to allow removal of the inner column. The upper bush simply pulls out.

13 The ignition switch is easily removed from the steering lock (9).

The steering lock can be cleaned and oiled while the switch itself can be renewed if faulty.

14 All parts of the column assembly can be cleaned and painted where necessary while being examined for damage prior to careful reassembly (10).

Renovating the Steering Wheel

Wire wool and fine grinding paste is both an effective rust remover and cleaner. Polish with wire wool and metal polish.

Leather damage can only be repaired by someone adept with needle and thread, but be careful who you go to lest the steering wheel comes back furry...

Steering Column Reassembly

Start by fitting the lower bush and its retainer clamp first, then fit the upper. Once the lower bush has been positioned it will be held in place making the rest of the job easier.

New bushes may prove to be to thick for the application for which they are intended. Bearing this in mind it may be worthwhile nipping the bushes slightly in a vice (once they have been oiled) to allow an improved fit.

The upper bush may even require trimming to allow a comfortable fit. Prepare to spend some time on this particular job.

Lower bush Fitting

1 With the outer column pushed right to the top of the inner column, fit the lower bush and retaining clamp over the inner column (1).

2 Use a strong clamp to compress the bush and retainer (2). Use a vice to compress the clamp (3), allowing the outer column to be drifted over the retainer in stages.

3 Ensure that the retainer springs out into the outer column cut out, thereby securing the bush in its correct position. (See illustration shown overleaf).

Upper Bush Fitting

You need a clamp and large washer. The washer needs to fit over the inner column. You also need a tool that can be used as a drift.

1 Arrange the columns so that only a few inches of the inner column shows at the top of the outer column.

2 Wrap the oiled upper bush around the inner column (4). Secure it with the clamp and then, little by little, push it downwards into the outer column and over the thin neck of the inner column (see also diagram overleaf).

3 Fit the washer and help to tap the bush into position (5). Use a drift to help the process.

4 Gradually force the outer column downwards so that 95mm of the inner column is exposed. Ensure that the upper bush remains in situ.

Once in place, the inner column should be able to turn. If not then the bushes are probably still a little tight. Remove them, nip them in the vice a bit and refit. Don't nip them up too tight however, otherwise the inner column will be able to vibrate when the car is driven.

Be careful not to damage the lower bush retainer.

Final Reassembly
1 Refit the indicator clip, using the marks made during disassembly (6).

2 If removed or replaced, the ignition switch may be refitted to the steering lock (7).

   The switch will only mount one way. Look for a small locating lobe in the lock casting which matches a cut-out in the switch.

3 The outer column boasts a small hole through which the steering lock extends to secure the inner column when locked (8). Ensure that through the hole you can see the knurled surface which butts against the lock mortise when it is engaged. If it can't be seen then the inner and outer columns are not correctly assembled and will need to be adjusted.

   Re-align the columns prior to installing the lock if necessary.

   Tighten and break off the shear bolt heads to ensure difficult removal.

4 Fit the horn ring to the centre boss (9). Note the hole through the boss which allows the horn brush to be fitted. The brass contact plate must be visible through the hole.

5 Ensure that the column splines at the head of the column are clean and smear some anti-seize lubricant onto them prior to fitting the centre boss (10). Secure with the locking nut.

6 Refit the outer column bracket - not forgetting the rubber anti-vibration pad (11).

7 Refit the indicator switch (12), connect horn push cable, refit the cowling and secure cable loom with wire tag.

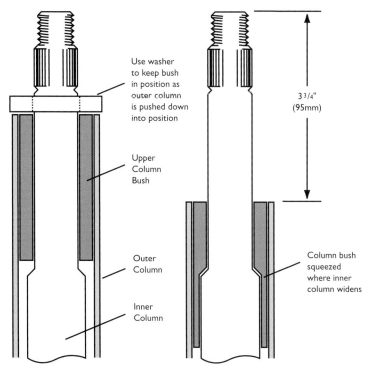

Use washer to keep bush in position as outer column is pushed down into position

Upper Column Bush

Outer Column

Inner Column

3 3/4" (95mm)

Column bush squeezed where inner column widens

Fitting and Positioning of the Upper Column Bush - 1275 Midget

Stiff Steering?

Steering is self-centring. This is to say that, should you be turning a corner or undertaking a bend and let go of the wheel the car will straighten up and steer in a straight line through the five bar gate and into the boggy field beyond.

The only replacement bushes available at the moment appear to be too thick for the purpose. Installation proved that once fitted any self-centring ability is lost. Replacements need to be lightly pinched in a vice to allow the inner column to turn freely.

Unless there is serious wear to the bushes you might prefer to stick with the originals.

Oiling Your Rack

The racks tend to last for ever. Even when they don't get oiled. The reason they don't get oiled is because nobody ever has a grease gun full of oil, and even if they do, they can't get the gun down to the grease nipple.

The alternative is to unclamp one of the gaiter ends, shove an oil can nozzle into the gaiter and squirt in between ten and fifteen steady strokes of motor oil before resealing the clamp.

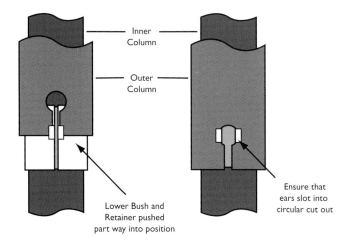

Inner Column

Outer Column

Lower Bush and Retainer pushed part way into position

Ensure that ears slot into circular cut out

Fitting the Lower Bush

Case Study: Steering Rack

There's actually not a lot you can do to restore a rack. It needs some specialist tools, experience, a lot of care and many parts which generally are not available. Still, without being driven by a merciless driver the racks have been known to be good for up to 200, 000 miles.

If you are looking for a replacement from a scrap yard I am reliably informed that the RHD steering rack is the same as Morris Minor LHD versions and vice versa. Not quite the straight swap that people think, but still there are plenty around. (This does not apply to Midget 1500 model which utilises the Triumph Spitfire rack).

The simplest and safest answer, should the rack appear worn, is to buy an exchange unit from a reputable rack specialist. However, there are a few things that you may be able to do yourself, especially if you believe the rack to be serviceable.

What can be done

1 Remove the whole rack from the car, clamps included, noting the shim which offers fine adjustment of the rack (1). For safe keeping attach the shim to the appropriate clamp with wire or string.

2 Clean thoroughly prior to dismantling (2).

3 Prior to removing the clamps for cleaning, mark their relative position to aid reassembly using a punch.

4 Note the paper gaskets (3) which wrap around the rack body beneath the clamps.

5 Note position of the braided wire (4) which provides earthing for the horn circuit.

6 Remove the track rod ends (5), making a note of the number of turns required to unscrew them. This will aid you during reassembly - even if fitting new ends. At the very least you'll get to the tyre specialist without scrubbing out the tyres completely.

Many garages have not heard of grease and are not renowned for any helpful application of such a useful substance. Its not unusual for track rod ends to be seized solid. A hacksaw and cold chisel may help with the removal of tricky nuts (6).

7 Remove the gaiters (7), clean rack components and examine gear mechanism for signs of wear.

As mentioned previously, there's really little that the average owner can do to renovate the steering gear. Should there be any signs of wear or foul play in the system, send the unit in for reconditioning or replacement.

If there is nothing wrong with the rack then beyond making sure that it is clean and, if necessary, that the outer casing has been repainted, it is best to put it back together for later use.

8 Ensure that the inner rack is correctly located in the outer casing.

9 Gaiter kits include plastic tie wraps. For complete originality however, wire clamps should be used. (8 & 9).

Grease heavily with a water proof grease to stop them seizing up, because they will suffer badly from road salt.

10 Clean and polish the mounting brackets and ensure that they have not been damaged or show signs of cracking (10).

11 During reassembly, reattach the mounting brackets using new paper gaskets (11).

12 If storing, remember to ensure that the shim has been secured to the appropriate clamp to avoid loss (12). Then affix a label to remind you to refill with oil during fitment.

13 Reattach the horn earthing strap (13).

14 Fit new track rod ends (14).

New track rod ends may differ slightly from the originals. At the earliest opportunity, get your tyre specialist to check out and adjust the tracking of the car.

Heading for a complete brakedown

There are some things that one just shouldn't do. This might include jumping from an aeroplane without a parachute, swimming in shark infested waters, climbing Ben Nevis during Easter, or replacing the seals in a brake calliper. Disc brakes are difficult to renovate, all the more so because the calliper should never be split. Only the pistons (which rust) and the seals (as fragile as butterfly wings) can be replaced.

The seals are notoriously difficult to replace without splitting the calliper. Now I don't know why the calipers shouldn't be split, but there must be a significant reason because I have never found a manual that explains how to do the job. There is clearly something mystical about the process; perhaps restoration is only possible following a powerful incantation to that omnipotent god of car restorers known as "SuuParGlu".

What I do know is that there are some parts, notably a crush washer, which sits between the two halves of the calliper, that remain suspiciously unavailable from any source. This is deliberate; if you can't buy parts you can't do the job. Bearing in mind how important your brakes are, perhaps it's best to bow down to the superior wisdom and benevolence of "SuuParGlu" and his descendent on Earth, "SuuParGlu III".

Front Axle Assembly

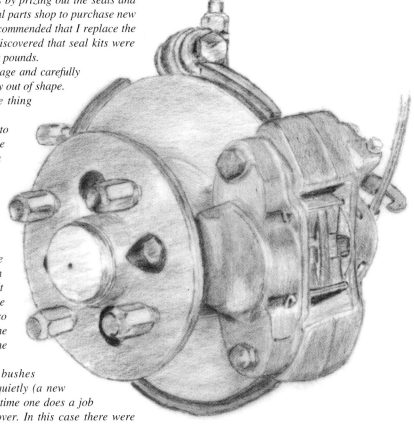

"SuuParGlu" has no respect for the ignorant. In my young and naive days this mercurial God watched over me while I attempted restoration of my own brake calipers. I started the process by prizing out the seals and removing the pistons. Then I went to the local parts shop to purchase new pistons and seal kits. Even the parts man recommended that I replace the calipers, but I was adamant; even when I discovered that seal kits were eight pounds each. A calliper only cost thirty pounds.

I got back home, whizzed down to the garage and carefully lined up the seal before bending it completely out of shape. I cursed, I tore it out, then I did the same thing again with the other seal.

You'd think I'd learn, but no, I went back to the shop, got another pair of seals, came home and did the same again. I had to get a lift to work every day for a week until I had a chance to buy new calipers. To this day I have one perfect calliper seal sitting on a shelf in the garage. I can feel "SuuParGlu" willing me to use it now.

And it's not just the callipers that can cause distress. Years ago, I had to replace the hub bearings, king pins and bushes on the Midget. Kath and I had just bought a rabbit hutch, by which I mean our first house. Like most first timers, we didn't have a garage, so we drove over to my parents and I spent the day in their garage working until late in the evening.

Finally, the king pins were fitted, the bushes replaced and the new hub bearings spun quietly (a new sound to my ears). Isn't it funny how every time one does a job like this, there are always some bolts left over. In this case there were eight of the things. I didn't think too much about it because I had replaced a lot of the old rusty bolts and nothing seemed loose.

It was only when Kath and I drove home that I realised that the eight bolts locked the hub and the brake disc together - and I only realised it as I braked for a junction. The discs stopped turning, the wheels, and the car hurtled on.

It's amazing how ineffectual a Midget handbrake can be when one approaches a red light.

Some History:
Stub Axle & Front Brakes

The front stub axle, as found on the Austin A30/A35 range changed little over the course of its life, being updated only to include necessary improvements to steering, brakes or wheels. The first revision, being to the steering arms at HAN5 4800, was perhaps due to the originals not being up to the job in hand.

The front stub axle was not handed, fitting either side of the car. The trend continued even when the stub axles were revised at HAN5 6433. This revised stub axle set was fitted intermittently at first on a number of Sprites, as listed in the parts book at the time, presumably while stocks of the early version were depleted.

Lower wishbone pans were revised and uprated at HAN5 27912. Up to that point, anti roll bar kits with 5/8in and 11/16in diameter bars had been offered as Special Tuning options (from the Competitions Department at Abingdon). A more sedate and road friendly version incorporating a 9/16in bar was now offered as an optional extra. When fitted, handed wishbone pans were used. The ARB fitting holes were drilled only on the forward facing part of the wishbone pan. Eventually somebody suffered from a bright idea because the handed versions were replaced by a single pan which could be used on the left or right of the car.

Drum brakes were fitted to HAN6 24731 / GAN1 16183, with disc brakes then being fitted from HAN7 24732 / GAN2 16184 on. Following fitment of the discs, no further changes were made to the front brakes throughout the life of the car.

The stub axle was revised again at HAN7 24732 / GAN2 16184, now handed (left and right), the assemblies supporting the disc brake calipers. New hubs were fitted at the time.

Wire wheels (including the appropriate hubs) were available from HAN7 29812 / GAN2 16780, although a conversion had been available from the early days if ordered from the Healey Motor Company.

Steering arms were again revised at HAN7 28368 / GAN2 18472. Used in pairs these new arms can be fitted retrospectively to earlier Sprites.

Wire wheel hub nuts came in two types, two eared (mostly UK market) or octagonal spinners (where safety legislation demanded it). These hub nuts were revised at HAN8 38829 / GAN3 25788.

Hub nuts were revised again at an unspecified point during Sprite IV / Midget III production to cater for a coarse thread. The change points are a little confused because part numbers of the hubs conflict between Sprite II / Midget I and Sprite IV / Midget III parts books. Tip; measuring the number of threads per inch (tpi) on the original hubs will help to ascertain your requirements if ordering hub nuts or new hubs.

The road springs were revised for all markets (except USA) from HAN8 60260. In the USA they were changed from HAN8 58381.

Steering arms were revised again at GAN5 114643, when the Triumph Spitfire rack was fitted, remaining unchanged to the end of Midget production.

Road springs were revised again mid way through 1977 model year 1500 production at GAN6 171478.

Shock absorbers, mounted over the coil spring, remained unchanged all the way through production and, despite unfeeling protests, are probably still the best things to fit.

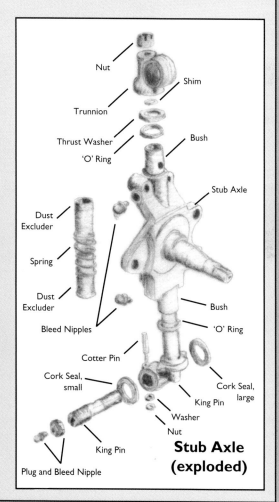

Nut
Shim
Trunnion
Thrust Washer
'O' Ring
Bush
Stub Axle
Dust Excluder
Spring
Dust Excluder
Bleed Nipples
Bush
'O' Ring
Cotter Pin
Cork Seal, small
Cork Seal, large
King Pin
Washer
Nut
King Pin
Plug and Bleed Nipple

Stub Axle (exploded)

Front Suspension Assembly (exploded)

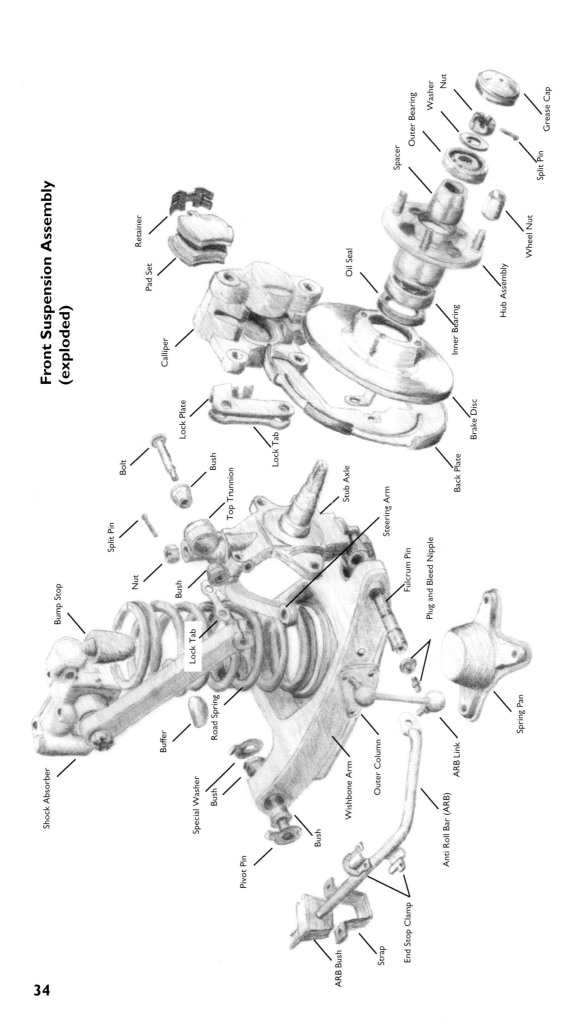

Retainer

Pad Set

Calliper

Lock Plate

Bolt

Bush

Lock Tab

Split Pin

Nut

Top Trunnion

Bush

Bump Stop

Lock Tab

Shock Absorber

Buffer

Road Spring

Special Washer

Bush

Pivot Pin

Bush

Wishbone Arm

Outer Column

Anti Roll Bar (ARB)

ARB Bush

Strap

End Stop Clamp

ARB Link

Spring Pan

Plug and Bleed Nipple

Fulcrum Pin

Steering Arm

Stub Axle

Back Plate

Brake Disc

Inner Bearing

Hub Assembly

Oil Seal

Spacer

Outer Bearing

Washer

Nut

Grease Cap

Split Pin

Wheel Nut

The Front Axle Assembly

The front axle assembly includes the suspension, steering, wheel hub and braking components all in one. To make things easier for restoration, the whole lot is held in place at only three points - where the damper meets the top trunnion, and at the two inner fulcrum pins which join the wishbone arm to the chassis.

If you are rebuilding or reshelling the car, you'll want to dismantle the whole unit anyway - and believe me, it's best to do the job on a work bench. It's a nicely designed unit, based on a suspension developed by BMC engineers and first used on the MG Y type saloon a generation before the Sprite. Variations also appeared on the MGA and MGB.

The only drawback is that the suspension requires the continuous maintenance of a grease gun, without which the front suspension will often start to show signs of wear after only a short distance - read less than 10, 000 miles!

Be Prepared

Units that have worn badly or have not been touched for some time will prove really difficult to deal with. The assembly suffers terribly if neglected - a good dose of winter road salt causes seized nuts, broken split pins and painful trunnions! Start disassembly by dousing everything with some penetrating oil.

During reassembly use anti-seize lube, which will make the job much easier to do the next time.

Stub Axle, King Pin and Wishbone Assembly

Apart from the constant need for greasing, the most annoying aspect of the whole axle assembly is that one cannot separate the king pin from the stub axle until the whole unit has been dismantled. Why, because the back plate stops the stub from separating away from the king pin - and the back plate can't be unbolted until the hub has been removed. Despite twenty years of production, warranty work and service repair, nobody ever thought to resolve that one.

Normally any rebuild guide will describe and examine each part of the assembly as a separate entity. The reality is that to undertake any restoration to the hub or stub axle requires a complete dismantling process. **It's for this reason that I have written the following examination and rebuild case study to include the complete axle assembly.**

Note: I couldn't undo one of the fulcrum pins during dismantling, quite a common problem. Once on the bench, one thing became apparent straight away - the wishbone had actually cracked, explaining why the fulcrum pin had locked itself into position. The answer was to cut the wishbone off and replace with a new unit. This may seem drastic, but with an un-repairable pan, its the only option.

Examination and Reassembly

The core of the unit is the stub axle and king pin. The king pin is prone to wear and needs to be replaced along with the bushes that fit inside the stub axle.

You could buy a kit which includes the king pin, bushes, cork seals (which fit in position between the king pin and the wishbone pan), shims (needed to adjust the trunnion) and the rubber 'O' rings used to keep the grease in. Many of the individual parts are difficult to buy on their own - so a kit is good value.

However, the king pin bushes must be pressed carefully into position and then reamed to allow a good fit. This is a problem, you will need a king pin reamer which costs a great deal of money (many places will hire them out), or a good workshop may fit and ream the bushes for you - which is frankly the easy option.

If you don't want to do that, then the alternative is an exchange stub axle. Exchange units will be fitted with a new king pin, cotter pin, upper and lower 'O' rings, shims and a new trunnion nut. If you hunt around you might get the assembly complete with trunnion (so no adjustment will be necessary). Even complete units with the wishbone pan and fulcrum pin fitted are available.

Case Study:
Front Suspension Renovation
Safe Road Spring Removal
There are various methods of removing the stub axle assembly and the key to it is to remove the spring first. This takes all of the tension out of the system and to do it safely you need a block of wood, two lengths of threaded rod or two bolts (at least 8 cm long) and some nuts.

1. With the car on axle stands, remove the road wheel.

   With the suspension dangling, the shock absorber arm is pressed against its rebound buffer.

2. Jack up the suspension using a jack under the king pin (1) until the shock absorber arm has lifted up about 3 or 4cm from the buffer (2). Place the block of wood between the shock absorber arm and the chassis (arrowed). Remove the jack.

   The wood block locks the wishbone arm almost parallel to the ground, allowing easy spring removal.

3. The bottom of the spring locates into a pan, held in by four bolts. Remove two opposite bolts, and replace with the long bolts (3). Fit the nuts finger tight (4), then remove the other two bolts.

4. Now a bit at a time, undo the two long bolts. Gradually, the spring pan is lowered down, all the tension is removed from the spring, allowing its safe removal (5).

Though time consuming, this method of spring removal is very safe, though not spectacular.

Removing the Stub Assembly
1. Remove (or cut through) the brake hose, carefully collecting waste brake fluid. Then separate the steering arm from the rack by undoing the track rod end.

2. Disconnect the anti-roll bar link (if fitted).

3. Undo (but don't remove) the top trunnion bolt (6) which secures the damper arm to the trunnion.

general view of the stub axle assembly

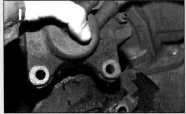

5. Undo the two inner fulcrum pins (7), prise out the outer bushes, and, with some assistance the wishbone will drop out.

   At this point the assembly will be hanging by the trunnion.

6. Simply slide the unit off of the shock absorber arm. The unit is quite heavy, so take care when releasing it from the trunnion.

Hey presto, one front stub axle assembly, removed, ready to clean and strip.

On the Bench
Remove all of the excess dirt and grease. In fact usually there isn't much grease - which is why it's now on the bench. Make a mental note to grease the steering and suspension at least every three thousand miles, and then you won't have to do this again...well, not for a long time anyway.

Some owners will tell you that the stub axle should be greased every weekend without fail, but these are generally very sad people with nothing better to do

Stub Axle Disassembly
1. Remove the top trunnion and shims, thrust washer and 'O' ring (8).

   The trunnion generally does not want to move, which explains why stub axle exchanges sometimes come with the trunnion fitted, it is all for your benefit. Why not try the application of some heat, penetrating fluid, a chisel, some variation of hub puller vice and club hammer- choose your weapon.

2. Undo the calliper bolts (9) to remove the hose clamp and calliper (10).

3. Knock out the hub grease cap and undo the retaining nut. Using a hub puller, carefully remove the hub (11) and brake disc assembly as one unit (12).

4. Remove the brake backplate which is held in position by one bolt (13).

5. The stub axle can now be withdrawn from the king pin and put to one side.

6. Now you should have just the king pin and wishbone. Separating the king pin from the arm is a simple task of removing the fulcrum pin.

The pin is usually seized into position and will often prove difficult to remove, especially since you'll probably not have a screwdriver blade big enough to get a good grip. Good luck. It might pay to make a tool which incorporates a wide blade suitable for unscrewing the fulcrum pin. There again, it might not...

7. Methodically clean all components and examine for wear (assuming any components have survived the dismantling process...or the last few thousand miles without grease).

One of the things I noticed during dismantling, was the absence of the 'O' ring which should be fitted under the top trunnion. This omission does, of course, help the ingress of water and damages the unit and I'm not in any way assuming that the stub axle restorer had intended to leave it out when he sold them...

King Pin Reassembly

1 Fit a new 'O' Ring into the base of the stub axle (14) - note that it is has a circular cross section, the upper seal (which fits under the trunnion) has a square cross section.

2 Locate the dust tube and spring assembly (15 & 16). Smear some water repellent grease (i.e. Duckhams Keenol) onto the kingpin and then fit into the stub axle.

Ensure that the lugs at the base of the king pin seat correctly (17), they limit the turning circle of the assembly, stopping damage to the road wheels and wheel arches as well as stopping you from having an unfair advantage while trying to park in any London street.

3 Fit the upper 'O' ring, thrust washer, shims and top trunnion. This is best done with the assembly mounted in a vice. Firstly put on some of the shims (say 3 off 0.003in or 0.009in), fit the trunnion and rubber seal and, using the old nut (if nyloc type) tighten down the trunnion (18).

If the assembly locks add more shims. If the assembly is loose and the stub can be felt to move up and down on the king pin, remove some shims. When there is slight resistance you've got it about right.

Once you're sure you've got it right lock the nut into position with a split pin (castellated nuts) or fit a new nyloc nut.

Early Front Drum
Brake Assembly (exploded)

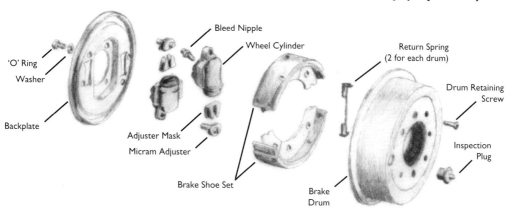

'O' Ring

Washer

Backplate

Bleed Nipple

Wheel Cylinder

Adjuster Mask

Micram Adjuster

Brake Shoe Set

Return Spring
(2 for each drum)

Drum Retaining
Screw

Inspection
Plug

Brake
Drum

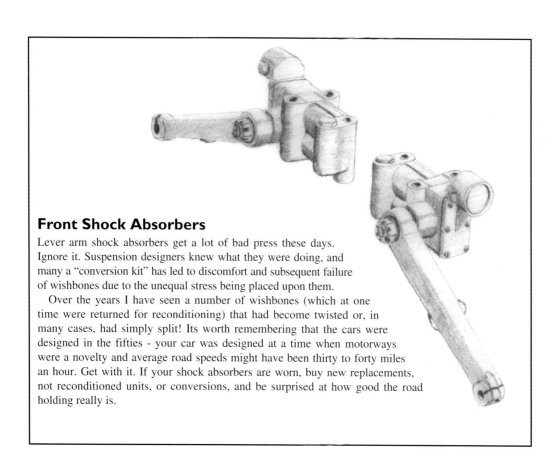

Front Shock Absorbers

Lever arm shock absorbers get a lot of bad press these days.
Ignore it. Suspension designers knew what they were doing, and
many a "conversion kit" has led to discomfort and subsequent failure
of wishbones due to the unequal stress being placed upon them.

Over the years I have seen a number of wishbones (which at one
time were returned for reconditioning) that had become twisted or, in
many cases, had simply split! Its worth remembering that the cars were
designed in the fifties - your car was designed at a time when motorways
were a novelty and average road speeds might have been thirty to forty miles
an hour. Get with it. If your shock absorbers are worn, buy new replacements,
not reconditioned units, or conversions, and be surprised at how good the road
holding really is.

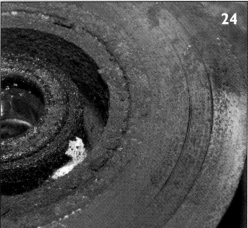

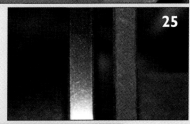

Front Brakes

1   Pull out and discard the old retaining pins (21). It really is sad that people use such a cheap consumable component twice - especially when the pads that are held in place by the pins are so important.

2   Allow the spring plate to fly across the room.

3   Pull out the brake pads and anti-squeal shims. You can see from the picture (22) how worn the pads can get. (Yes that is a pad on the left, not a pancake). Replace if necessary, especially if worn or showing signs of oil contamination.

4. Examine the callipers for signs of wear or leakage - especially around the calliper seals (23). The pistons often suffer from corrosion and if badly damaged, will require replacement.

If the pistons are rusted, they will almost certainly damage the seals when pressed back into the calliper to allow fitment of new pads. (I would like to take the opportunity or referring you back to my remarks regarding replacement at the beginning of this section).

Wheel Hub

1   The hub and disc are attached by four bolts visible on the outside face of the hub. Remove the bolts (26) and separate the brake disc and hub using a hub puller.

It's not the ideal way, because there is always the chance that the disc might warp or shatter. To be honest though, most Midget brake discs seem to look like a cross section of the Alps (24). Mine were so worn out that in places they were down to only two thirds original thickness (25).

It helps to gently apply pressure with the hub puller and then tap the hub (not the disc) with a lead hammer, tighten up the puller again and tap, tighten up... and so on. Because the pressure is applied more gently the risk of damage is greatly reduced if not eradicated.

Eventually the two parts separate. Sometimes...

2   If the disc is scored it should be machined.

In practice the discs, like the rear drums, are freely available as new items. It's cheaper and less time consuming to replace them.

Replacement means that the thickness of the discs are retained. Thicker discs dissipate more heat which reduces brake fade.

3 Prise out the oil seal from the inner face of the hub (27).

4 Drift out the outer bearing using a suitable wooden drift (28).

5 Remove the spacer and then drift out the inner bearing.

   Very often the inner races knock out, leaving the outer races in-situ. Carefully knock out the remaining outer race.

TIP Don't damage the spacer which sits between the bearings. It is of vital importance and accurately spaces the outer and inner bearings. If this is damaged, shortened or squashed then the bearings will never sit square and you will be plagued forever after with fast wearing wheel bearings requiring replacement on a regular basis.

6 Clean and examine all components for wear and replace damaged or worn parts as necessary. In fact, since you've pulled it apart, just replace the bearings anyway.

Wheel Hub Reassembly

1 Fit the new outer bearing first. One side of the bearing should be marked THRUST and this face should be fitted inmost.

   The old outer race can be used to drift the bearing in part of the way (29) - but be careful not to wedge it inside the hub. To finish the job off, a piece of copper pipe, two or three inches long, flattened and then shaped at one end, makes an ideal drift (30). Gently tapping around the outer race of the bearing slowly pushes it home without damage.

2 Drop the spacer into position and pack the hub with grease (31).

3 Fit a new inner bearing. Again ensure that the face marked Thrust faces inwards.

   Once the inner bearing has been positioned correctly, the spacer should be held in position between the two bearings but without the assembly being locked solid.

4 Finally refit the oil seal, felt side outermost (32). Cautiously drift into place using one of the old outer races.

Do not attempt to push home one side before the other. The seal will simply collapse unless equal pressure is applied all round.

5 Prior to fitment onto the stub axle, the felt seal should be oiled (33).

Stub Axle Reassembly
New brake discs are often coated in grease to stop them rusting. It seems obvious to surprisingly few people that all of the grease should be removed (34).

My old boss used regularly to go a funny shade of purple if ever the words "Frenchman" and "brake discs" were used in the same sentence. A protracted argument had developed one day between him and a Gallic visitor who was requesting a refund after his brake pads had become contaminated with grease following the fitment of new discs. These things are sold swimming in grease to protect them against rust, yet the customer apparently failed to notice the slippery, sticky substance during fitting and demanded compensation.

Clearly, failure to think could invalidate your lifetime warranty for living....

Guard against future misery, use anti-seize grease on all of the bolts and nuts, on the hub (where it comes in contact with the disc - without contaminating the braking surface) and so on.

1 Fit the wheel studs, which need to be pressed into position (35).

The wheel studs fit in the assembly at a slight angle. Over-tightening the wheel nuts leads to twisting and, ultimately they can snap. If the studs are removed for any reason, why not replace them. These studs (36) became deformed due to over-tightening.

2 Attach the disc to the hub. Don't forget to fit those high tensile steel bolts (mild steel just won't do).

3 Refit the brake disc back plate to the stub axle using a new shakeproof washer and bolt (37).

4 Drop the hub assembly onto the stub axle. Then fit the special washer (38) and nut (39).

5 The hub nut has to be torqued down to between 40 and 45ft / lbs before turning the nut back to the nearest split pin hole.

Do this by either mounting the assembly into a stout vice and torquing the nut down, or, wait until the stub is mounted back into position on the car.

6 Finally, fit a new split pin and smear liberally with grease (40) before refitting the grease cap (41).

Note: The disc hub bolts also are best left until the assembly is mounted in the car, because it's easier to get someone to hold their foot on the brake, locking the assembly solid while you tighten the bolts, rather than trying to stop the hub spinning round while on the work bench.

Attach a label to the assembly reminding you to torque the hub bolts (42). If you are rebuilding a car over a number of years you will almost certainly forget what needs doing unless you keep notes close to hand.

8 Attach the brake calliper. If, while you're tightening the bolts you notice that the disc has locked solid you have probably forgotten to attach the hose clamp. Remove the bolts, fit the hose, hose clamp and lock tab then refit the bolts (45 to 50ft / lbs) and apologise to yourself like I did.

Never forget to fit a new lock tab (43). As we all know, if a lock tab is fitted the bolts will seize solid and be unremovable, but without one the bolts will quickly unwind and fall out!

9 Refit the steering arm using a new lock tab (44).

10 Finally fit new brake pads, anti-squeal shims, retaining springs and split pins (45).

Ensure that the split pins are secured properly as shown here (46).

11 And that's about it really...

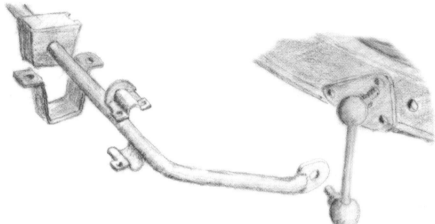

Anti-Roll Bar

More properly called a torsion bar, the anti roll bar is a simple device designed to limit body roll. The device is attached firmly to the body of the car (in this case at two points under the H Frame) and links the two stub axle assemblies. As you drive into a bend the body begins to roll due to the action of centrifugal force against the anchor-like effect of the tyres clinging on for dear life. The anti-roll bar twists in opposite directions as the body starts to roll.

What is happening here is that the bar is taking the strain placed upon it from one side of the car and applying it to the other side. As one side of the suspension compresses, the bar forcibly limits the decompressing action on the opposite side of the car. The result is that body roll is limited. The harder you corner, the greater the amount of force transferred from one stub axle to the other. Be warned however, as you reduce body roll you increase the chances that the front end will eventually break away from the road surface.

Early cars only had ARBs fitted as an option, and if you've never had one fitted to a Midget you might not worry about it. If you fit one you might still think nothing much of it, except that maybe the old speedo starts creeping up a bit. Leave it a couple of weeks and then take the bar off again - and you'll notice the difference on the first bend you come to.

The wishbones on early cars had no extra holes drilled to support the ARB, unless it was supplied as an option. Later cars had handed wishbones with holes drilled on the front facing side of each wishbone arm. Later still, one part number got superseded to the other, and a universal pan was supplied with holes at the front and rear, so that it could fit either side.

The most worthwhile suspension improvement for any Sprite or Midget, it's easy to fit and offers no adverse effect, so long as you stick to the standard road bar. For racing people there are thicker bars available, but be warned that there is a comfort cost - and maybe even long term damage could occur by uprating the ARB.

The bigger (thicker) bars are very stiff, being designed for good roads and smooth race tracks. Well it's not every day you get to drive on a race track, and I don't know about other countries but Britain does not have an abundance of good road surfaces. The thicker bars are very inflexible and cause considerable jarring. Undoubtedly it becomes more uncomfortable, with the vehicle more unpleasant to drive, and far more prone to "skipping" when hitting bad potholes (which are not infrequent). Without a doubt the worse the jarring becomes, the greater the strain on the suspension and with it comes more rapid wear. They can tell you what they like, but it doesn't take a rocket ship scientist to realise that there is no gain without pain.

1   The ARB is attached to the front face of the wishbone arm via a link which incorporates a rubber bush at each end. These wear and often require replacement after a number of bends. The links are handed left and right.

2   The ARB is attached firmly to the H Frame via rubber bushes and stiff brackets. The standard bar uses a clamp to retain its position against the rubber bushes during cornering. The correct brackets don't seem to be available for the larger diameter bars.

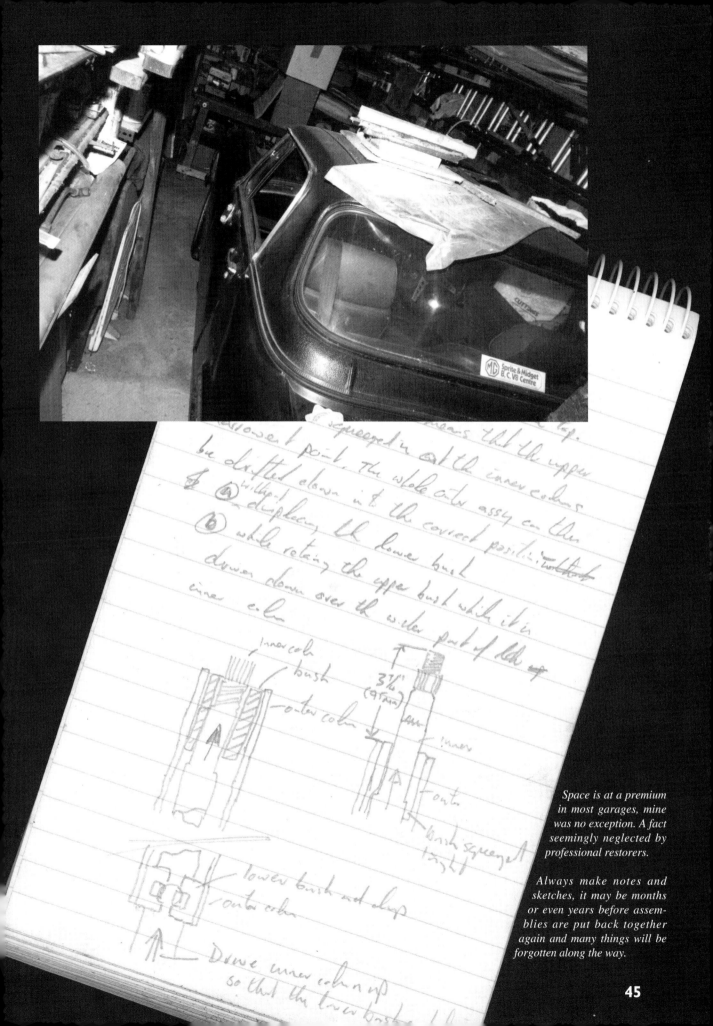

Space is at a premium in most garages, mine was no exception. A fact seemingly neglected by professional restorers.

Always make notes and sketches, it may be months or even years before assemblies are put back together again and many things will be forgotten along the way.

Aggravated circlip syndrome

I'm not an adept mechanic but I'm more or less proficient at most jobs. It is the simple jobs however, that cause me most trouble. Circlips for example, seemingly innocent and harmless, have given me hours of anguish, with time spent kneeling on the ground searching dark recesses for escapees or, in two sad and pathetic cases, a visit to hospital.

On one occasion I had spent a few days getting nowhere with some other annoying problem and by the time it came to working on my car, I was already in a "high old state". I had simply to replace a wheel cylinder but its removal caused the brake pipe to shear, so I had to visit the local shop for a replacement and I was running out of time and patience. As I fitted the new cylinder I found that the circlip which held it in position just would not fit.

Rear Suspension, Brakes Rear Axle and Propshaft

Eventually, and knowing that all tools have multiple uses, I found a broad bladed screw driver, wedged the blade against the circlip and pushed hard. The circlip started to go home when suddenly, and without warning it flew across the garage. The screwdriver slipped, my thumb smashed against the brake back plate ripping my thumbnail half out - though at the time I was too angry to feel anything.

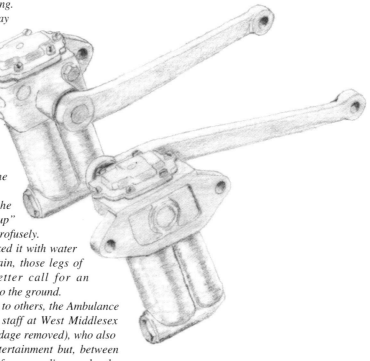

My mental state would have got me a one way ticket to the nearest institution and I threw down the screwdriver unable to think of any worthwhile blasphemies to utter. I looked dumb-struck at my thumb and found that my whole hand was shaking uncontrollably. I stomped up to the house where I met my mother in the kitchen. Strangely I could still feel no pain, yet my hand continued to vibrate as if being electrocuted.

"What's up dear, having some trouble" she murmured, busily cutting vegetables at the sink.

"Look..." I said. "Look at this". I held the trembling thumb aloft. "I need to get it cleaned up" I ranted. By now the greasy digit was bleeding profusely.

Mum, patient as ever, got out the Dettol, mixed it with water in a bowl, and I put my thumb in. Ahh..the pain, those legs of jelly, my tongue felt like a balloon. "Better call for an Ambulance!" I said sinking none too delicately to the ground.

I suppose it must be my lot in life to bring joy to others, the Ambulance driver suffered near hysteria, as did the duty staff at West Middlesex A&E. I saw my G.P. soon after (to have the bandage removed), who also believed my story to be a matter of joyous entertainment but, between sobs of laughter, explained that there are a lot of nerve endings under the thumb.

You'd think I'd learn, but no. Some years later I was refitting a sprocket onto a motorcycle wheel. The circlip holding the sprocket in place was one of the largest I'd ever seen and I couldn't get circlip pliers big enough to open the clip. There I was, knee on the bench holding the wheel steady while I grappled with some broad bladed screwdrivers (see a pattern emerging here?) when the inevitable happened. My hand slipped, I caught the edge of the sprocket and my knuckle joint burst asunder.

I looked at my finger and the blood splattered wheel. My finger began to shake and I felt a little hot. I'd been here before. I took a deep breath and brought some inner calmness to bear. I'd avoid the Dettol this time.

I walked calmly up to the house, found Kath and showed her my bloody finger with the exposed knuckle joint waving at her.

"Do you think this needs a plaster?" I asked. "Ohh!, Hospital I think dear!" she said, in a knowing sort of way.

Here we go again.

Some History:
Rear Suspension & Rear Axle

When the Sprite was introduced its rear suspension consisted of a live rear axle, slung beneath the bodyshell on the end of a pair of quarter-elliptic springs. The axle ratio was 4.222:1 (using 9 x 32 teeth in the differential). To hold its position and stop undue flexing, the axle movement was further limited by the inclusion of a pair of radius arms, mounted above the springs. Mounted inboard lever arm shock absorbers helped to make the little car a lot of fun over short to medium distances.

Originally taking only steel disc wheels, wire wheel conversions became available as an option from the Donald Healey Motor Company.

The rear axle was revised from HAN5 4333 / GAN1 101. Newer design brake shoes were used from HAN6 12867 / GAN1 7897 onwards.

The axle was revised again at HAN6 20545 / GAN1 13555 *. Brake back plates were revised to fit the new axle. Brake shoes and wheel cylinders were also replaced, with double acting wheel cylinders now being fitted.

A variation to the new axle allowed fitment of wire wheels from HAN6 20812 / GAN2 16790, with a modified differential being fitted from HAN6 24732 / GAN1 16184 - retaining the original ratio.

The double acting wheel cylinders and brake shoes were again revised at HAN7 24732 / GAN2 16184 with the back plates being revised again at HAN7 26913 / GAN2 17835.

When the Sprite Mk III / Midget Mk II arrived, revisions to the rear boot floor (including the fitment of extended chassis legs), allowed for the inclusion of semi-elliptic springs. A revised axle, slung centrally over the springs, did away with the need for radius arms. Shock absorbers, appropriately revised, were moved above the assembly and mounted inside the gusset panels of the wheel arches.

Even the propshaft got revised at HAN8 52665 / GAN3 40086. Since nobody ever bothered greasing them, the revision incorporated non-greaseable universal joints.

The axle ratio was revised to 3.90:1 at HAN9 77591 / GAN4 66226. The carrier assembly remained unchanged, though the half shafts were altered to suit the new requirements.

The propshaft was revised again at some unspecified point during the run of HAN9 / GAN4 models.

No other changes occurred until the introduction of the 1500 models, when the heavier car received new back plates, shoes and more powerful wheel cylinders to assist in dealing with the extra momentum caused by the black bumpers.

To cater for the extra weight and increased ride height, the springs were uprated for the 1500 models. Rebound straps were revised as appropriate. The springs themselves did not account for all of the ride height increase, plates welded to the spring mount area made a difference. Some unscrupulous dealers have tended to sell 1500 springs to 1275 owners leading to an unsightly raised rear end.

The propshaft was altered again, corresponding to the new gearbox fitted with the introduction of the Midget 1500 model.

The shock absorber links were altered at GAN6 157672. Then, at GAN6 182001, the perfectly efficient and simple hand-braking mechanism was replaced by several bolts, some floppy rubberised material and a complex arrangement of cables and clamps which probably saved the company a couple of new pence - but took five times longer to fit...why?

The axle ratio was revised again at GAN6 200001 to a ratio of 3.7:1, something worth remembering if you ever want to make your 1275 a bit more long legged because the later differential will fit the earlier cars.

* Note: *Some stocks of the older axle and appropriate brake fittings found its way onto the following Sprites:- HAN6 20580, 20582, 20583, 20595, 20596, 20692 to 96, 20741 to 57, 20760 and 20788 to 92 inclusive.*

Rear Axle and Rear Suspension Assembly

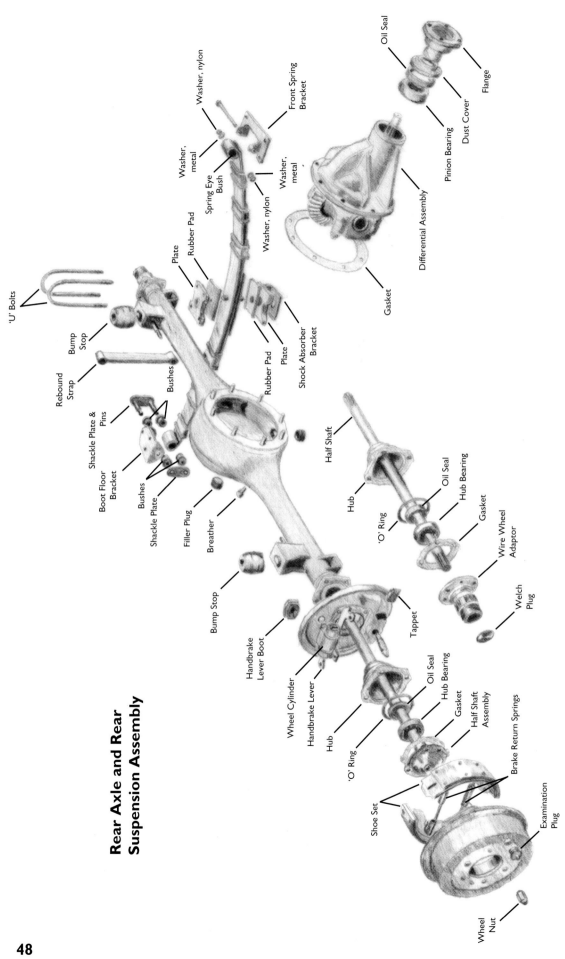

'U' Bolts

Washer, nylon

Front Spring Bracket

Washer, metal

Spring Eye Bush

Washer, metal

Washer, nylon

Oil Seal

Flange

Dust Cover

Pinion Bearing

Differential Assembly

Gasket

Plate

Rubber Pad

Rubber Pad

Plate

Shock Absorber Bracket

Rebound Strap

Bump Stop

Bushes

Shackle Plate & Pins

Boot Floor Bracket

Bushes

Shackle Plate

Filler Plug

Breather

Bump Stop

Half Shaft

Hub

Oil Seal

Hub Bearing

Gasket

'O' Ring

Wire Wheel Adaptor

Welch Plug

Handbrake Lever Boot

Wheel Cylinder

Handbrake Lever

Hub

'O' Ring

Tappet

Oil Seal

Hub Bearing

Gasket

Half Shaft Assembly

Brake Return Springs

Shoe Set

Examination Plug

Wheel Nut

Early Handbrake Operating Mechanism

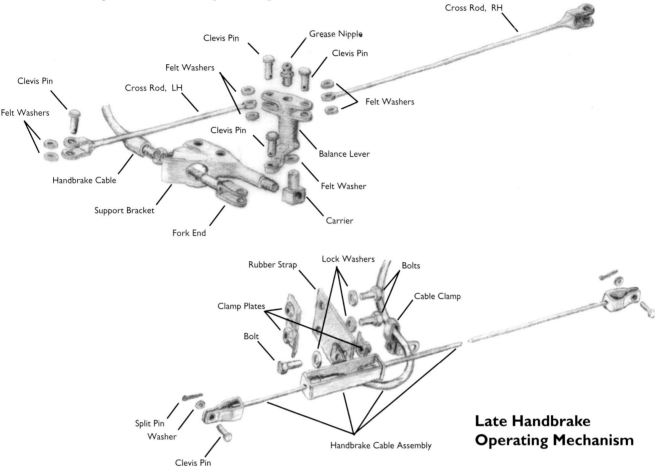

Clevis Pin
Grease Nipple
Clevis Pin
Felt Washers
Cross Rod, RH
Clevis Pin
Cross Rod, LH
Felt Washers
Felt Washers
Clevis Pin
Balance Lever
Handbrake Cable
Felt Washer
Support Bracket
Carrier
Fork End

Rubber Strap
Lock Washers
Bolts
Clamp Plates
Cable Clamp
Bolt
Late Handbrake Operating Mechanism
Split Pin
Washer
Handbrake Cable Assembly
Clevis Pin

A Few Tips About Rear Suspension and Rear Axle Assemblies

Seized bolts: Like many other old suspension systems, Sprites and Midgets suffer from seized bolts, making it difficult to dismantle the suspension assembly. Begin the removal procedure the night before you intend to start work by spraying the nuts and bolts with a good penetrating lubricant.

When you do attack the bolts try doing them up a bit. Often, the rusty seal can be broken without damage to that part of the bolt head needed to release it. Then, slowly and by small amounts begin to unscrew the bolt, tightening it up again by degrees to relax and clear the threads. If necessary, apply a bit more oil and retire to a good book for a while.

During reassembly, the application of some grease on all of the nuts and bolts makes it easier to restore the suspension the second time around - even, as I found, after 75,000 miles of all weather driving.

Spring eye bushes are frequently worn and seized, requiring replacement. In fact, it is the bush that is likely to squeak noisily. To test the hypothesis, spray some WD40 into the bush area and leave it to penetrate. If the spring still squeaks, well, at least you know its not the bush.

Though telescopic conversion kits are available the original set up is still hard to beat. If your old shock absorbers are worn, buy new replacements, not reconditioned. New lever arms are readily available, so use them and be surprised at how efficient they really are, while being pleasantly pleased at the high level of comfort offered. Be kind to your back, it has to last you a lifetime.

Rattling Rear Axles. If, with the hood down, you notice that the rear axle is rattling, don't be too alarmed. Have a good look at the handbrake crossrods, chances are the felt washers are worn or missing, causing alarming, but safe rattles.

Finally, if your rear axle suddenly sounds like it is wearing out make sure that the spare wheel is in the boot and clamped into position. Unsecured or missing spare wheels allow the boot floor to vibrate, often sounding like a whining axle.

Case Study:
Rear Suspension

It all sounds so simple to do, but with seized nuts and bolts, limited access behind the seats, and dirty gritty components, accessed only from below, this is one of the most unpleasant and intolerable jobs on any Sprite or Midget.

The rear suspension commonly squeals and groans (due to worn interleaves or bushes) and every nut, bolt and bush is usually seized solid. Start this job the day before by spraying everything with penetrating fluid.

Rear Shock Absorbers

Simply secured by two bolts to the side gussets, the shock absorbers are linked to the rear axle by a short link rod with integral rubber bushes. As mentioned previously, keep your car friendly and original by refitting the lever arm shock absorbers designed for car.

1   Disconnect link rod from axle at "A" (1).

2   Undo the bolts attaching the shock absorber to the gusset (2).

Dropping The Axle Assembly...

The axle is supported by the rebound straps and you can either leave it hanging by removing one spring at a time, or support the axle, undo the rebound straps, shock absorber links and both springs and pull out the whole assembly complete with propshaft. The latter way is macho, quite neat but otherwise unwieldy - although by leaving the wheels attached you could drop the axle/spring assembly and roll it out from under the car in a nonchalant manner.

Remember to drain the gearbox oil before removing the propshaft!

...(or) Removing Springs Only

1   Undo the "U" bolts shown here (3).

2   Undo and remove the rear shackles (4).

3   Let the spring drop then undo the front shackle plate (5). Two bolts are accessed from behind the seats, and two from below the car.

4   Clean springs and examine for broken leaves and missing clamps. Worn bushes (6) can be replaced but damaged or weak springs should be discarded and replaced as a pair.

Also replace the springs if you know that the car is sagging at the rear. This is obvious if, when viewed from the side, the sills are running downwards towards the rear of the car.

Removing a spring eye bush

Can't get the bushes out? This works!

1. Heat the bush with a blow torch (7). The rubber melts and all of the inner section will simply push out (8), leaving the outer metal casing in situ. Smells a bit though...

2. With the spring locked in a vice, insert a saw blade through the eye and attach it to a saw, then cut a neat line, or two lines, through the outer casing of the bush (9 & 10) - but not through the spring itself please.

3. Chisel (or drift) the casing out. It will come out quite easily now. A bolt of appropriate diameter head makes a convenient drift (11).

Replacing a Spring Eye Bush

1. Put some anti-seize lubricant inside the spring eye.

2. Use a drift to press in the new spring eye bush. A vice is wonderfully supportive and helpful during this act of cruelty (12 & 13).

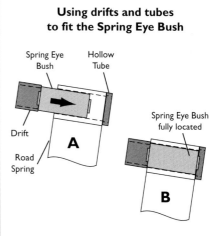

Using drifts and tubes to fit the Spring Eye Bush

A   Use a drift to push the bush into the spring eye.

B   The bush sits proud of the spring eye, so position a hollow tube allowing the bush to be pressed fully into place with the inner part of the bush sitting proud of the spring on both sides.

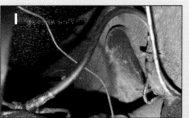

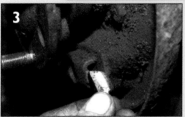

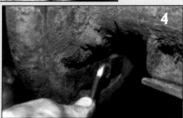

Case Study: Rear Axle

Removal

1 Drain the axle (before removal)

2 Disconnect or cut off the brake hose connecting the rear axle brake pipe to the gearbox tunnel pipe (1)

3 Disconnect the handbrake cable from the actuation balance lever assembly

4 Disconnect propshaft - but ensure that it is marked in some way so that it can be refitted correctly. There should be a nick in both the propshaft flange and differential flange, but this is often difficult to see (2).

TIP: Prior to disconnecting the unit from the rubber straps that secure it to the car it may prove worthwhile supporting the front of the diff on an axle stand to stop it from swinging down.

The axle is light enough to drop to the floor without too much effort, by releasing one strap at a time.

Once cleaned

1 Remove the brake pipes, but store them to use as templates for replacements.

2 Remove straps (if attached), bump stops, handbrake actuator, and so on.

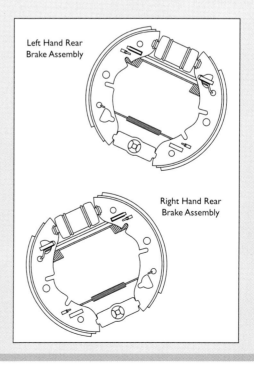

Left Hand Rear Brake Assembly

Right Hand Rear Brake Assembly

Dismantling the rear brakes

1 Remove the brake drum.

Two screws secure the brake drum, but expect real problems if the shoes have seized into position or if the drum itself is worn. If the car has been stored for a long time it is not uncommon for the brake shoes to have stuck to the drum, especially if the hand brake has been applied.

NEVER EVER store a car with the hand brake applied!

If the drums are seized be warned that whacking the cast drum may cause it to shatter (or worse still to fracture without appearing damaged). Try tapping with a wood block, or heating gently, to get them moving.

2 Examine the drums for wear to the friction surfaces. The drums should be free from scoring. If worn or scored it will be cheaper to buy new rather than skim the originals.

3 Note the position of the brake springs (see illustration on previous page). Then remove the shoes and discard. You may just as well buy and fit new replacements if you are going to the effort of restoring the rest of the assembly.

4 Remove the shoe adjusting tappets (3), which may just fall out in any case.

5 The adjusting wedge may prove difficult to release, but some penetrating fluid will help get things moving. Screw it into the brake backplate (4) to draw it out through the tappet case (5).

6 Remove the wheel cylinder by prizing off the circlip (6) and pulling it away from the back-plate.

7 Remove the dust cover (7) to allow removal of the handbrake lever - RH shown - (8).

Make a note of which lever is which since this will otherwise cause problems during reassembly.

Half shafts and Hub Assembly

1 A single screw secures the halfshaft (9). Withdraw, clean and label the halfshaft (10). Examine for distortion or wear to the splines.

2 Remove the hub assembly by unscrewing the hub nut (11) - you need a 1 7/8in socket. **Note that the right hand hub nut has a left hand thread, the left hand hub nut has a right hand thread.** This stops them spinning undone while the car is moving forward.

You can unscrew a left hand threaded nut with a right hand action and a four foot lever but, as I discovered, this is not a very sensible approach. Good axle casings, I later found, are hard to find, and once the thread is stripped there is no way of restoring the casing. It's then only good for cutting up (12).

3 Note that the back plates are handed, mark them accordingly prior to removal. Simply unbolt to remove them once the hub assembly has been withdrawn.

The backplates are stamped LH or RH, but usually rusted, these marks are revealed only by grit blasting. For reference, the left hand backplate is shown here (13).

Dismantling the Hub

1 A paper gasket is sandwiched between the hub and halfshaft. This should be removed to reveal an 'O' ring which fits into a groove on the face of the hub assembly.

Remove the gasket and 'O' ring (which needs to be prised out).

2 Remove the bearing (14) and oil seal (15).

3 Clean the hub (16), examine for damage and then reassemble using new components.

4 During fitting, the oil seal must not become warped. An old tin of primer made a perfect drift (17), though I have to say, an empty one works best!

5 The new bearing can be pressed in using the old bearing shell and a vice. The old bearing can be seen, with the new bearing already pressed into position (18).

6 Pack the assembly with grease, fit a new 'O' ring and gasket (19), and keep to one side.

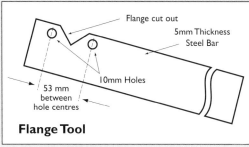

Flange Tool

Flange cut out

5mm Thickness
Steel Bar

10mm Holes

53 mm
between
hole centres

Fiddling with the differential

The rear differential unit is an expensive, rare and sought after unit

About all that you can do easily (and without accurate gauges and a variety of special tools) is to replace the flange oil seal which often wears.

The crown wheel, pinion and differential bearings have to be located accurately into position using shims selected by a careful process of measurement and mathematics. Variations between bearing thicknesses, damage to the collapsible spacers and other factors make "do it yourself" restoration difficult.

If it ain't broke, don't fix it.

Differential Pinion Seal

If the axle looks like an advert for Triumph Motorcycles (ie it's covered in filthy oil) then either the axle has started to leak (not unlikely - they rust) or the pinion oil seal has gone. The seals do just wear out, but it might also be a sign that the diff bearings are worn and this has caused damage to the seal. There is nothing you can do about the bearings (it needs specialist help) but you can replace the seal.

1 Make a flange tool to lock the differential drive flange into position (see illustration). Attach it to the flange and lock the end in a vice (20). Undo the nut with a long bar and socket.

2 Remove the nut and washer and withdraw the flange (21). Then remove, but do not lose the the dust cover (22) and prise out the old seal.

3 Fit new seal (23). Be careful not to damage the face of the seal during fitting by using a suitable drift, the hub nut socket works well.(24).

4 Lightly lubricate the lip of the seal (25) and refit the dust seal, followed by the flange, washer and nut. Now, using the special tool you made earlier, lock it up in the vice again.

5 Make sure its locked in really tight. I mean REALLY tight.

6 No, tighter still.

7 Now, using a big torque wrench, tighten the nut up to 135lbs/ft.

Once your up to about 110lbs/ft and the bench legs are lifting off the floor you'll understand why the vice needs to be REALLY tight.

Rear Axle Casing Preparation

To protect the differential against damage caused by the ingress of sand during grit blasting, I made up a wooden plate to cover the diff hole (26) filled the hub ends with plenty of rag and bound them with strong tape (27).

I also refitted the drain and filling plugs and plugged the vent hole with a small bolt.

Reassembly

1 Refit the brake back plates (remembering that they are handed).

2 Fit the lever assemblies using a new dust excluder in each backplate.

   The lever assembly is in two parts, connected by a pin. The longer, straighter arm extends under the wheel cylinder. The shorter dog leg sits above the straight arm and feeds through the backplate. The right hand backplate and assembly is shown here (28)

3 Fit the wheel cylinder by holding it against the backplate and fitting the circlip. See "Using a circlip tool" overleaf.

   Don't forget to fit a new gasket under the wheel cylinder (29). What do you mean there wasn't one there to start with - there should have been!

   Wheel cylinders are so cheap, why not fit new ones rather than reseal the originals. It will save time and expense in the future.

4 Temporarily refit the dust excluder (if removed) to the fluid inlet, and fit a dust cover over the bleed nipple.

5 Install the brake adjuster and tappets (30).

6 Refit the handbrake lever assembly* (31) and actuating rods. Note felt washers (arrowed) which stop the rods and pins from rattling (32).

   * Ensure that the lever is fitted correctly as shown, otherwise the cable won't reach.

   Hillman Imps use thackery washers instead of felt washers, providing a quieter, longer lasting and superior handbrake.

7 Struggle to refit the brake shoes (33) - left side shown noting the correct position of the springs (see also earlier diagram).

8 Drift the hub into position, fit new lock tabs and the correct handed hub nuts - right side shown (34).

Note: the nut for the right hand hub has a left hand thread. Torque to 45ft/lbs.

9 Install the rear differential, trying not to rip the new gasket (35). Buy a few gaskets because they tend to tear easily.

Rear Axle - The final assembly

10 Insert half shafts, securing with locating screws (36)

11 Install support straps and bump stops (37).

12 Fit brake drums, remembering to degrease and paint new drums. Use anti-seize lubricant on the securing screws. Remember to fit the inspection hole grommets.

13 Fit the three-way connector, brake pipes and a new hose (38), using new securing straps as shown (39).

14 Adjust rear brakes by turning the brake back-plate adjusting screws in until the hub is locked. Then unscrew each adjuster three "clicks" - at which point the hubs should be free to rotate.

Allow, however, for some surface imperfections in the brake shoe linings. The car will need to be run for about one hundred miles, allowing the brakes to be run in, before re-adjusting them.

15 Store assembly in your father's attic until required and always change the subject if he starts talking about strange groaning sounds coming from the roof at night.

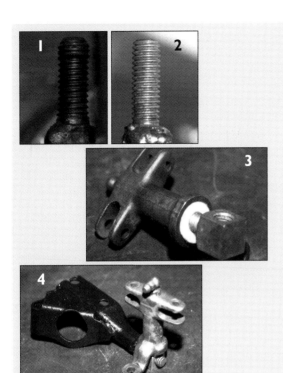

Handbrake Actuating Lever

The early axles (until mid-1500 models) used a balance lever mechanism which, once twisted, pulled on both rear brakes via control rods. The balance lever has a grease nipple to limit wear. Later 1500s replaced this simple and effective mechanism with a twin brake cable, some floppy plastic strips and a load of bolts - make of that what you will.

Due to a lack of grease the threaded portion of the actuator bracket often wears alarmingly and leads to slackness in the handbrake system while giving potential for future disaster (1).

Replacements are currently unavailable so I restored mine by cutting the thread off, filing the end square and having a new threaded length welded into position (2).

I grit blasted and repainted the bracket, cleaned the balance lever and fitted a new carrier and felt washer (3).

Picture 4 shows how it fits to the car, the cable fits through the large hole in the bracket and attaches to the bottom of the lever.

Using a Circlip Tool

Anybody who has tried fitting a wheel cylinder will know what a difficult job it can be. A wheel cylinder tool makes light work of the job (1).

The tool consists of a hollow barrel, a cone, a threaded rod and nut.

Screw the threaded rod into the wheel cylinder fluid inlet.

Slip the cone onto the rod, followed by the circlip and barrel. Finally, screw the nut onto the end of the rod (2).

As the nut is turned, the barrel pushes against the cone, forcing the 'E' clip to open (3) until it slips over the cone and onto the wheel cylinder (4).

Undo the nut and unscrew the tool. Stand back and admire (5).

Stud Fitting Tip

The axle studs securing the diff are a problem. They need pressing into position, but you can't get anything inside the casing to do the job.

Push them in by hand so that the thread pokes through the hole. Place an oversized nut over the thread (fig A), followed by a flat washer and the proper nut.

Then, simply tighten the nut. The stud is pulled through the oversized nut (fig.B) and into position.

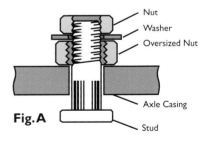

Nut
Washer
Oversized Nut
Axle Casing
Fig.A
Stud

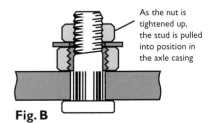

As the nut is tightened up, the stud is pulled into position in the axle casing

Fig. B

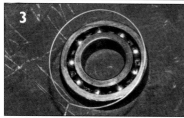

How To Get New Bearings In The Desert...

We take things pretty much for granted in England. If we need a bearing for a hub or axle, it is simply a matter of looking in a parts catalogue, phoning a specialist or popping into the local motor factor and waiting for several days before the wrong part arrives. When we do have the right part, fitting is something we do over the weekend if the weather's fine.

In many parts of Africa this is not so simple. With huge wilderness areas and scattered towns and villages, the nearest factor might be hundreds of miles away. Roads are often very bad, sometimes impassable by anything other than trucks. The roads are strewn with forgotten cars and trucks, laid waste by the roads and weather.

What's more, there's no AA. Vehicles are often so battered and bodged, their pedigree may only be guessed at. Imagine trying to get the right bearing to fix a damaged vehicle of indeterminate breed, and bearings suffer badly from the insensitive conditions.

So how do they do it. Many of the drivers / owners have no written documentation for the vehicles they own (a bit like the average new age traveller - but without the whippets) and, though they often know their vehicles inside out (unlike the average new age traveller), they may have to rely upon more rough and ready techniques to get the right replacement parts.

Getting bearings in Africa is a good example of ingenuity, and it's a trick worth learning if you travel beyond the realms of sanity in your MG.

Here's how they do it

Having removed the damaged bearing, they get a long length of wire, wrap it around the outside shell (1) and tighten it up (2). Then they slip the bearing out (3), leaving a neat circle in the wire.

Then they take the other end of the wire, wrap it round the exposed hub or shaft, tighten it up and slip it off (4), leaving another perfect circle (5) - accurate measurements for a new bearing. Finally they simply walk forty miles wearing flip flops to the nearest town and secure a replacement bearing!

Exercise 53 - at the specialist store. *Take a wire constructed as shown above to your local specialist, ask for a bearing and see what happens!*

Let's Twist Again

While working for a UK MG specialist I had some dealings with a Canadian Midget enthusiast and circuit racer. He had been getting real problems getting hold of good quality head gaskets and other genuine parts and for a while, during the racing season, he became a good customer of mine. The 'A' series engine on which his racing Midget was based is ideal for tuning.

On the rolling road his bored out 1275cc engine was giving 130bhp+.

He took his racing seriously, dismantling and examining certain components for wear following races. The rear axle came in for close scrutiny and along the length of the half shafts he painted a white line so that he could check to see if the half shafts were deforming under the stress of racing. One season he went through a few sets of half shafts, but one set in particular twisted up so badly that they actually ended up looking like a barber shop pole, with a spiral white line running all the way along their length...

Case Study: Propshaft

1   It is possible that oil will begin to seep out of the gearbox when the propshaft is removed. So, prior to removal, drain the oil from the gearbox.

This instruction applies particularly when hoisting the engine and gearbox out from the engine bay. As the assembled units are lifted out at a steep angle the oil is able to discharge all over the garage floor.

2   The flanges of the both the diff and shaft have been marked and should be fitted together that way during re-installation (1).

Early cars were fitted with greaseable UJs, later superseded by the "sealed for life" variety which lasted about as long as the ordinary greaseable ones. Nobody ever seems to grease them anyway, and let's face it if the one closest (and most visible) to the axle doesn't see much grease then the one up the tunnel has no chance. I imagine that BL probably realised that if nobody was going to use the grease nipples provided they might as well save some money.

Tip: Always replace both UJs. They're cheap and you don't want to have to go through this palaver again in a few months time - and you will - after all both ends are subject to the same forces, they really ought to be equally worn.

Removing and replacing a UJ.

Note: The prop and yoke should be re-aligned exactly as disassembled. Mark accordingly.

Most authoritative rebuild books suggest stripping down UJs and examining them for wear. I have always found this impossible to do because inevitably I end up with a pile of needle bearings under the bench, broken caps, absent circlips and dysfunctional rubber seals. Good luck if you can do it. I just start by buying new UJs.

Identify the UJ you want to remove first.

1   Remove all of the circlips (2) and then...

2   Tap the yoke downwards (3). This forces one of the caps outward.

3   Turn the unit over and attack from the opposite direction. Suitable drifts (4) or tubes (5) may help - okay, okay, so I use sockets, they are really very versatile you know. You can even use them for undoing nuts and things.

General view of the U.J. in position

Eventually the caps are pushed so far apart that the UJ should be able to twist out, leaving only the caps still attached to the yoke or shaft.

All those shiny bits that have fallen out on the floor (and are now lost forever amongst the grit and dust) were the roller bearings. That's why I always start by buying new UJs - better pop down to the local garage before it closes.

Repeat the procedure to remove the UJ from the prop body.

Fitting a new UJ.

1　Start by smearing a little anti-seize lubricant into the mounts on the end of the propshaft and yokes. This may aid removal of the UJs. next time around.

2　Remove two opposite cups from the new UJ. Ensure that the roller bearings are not dislodged. The grease should hold them in place, but check anyway.

3　Either tap or press the caps into place with care (6). Not all the way in - just enough to hold them in position.

4　Fit the UJ into one of the caps (7 & 8), then squeeze or drift the caps slowly together so that the UJ is held in position. A socket may help drift the caps into position (9).

Ensure that the roller bearings remain in place. To be sure, once the UJ is trapped you should be able to swing it freely backwards and forwards. If the bearings have slipped out of position, the UJ will not be able to move into the caps. (If so, remove the caps, re-align the needles and try again).

5　Push the caps completely into place and fit the circlips (10).

6　Once the UJ has been located and held in place with circlips, follow the same procedure to join the yoke with the main body of the propshaft (11 & 12).

Tip. If the UJ feels stiff once fitted then maybe the caps have been pushed in too far. When the assembly is fully built up, simply knock the yoke and prop gently to push the caps back against the circlips, thus releasing the UJ to work freely.

Some History: Road Wheels

Similar in design to the old Midget TD, the new Sprite disc wheels had circular perforations (1) running around the rim. Maybe the wheel wasn't too strong because a revised version was fitted from HAN5 15150 and revised again from HAN5 39223. I guess this must have cracked the problem because the later version continued to be fitted until HAN7 26239 and GAN2 17165, when it was replaced with a seemingly more modern slotted disc wheel (2).

The spare was secured to the boot floor of the Sprite with a webbing strap. With the arrival of the Mk II Sprite and Midget Mk I, the strap was replaced with a bolt and securing cone. Oh, and a boot lid helped one to get it out.

Both the perforated and slotted wheels were finished with chrome hub caps (3), the Sprite cap incorporating a debossed AH in the centre, the Midget version being unadorned.

The Sprite Mk II and Midget Mk I were also offered with optional wheel trims (4) in three styles. One was an imitation knock-on with 'S' logo, another incorporated an imitation hub nut, the third, a hub nut with MG logo. Many of these chrome trims would have been found at any time during the early to mid 1960s along embankments or in ditches just by the roadside, or more likely near the edges of high kerbs and would have been easily spotted by observant road users.

Wire wheels, painted, never chromed, appeared from HAN7 20812 / GAN2 16780 (though they had been offered from an early date for the Sprite Mk I by the Donald Healey Motor Company). The Octagonal (5) or two-eared (6) knock-ons were supplied depending upon the safety requirements of the country concerned.

Disc wheels continued to be fitted until late on in Sprite III and Midget Mk II production whereupon at some point, Rostyle wheels (7) were offered as an optional extra. (HAN9 / GAN4).

By the way, the name "Rostyle" belongs to the Birmingham based manufacturer Rubery Owen. The rim of a Rostyle wheel is usually stamped with the words RO&Co. So now you know. These difficult to paint wheels were finished using a small stainless steel centrepiece (8) and chromed wheel nuts.

The Rostyle design was replaced at GAN5 105501 with a later style (9), in keeping with the MGB model. This later design continued to be used until the demise of the Midget 1500 model.

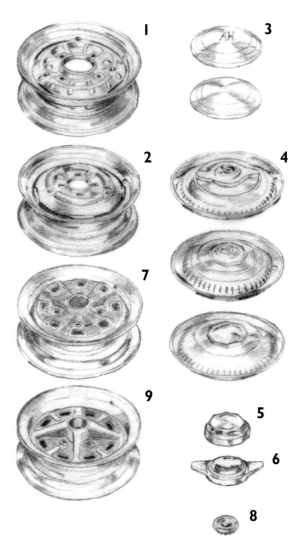

Case Study: Wheel Restoration

Wheels make a lot of difference to any restoration. Without them, where would you be. Stuck at home with your car on blocks I suppose. Over the years I have seen many a fine restoration spoilt by poorly finished wheels. The "norm" being a cursory spray over with cheap silver paint which later takes on a distinctly reddish hue after some wet autumnal motoring.

Wire wheels are best left to being restored by professional wheel specialists, after all, fitting new spokes is quite an art. Often, replacing some spokes leads to extra stress being placed on the others and eventually more spokes require replacement. New and reconditioned wire wheels are easily available at the moment. For a genuine look, replace them with painted wheels, not gaudy chrome. That's my opinion!

Early steel wheels simply require repainting. The later "rostyle wheels" need a bit more effort. Here's how I did mine...

1. I had the wheels grit blasted, far and away the easiest method of removing chipped paint and unwanted rust (1), and then had them electro-coated (2) to guard against corrosion.

2. I built a turntable using a circular piece of wood and a wooden bar (to help take the weight of the wheel). A long bolt, washer and some nuts made an axle (3). A vice held it all in position and allowed the assembly to spin.

3. I sprayed the inside faces with Finnigan's Smoothrite. I think that two cans proved more than adequate for the five wheels.

4. Having left them to dry, I then turned them over and sprayed the wheel faces silver (4) with three coats of paint. I then masked the wheels with masking tape and paper (5) and sprayed three coats of black silk finish paint over the exposed parts.

5. I left the wheels to cure before removing the masking tape (6) and then smoothed down any irregularities, before finally giving them a good polish.

   If you have not treated the wheels in any way to guard against corrosion, it may be worth lacquering the wheels; otherwise they will go rusty again very quickly.

6. Finish off with a set of matching tyres (7).

Take A Brake!

A few years ago I owned a bike, it was black, it was old and I called it, appropriately I felt at the time, the black dog. Old and Japanese is not a mixture to tinker with too much and evidently this was a view similar to that held by its last twelve owners. By the time I purchased the machine it bore little resemblance to its original shape, colour or mechanical background. It was not so much a bike as a collection of parts which would, with some coaxing, head off in a roughly similar direction. Generally speaking however, this was a bike which knew and understood its master in most things. It started when necessary, it performed a stunning array of feats in most gears, but braking was a department in which it failed most often to perform with any degree of certainty.

As common with many other bikes of the period, the front brakes had fluid supplied from a master cylinder on the handle bars, down a long hose pipe, a union made of some curious metal not known to Western civilisation and then two more hoses to the callipers. Genuine hoses are expensive items and mine had thus been replaced by a longer and more economic alternative. In fact I think it fair to say that there was more hose pipe on my bike than in my garden shed. The hoses, like many a jazz trumpeters' cheeks, had seen better days. Whenever I hit the front brakes, the lower hoses performed a remarkable impression of a bullfrog.

Brake & Clutch Hydraulics

Surprisingly, this slight defect failed to concern my wife who, upon one occasion actually managed to doze off while riding pillion. We were returning from a folk festival and I spent most off the journey home across the Cotswolds steering with one hand and holding her on with the other!

Brake hydraulics are difficult things, being one of the few jobs you really can't do on your own, an assistant is always useful when trying to get that last bubble out of system, only to find that others are being sucked in through imperfect seals elsewhere. I have tried a number of "one man" bleeding systems with various degrees of failure. Many's the bleed valve that's dropped off bleed nipples and on one memorable occasion I used jet propulsion to fire an Eazibleed across the garage. Apparently you are supposed to deflate the tyre to about 18lb/ft/in before attaching the tube. I agree that 36lb/ft/in may have been a little too high. Impressive though!

Some years ago I noticed that whenever I depressed the brake pedal in the Midget it stayed down. I came to the conclusion that the problem was caused by sticking wheel cylinders or callipers and that the only recourse would be to strip down, clean and rebuild the offending units. My theory being that as the pistons were sticking open, the fluid remained in the piston chambers and couldn't return - the pedal thus being "sucked down". I examined and resealed the wheel cylinders. Examined, fitted new seals into the callipers (which I broke), fitted more new seals (which I broke again) and then purchased new callipers. I installed the units, bled the brakes and presto! The brake pedal continued to stay down. The problem proved to be nothing more than the pedal bolt which had seized to the pedal.

The answer: - just two pennyworth of WD40....still, the brakes worked really well afterwards!

Some History:
The Hydraulic System

The brake hydraulic system for the original Sprite was a straightforward affair. A master cylinder, controlling the brakes and clutch, sat in a pedal box on either the left or right hand footwell of the car. The opposite footwell was fitted with a blanking plate to fill the otherwise gaping hole.

The master cylinder was uprated and improved from HAN5 50116 and at some point the original metal caps were replaced by a neat plastic equivalent which could usually be undone without the need of Mole Grips.

From HAN9 64755 / GAN4 52390 a new pedal box was used, into which was mounted separate brake and clutch master cylinders, a move which rendered later repair or replacement no less tricky. At least restoration became a more inexpensive prospect.

Due to improved safety regulations, France and the Benelux countries were given an extension to screw into the top of the brake master cylinder. A translucent tube allowed Gallic owners the opportunity to see that the brake fluid had run out without unscrewing the cap and looking inside. "So, this is why it crashed Huh!!!"

Serious measures were meanwhile being undertaken in North America and Canada to reduce accidents. A dual line braking system was incorporated at HAN9 72034 / GAN4 60441. The brake lights had been operated by a hydraulically operated switch, but at this point, North American cars were fitted with a mechanical switch attached to the pedal box casing. The brake pedal was revised by adding a short tongue to operate the switch at the appropriate moment.

Back in Blighty and Europe things went on pretty much unchanged until the introduction of the 1500 model, when the brake master cylinder was altered internally. The later master cylinder was offered as a direct replacement for the earlier unit. Watch out when renovating this type of cylinder. The later type has concentric circles stamped on its body and uses a different repair kit (shown elsewhere).

A banjo adaptor fitted to the back of this assembly split the hydraulic system, doing away with the four way union fitted to earlier cars. From now on, a separate pipe provided fluid to one front wheel. The other pipe fed the other front wheel and both rear wheels, via the rear axle.

At GAN6 200001 a tubular cylinder with separate reservoir was fitted. Like the earlier European extension, the translucent reservoir allowed easy viewing of the contents without unpleasant bending.

Finally, at GAN6 212001, Europe and the UK caught up with the USA market and got the same dual line system that had preserved many an American life years before...they say that once we led the world..

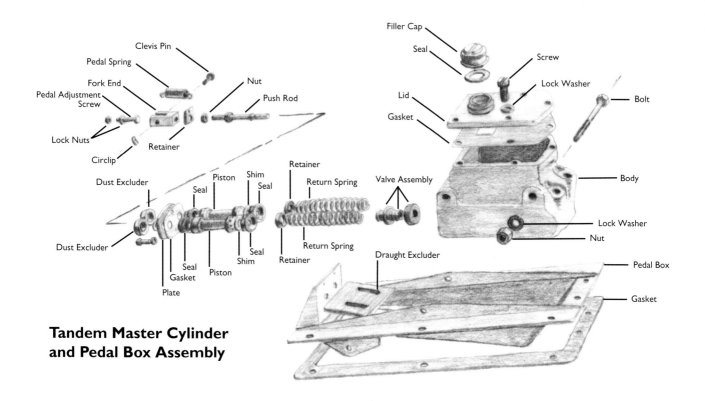

Tandem Master Cylinder and Pedal Box Assembly

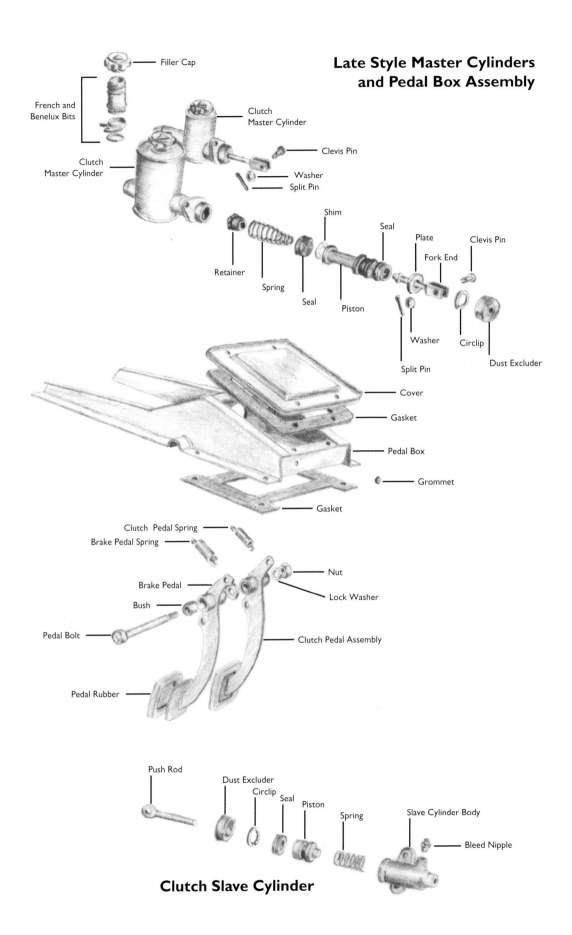

Late Style Master Cylinders and Pedal Box Assembly

Filler Cap

French and Benelux Bits

Clutch Master Cylinder

Clutch Master Cylinder

Clevis Pin

Washer

Split Pin

Retainer

Spring

Seal

Shim

Seal

Piston

Seal

Plate

Fork End

Clevis Pin

Washer

Circlip

Dust Excluder

Split Pin

Cover

Gasket

Pedal Box

Grommet

Gasket

Clutch Pedal Spring

Brake Pedal Spring

Brake Pedal

Bush

Pedal Bolt

Pedal Rubber

Nut

Lock Washer

Clutch Pedal Assembly

Push Rod

Dust Excluder

Circlip

Seal

Piston

Spring

Slave Cylinder Body

Bleed Nipple

Clutch Slave Cylinder

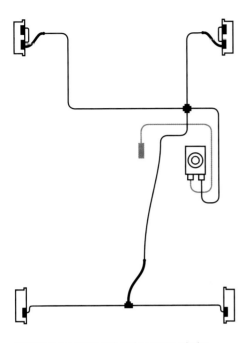

Early single line system with tandem master cylinder and drum front brakes.

Clutch pipe on tandem cylinder crossed over the brake pipe and followed the same course around the pedal box assembly.

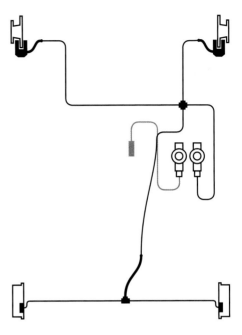

Late single line system showing disc brakes and individual master cylinders for clutch and brake.

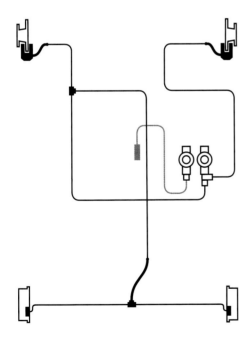

Last single line system with adaptor fitted to brake master doing away with the need for the four-way footwell mounted union.

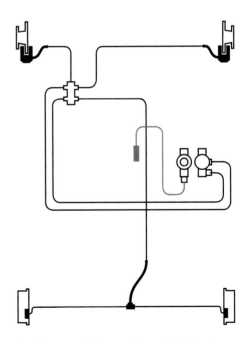

Dual line system offering some degree of braking in the event of leakage.

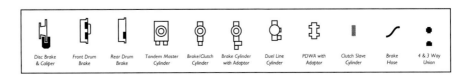

| Disc Brake & Caliper | Front Drum Brake | Rear Drum Brake | Tandem Master Cylinder | Brake/Clutch Cylinder | Brake Cylinder with Adaptor | Duel Line Cylinder | PDWA with Adaptor | Clutch Slave Cylinder | Brake Hose | 4 & 3 Way Union |

Case Study:
Brake & Clutch Pedal Box

You'll have noticed that on the footwell opposite the pedal box is a plate (1). It's there for cars that drive on the wrong side of the road. There is also a fitting above, blocked with sealant. That would be for the accelerator cable - if you were driving on the other side of the road that is.

Warning - Paint Work Damage

It is important to remember that hydraulic fluid will be spilt when you attempt to remove the master cylinder. Even if you drain the circuit beforehand there is still a good chance that some fluid will remain in the system, ready to drip out at an inappropriate moment. Have some soapy water handy just in case!

In my case, the shell was scrap anyway and, having let the car stand for five years there was little fluid left in the brakes at any event. Spilling the fluid may even have stabilised the rust problem.

Removing The Pedal Box

1. Begin by draining as much of the fluid from the system as possible by opening the bleed nipples on the callipers and wheel cylinders (one after another) and forcing fluid out of the system or by letting it drain naturally away.

2. Get some access to the pedal box by folding back the securing tags and pulling the wiring loom out of the way.

3. Remove the pedal box cover - assuming you can get the four screws undone.

4. Disengage the fork ends from the foot pedals by removing the split pins and clevis pins.

5. Undo the pipes connected to the brake and clutch cylinder outlets (2) and gently pull them away from the cylinders.

   Steel brake pipes suffer badly from corrosion. It's not uncommon to start undoing a pipe union, only to find that the pipe turns as well. Any damaged or corroded pipes should be replaced as a matter of course.

6. Undo the nuts and bolts securing the master cylinder(s) to the pedal box (3) and remove them from the assembly (4).

   Access to the nuts and bolts is difficult. An alternative is to leave the cylinders in situ to be removed with the entire pedal box.

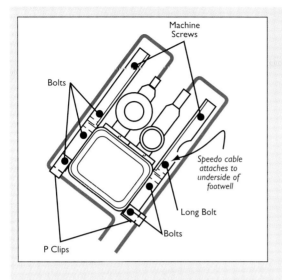

Machine Screws

Bolts

Speedo cable attaches to underside of footwell

Long Bolt

Bolts

P Clips

7 Undo the mixture of bolts that secure the pedal box assembly (see diagram left).

Note the position of "P" clips which secure the pipes to the footwell.
Also note that a longer bolt is required to help anchor the speedo cable inside the footwell (5 - arrowed).

8 From inside the footwell remove the two pedal springs.

Note: The clutch return spring is sometimes missing (6), making gear changes easier. This shouldn't cause any problem unless you have a tendency to "ride" (leave your foot resting on) the clutch.

9 Undo the bolt and nut which secures the pedals. Then, from the engine bay, lift the pedal box assembly upwards slightly to withdraw the securing bolt and listen as the pedals fall to the rusty floor below.

The pedals must be removed because it is not possible to withdraw the pedal box assembly with the pedals attached.

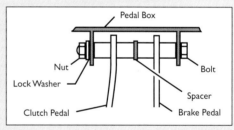

Pedal Box

Nut

Lock Washer

Clutch Pedal

Bolt

Spacer

Brake Pedal

10 If undertaking a full restoration of the pedal box note the grommet (7) which fits in the rear of the pedal box. This hole takes a brake light switch where demanded by market requirements.

Some Of Them There Pointy Bolts Please...

Many of the bolts fitted into the bulkhead area (i.e. wiper motor, brake and clutch master cylinder box etc.) are machined to have a pointed end. I don't know why that should be, but it seems that these were intended only to be used where the bolts entered the cockpit area.

Perhaps some unfeeling engineer took pleasure in people scratching themselves while they were rooting around the parcel shelf, or maybe a very sad marketing man felt that customers would prefer pointy bits jutting into the habitable parts of the car. Maybe there is some perfectly rational engineering reason. I wasn't sure that I wanted to enter into a long lecture about pointy bolts with an all knowing engineer and thus, I'm afraid, I have no enlightening news to give you on the subject.

What is certain however, is that this is not the kind of bolt carried by any parts specialist that I know of. You might try a screw or bolt specialist (yes, they do exist). Alternatively, use the originals or find someone with a lathe.

Case Study:
Master Cylinder Restoration

1 Over a suitable container, drain the remaining fluid from the brake master cylinder and carefully clean the body prior to disassembly.

2 Pull back the fork end gaiter (1) to release the circlip and remove the actuating fork (2).

3 Remove the piston (3) - noting the shim behind it, rubber seal, spring and valve (4).

With regard to this case study note that two visually similar brake master cylinder kits were fitted to Sprites and Midget at around the same time. The inner assemblies are not interchangeable and use different repair kits.

One master cylinder had concentric rings marked on its body. The kit shown in picture 5 is for the plain body type, the kit shown in picture 6 is for the cylinder with concentric grooves.

4 Clean the body scrupulously using fresh hydraulic fluid. If you intend changing over to silicon fluid then use silicon fluid to clean and wash the chambers out. *DO NOT USE METHYLATED SPIRITS.*

5 Examine the barrel for scoring. Discard if there are obvious signs of damage or restore if possible.

Owners of the earlier twin master cylinder assemblies should make every effort to salvage old units since suitable replacements are now difficult to get hold of.

6 Fit a new seal onto the piston (7). Smear a small amount of rubber grease onto the seal to protect it from damage and to assist with reassembly. Then fit the valve, spring and cup into the piston chamber (8).

7 Fit the shim and piston (9), fork end, spacer and circlip (10) using wire to hold the fork in position while the circlip is attached (11).

Tip: The piston seal is larger than the chamber. Using your finger nail, gently work around the seal until all of the lip has been pushed inside the chamber, then push the piston home.

8 Fill the aperture with rubber grease and fit the rubber boot.

Clutch Master Cylinder

The clutch master cylinder is very similar to the brake master cylinder, in both construction and appearance. The bore size is slightly different and the cylinder does not utilise a valve at the rear end of the assembly (see overhead shot shown below).

Disassembly and reassembly is just the same as for the brake master cylinder.

brake cylinder

clutch cylinder

How A Master Cylinder Operates

1 While at rest both chambers A and B are full of fluid.

2 As the piston is depressed chamber A is sealed. Fluid in chamber A is forced into the pipe making the wheel cylinders and callipers operate.

3 Chamber A incorporates a powerful spring (not shown) which helps force the piston back to its rest position. Brake fluid is sucked back up the pipes, releasing pressure on the wheel cylinders and callipers.

4 Inevitably, brake fluid escapes from the reservoir into the piston area as the brake pedal is depressed. While at rest, the trapped fluid could expand and burst the seals allowing seepage of fluid. To alleviate this problem a large vent hole (C) effectively stops the build up of pressure in the piston area.

Note: The filler cap boasts a tiny hole allowing air to seep in and out of the chamber. If the hole becomes blocked a vacuum will develop inside the chamber which may cause operating difficulties and even damage the chamber or seals. Ensure that the airway is clear.

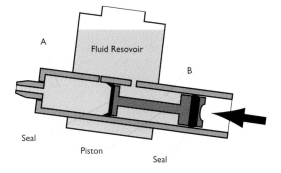

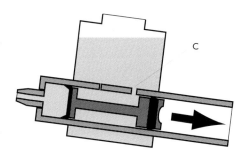

Case Study:
Pedal Box Restoration

The pedal box itself is prone to rust. However, being of sturdy construction, it is ideally suited to grit blasting. The lid itself is lighter and requires more careful treatment during cleaning. Both should be sprayed black once cleaned and new screws should be used to secure the cover.

A gasket normally fits below the cover to guard against the ingress of water (1).

A further gasket fits between the pedal box assembly and the footwell. Both are available and should be replaced as a matter of course.

The closing plate fitted to the passenger footwell is also restorable. Again, use new screws and a new gasket (2) to guard against water ingress onto passengers legs, for some reason they don't like getting wet.

Finally, the bolts and machine screws that secure the assembly to the footwell should have pointed ends. Hunt around because these bolts are sometimes available.

The brake and clutch pedals should be painted black and both have rubber pedal covers.

The pedals are fitted with phosphor bronze bushes. If worn they should be replaced with new bushes, pre-soaked in motor oil for 24 hours prior to installation.

1. Mount the brake and clutch master cylinders into the pedal box (3).

2 Temporarily fit the lid and new gasket.

3 Where applicable fit the rubber plug to the front face of the pedal box (4). The hole is there for US specification models which have a brake switch operating off the pedal (just thought you Europeans would like to know!)

4. Temporarily fit the pedals into the assembly (5 and also the diagram shown previously) for storage purposes - though they will need to be removed later to allow fitment of the assembly onto the car.

Making Better Brakes

Sprite and Midget brakes are not renowned for their effectiveness. Even the disc brake set up used from the early days seem to leave a little to be desired. Before looking at expensive conversion jobs however, there are many ways of improving the performance of standard brakes.

In many cases braking problems are caused by wear and tear rather than the system not being up to the job. Here's a quick check list to go through...

1. What are the pads and shoes like? Worn linings dissipate less heat. Harder braking will make the linings overheat - causing brake fade.

   If the linings are worn try replacing them with new pad and shoe sets. Make sure you buy good quality pads and shoes, since cheaper brands often have inferior quality linings.

2. What are the discs and brake drums like? It's not uncommon for them to be worn due to grit or even rust. The swept surfaces should be smooth and clean.

   Any ridges or grooves will mean that much less of the linings will be in contact with the surface and so braking efficiency will drop off.

   Replace worn discs and drums rather than re-machine them. Like the pads and shoes, discs and drums will dissipate heat more rapidly if they are thicker.

3. Are the callipers, wheel cylinders and master cylinder working effectively.? It's not uncommon for wheel cylinders to be found leaking or to have a seized piston. The same is true of the callipers where the chromed pistons corrode causing damage to the seals.

   A leaking master cylinder may only be noticed as fluid is lost and will again reduce braking ability.

4 Tired hoses expand under pressure, making the brakes spongy as the pressurised fluid forces them to balloon outward.

   Fit braided hoses, or those with spring steel sheaths. The corset like nature of the braiding stops them expanding, so that the only way the fluid can escape from your vicious right foot is by pumping fluid into the calliper and cylinder pistons.

5 Make sure that all of the pipes are sound and that there are no leaks (however slight) from unions.

   Replace any worn or damaged pipes, especially if there are any signs of corrosion.

6 Depress the pedal harder.

Brake Fluids

Brake fluid is hygroscopic - that is, it soaks up water like a sponge. Older fluid can be full of water causing two distinct problems.

The first is rust. Steel pipes will literally rust out from the inside while wheel cylinders fail due to corrosion. Secondly, the water boils off during heavy braking and bubbles develop in the system. These bubbles can be compressed causing the brakes to turn spongy.

It is essential that brake fluid in any vehicle is replaced every eighteen months to two years.

An alternative is to use silicon fluid which is non-hygroscopic. It is best to start by removing all traces of the original fluid. I would recommend using it when fitting all new components, fine if you are restoring a vehicle anyway. The results will be rust free brakes and pipes with no water contamination. The fluid and hydraulic system should last a lifetime...and it won't damage paint work.

Brake Pipes

Sprites and Midgets were fitted with steel brake pipes and would have been originally supplied pre-formed, great for the customer but not for the shop owner.

Steel pipes inevitably rust and a common alternative is to fit a copper pipe kit. These pipes are easy to bend to shape, but be warned; too much bending makes them brittle and susceptible to damage through vibration.

Another alternative is to fit "Kunifer" pipe. More expensive than steel or copper pipe, Kunifer is flexible, easily worked and of enormous durability. Manufactured from a cupro-nickel alloy, it offers greater resistance to vibration, looks like steel pipe and lasts.

Notes on Using Braided Hoses

Steel braided hoses are highly recommended for racing. That's not to say that you can't use them for road use but take careful note of the following points.

a. Ensure that hoses are not kinked or twisted, that the unions are secure, and that the hoses are not stretched when the suspension is at full travel. Above all do not overtighten the unions.

b. Inspect the hoses regularly for signs of decay, damage, leaks or signs of burning or scuffing.

c. It is not unknown (though rare) for the braiding to act as an earthing point for the starter motor leading to damage to the hose. Ensure that the engine earthing straps are in good condition. You'll notice that though once common, steel braided hoses are rarely fitted as standard to modern production vehicles.

There are ways of uprating the system:- fitting a servo, uprating callipers (make sure the wheels still fit), vented discs, etc. I've never bothered myself. Well maintained brakes and sensible driving works for me, it will also work for you to.

Start Your Engines, Perhaps

I think that a good place to start the electrical section is with the starter motor. Without it, what is a modern car but street furniture. After all, there's no hole to put your starting handle in these days, so if the starter stops, you're going to go nowhere. Also, the starter motor is surely the truest gauge your partner has of your temperament. After all, that painful excursion where you, the car owner, cowers in the passenger seat while your companion steers the car ever onward through apparently unseen and untested danger begins with the first turn of the key. That's when they know what kind of mood your going to be in. The pain increases tenfold when you have rebuilt the car yourself - only you will recognise that the grinding, wheezing and whirring noises that echo and rattle around the engine bay is the result of two toothed wheels smashing together and that the larger of the two - the ring gear - is the mother of big jobs to replace.

It was while allowing Kathryn to practice driving (I refused point blank to teach her, knowing this was the surest way to an early and hostile separation) that the starter motor packed up on the Midget. When I say packed up, that's not strictly true. It just became a bit difficult. For example, it would work perfectly for days on end and then, having stopped outside a shop or a crowded bar, would refuse to operate. The only thing to do then, much to the crowds amusement (there's always a crowd isn't there), was to stick the car in gear,

Starter Motor and the Starter Circuit

leap out and give it a good shake, by that I mean I had to grab the bumper and rock the car back and forth in the hope that it would free up the pinion.

A few years later I purchased a Citroen 2CV6, I'd only had it for a few hours, and keen to show it off Kathryn, I and two friends went to the pub. Kathryn wanted to drive and I was keen to let her have a crack at this untamed beast. For those who don't know, a 2CV has a dash mounted gear lever resembling a bent bicycle pump and an umbrella for a hand-brake, it can get a bit confusing until you get used to it. We had to turn off a fast dual carriageway to reach the pub. Cutting majestically across to the safety island on the right, we stopped to await a suitable gap in the oncoming traffic. I should mention that the car only has a 602cc engine, so as you can imagine, driving four up is a lot of work for it.

When the gap came, Kath attempted take off, and not being used to it, stalled the car which then rolled across the carriageway.

"I'd hit the starter Kath....I'd really hit the starter... no leave the handbrake... j u s t t h e starter". The hushed passengers in the rear seats peered towards the oncoming cars as I began to open the door to push us to safety when Kathryn found the starter. The car, powered only by the starter motor and still in gear, jumped across the road to safety. Hoots of nervous laughter and a curious smell from one of the rear occupants filled the car, much to the embarrassment of Kathryn. To the day I sold the car, the starter motor never failed, which reinforced my opinion of French engineering no end.

Starter (exploded view)

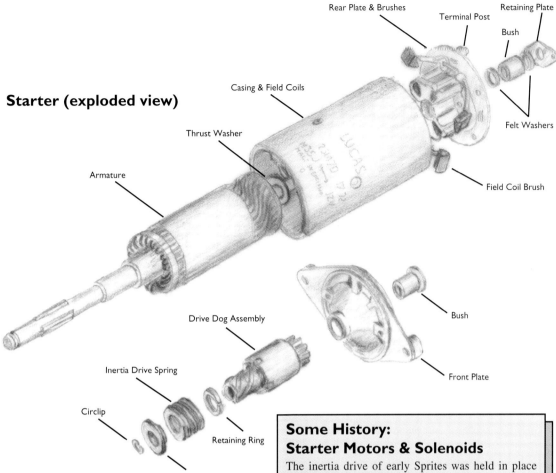

Rear Plate & Brushes

Terminal Post

Retaining Plate

Bush

Casing & Field Coils

Thrust Washer

Felt Washers

Armature

Field Coil Brush

Bush

Drive Dog Assembly

Front Plate

Inertia Drive Spring

Circlip

Retaining Ring

Retaining Ring

One more push and we'll be at the shops...

If you ever need to bump start a car, then select second gear rather than first, it's easier on the knees. I learned this painful lesson after years of push starting old British cars.

When you get the car up to a gentle running speed, it's going quite fast for first gear, especially in the Midget in which first is just meant to get you rolling. When your driver drops the clutch it locks the transmission, the car judders to a halt and you end up crushing your groin against the rear wing before flopping in an ungainly manner to the floor.

Having selected second gear, you'll often find the car will keep rolling along quite agreeably while the driver plays around with the pedals, rips the choke out, sets the windscreen wipers going along with all the other curious things that they do while you are turning red in the face and slipping up on icy roads.

Some History:
Starter Motors & Solenoids

The inertia drive of early Sprites was held in place with a split pin. Perhaps this method didn't work too well because, at some point during the time of the 9CG engined cars, the starter motor was replaced with a revised type which held the inertia drive in place with a circlip as detailed later.

This second type of starter was a Lucas M35G type, the case being stamped 25079 followed by a suffix ranging from A to H. This in turn was superseded by the M35J type, stamped 25149 on the casing. Change points are not clear, however both are interchangeable and probably will have been replaced by something similar by now anyway. Parts for both types are readily available, as are exchange units.

The dash mounted starter button and early switch were replaced at GAN3 25788 and HAN8 38829 with a starter solenoid remotely operated by the ignition switch. The solenoid was superseded with a more efficient design at GAN4 59608 and HAN9 71624. Another was fitted with the introduction of the 1500 model.

For a brief period of time (1973 to 1975) the USA models were fitted with a safety device stopping the starter from operating until the seat belts were used. This must have proved unpopular because after three years it was removed and the circuit reverted to its earlier incarnation.

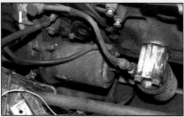

Case Study: Starter Motors

Unless you own an early Sprite, where the bonnet and wings lift away in one gut enhancing movement, access to the starter motor is difficult to say the least. If you are not removing the engine at all, then a helpful option is to remove the distributor. Simply undo the two bolts that hold the clamp plate to the block and pull the assembly free. This at least gives you a little more room (1).

Even then, undoing and withdrawing the two nuts and bolts are very tiresome, with the lower one being reached through the clutch slave cylinder access hole just above the floor in the right hand footwell (2). Removing the steering wheel helps provide more access.

Mostly the Sprites and Midgets were fitted with inertia drive starters (3), some, however, particularly from warmer climates, were fitted with pre-engaged starters, where the gear is already engaged with the starter ring prior to starting, and remains in situ. I don't know why.

Holding the unit firmly on the bench, the inertia drive starter (ie the one with the bendix and gear coming straight out of the end) can be checked for wear. That's easy, hold the unit steady and try to pull the armature upwards. Excessive play from worn bearings will be obvious. There will be some play, though trying to decide how much play is reasonable or excessive may require superhuman judgement.

Make sure the drive dog teeth are okay, otherwise it will need replacement. If the teeth are worn then wear is just as likely on the starter ring gear. Examine the ring gear through the bell housing and grimace quietly to yourself.

Dismantling

1. Dismantling is quite straightforward. Start by removing the two long bolts (4) and withdrawing the commutator assembly and front plate (5). A thrust washer will be found at the rear end of the armature (6). Don't lose it.

2. Examination of the rear plate will probably show wear to the commutator brushes (7), a consumable item readily available. Note the sealing gasket - more about that later.

3. Hold the bendix gear back out of the way with some tape and then use a spring compressor to compress the drive spring (8). Once compressed the circlip and lock washer can be removed and the assembly can be dismantled. Note carefully the position of the individual components (9).

Historical detail: The early units had springs and bendix gear held in place with a split pin, later units incorporated a cunning collar and circlip - yes, hours of endless fun hunting around the darkest corners of the garage for that wayward clip. Simply fit the compressor, compress the spring and the circlip can be removed.

4. Note carefully the complex arrangement of various washers and collars that are fitted to the terminal post.

    As well as securing the power cable, they act as insulators and the starter will short out if these are not correctly reassembled.

5. Examine the commutator assembly for sign of damage, particularly that the spindle is not deformed or bent and that the windings show no signs of being worn. The end shown (11) is in contact with the brushes and if necessary may be cleaned with a very fine abrasive paper.

6. The "business end" of the assembly will probably be covered in dust. This is most likely to be asbestos dust from the clutch so handle it with care. Once dismantled the parts should be thoroughly cleaned BUT NOT OILED OR GREASED.

    The unit operates correctly when it can move freely, grease limits the spinning action of the drive dog and attracts dust and muck like a white shirt on a visit to any good restaurant.

Front and Rear Bushes

The motor itself has 'Oilite' bushes front and rear, both mounted in the end plates. Made from phosphor bronze, these need to be pressed in to position (after having been soaked in oil for 24 hours).

1. The old front bearing can be driven out using a drift (ie a suitable socket) and a vice or hammer (12 & 13). The replacement can be fitted in the same way.

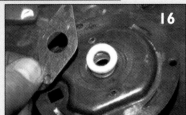

Exercise extreme caution when doing this - remember that the front plate is made of a light alloy.

2. The rear bearing cannot be removed using a drift, so it either needs to be broken up and removed or, a less damaging way, it can be pulled out.

Get a bolt, with a thread slightly greater than the internal diameter of the bearing. Cut across the threads so that it resembles a tap (14) and then screw it into the bush - as if you were tapping a hole. Lock the bolt in a vice and pull (15).

A point which often goes unnoticed is that the rear bearing should have a plate rivetted over it, under which is placed a felt washer. The felt washer is the means by which the bearing can occasionally be oiled. If your starter motor is a reconditioned unit then the chances are it will be missing. If you are reconditioning the unit yourself, why not replace it. Then at least you can partially service the unit in the future.

Reassembly

Having fitted new bushes its time to reassemble the unit.

1. Fit new brushes into the end plate (17). Make sure that the shims have been replaced at the rear of the armature, fit it into the body ensuring that the brushes locate correctly onto the commutator. Don't forget to use a new gasket, cut your own from gasket material if one is not available (18). Gasket material is available from most good motor factors.

2. Fit the front plate, ensuring that the guides on the plate and casing line up (19).

4. Reattach cable hardware, ensuring that the terminal post is properly insulated from the body (refer back to picture 10).

5. Refit the pinion, barrel and sleeve, spacer and bendix (20 and 21), making sure that there is no grease or grit on the assembly and that the barrel moves freely.

6. Using the spring compressor, refit the collar and circlip (22 and 23).

Tip: For easy circlip fitment, place a 1/2in socket over the circlip and gently tap the circlip down. The circlip will expand equally over the armature and fall into its correct position.

7. Check free movement of the armature to ensure that everything feels okay. Finally, bench test it.

Bench test procedure

Connect the negative cable from battery to starter body, and touch the terminal with the positive. The armature should spin freely with the inertia forcing the barrel to move along the shaft.

If the unit does not spin freely, there will be something wrong. Having removed the power examine the components, particularly ensuring that the gear is able to move freely along the shaft. If the assembly worked before dismantling, it should work now.

The assembly may need to be examined closely for damage or missing parts.

A Simple Spring Compressor

To dismantle the commutator assembly you will need a spring compressor. If you don't own one, then one is fairly easy to make. It's nothing special, just two thick rectangles of steel, each with a semi-circular cut-out which will fit just snugly onto the of the spring while not trapping the collars. Two smaller holes take two long nuts and bolts.

As the spring is compressed, the collar drops free of the circlip which can then be removed with ease. You'll see mine is not a very elegant device, but it does the trick and cost only some time, effort and some unpleasant filing.

Starter Motor Circuits

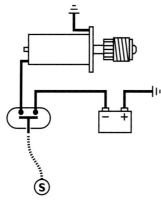

Circuit 1

Sprite Mk I, II, III, Midget Mk I, II
To GAN3 25787 and HAN8 38828

The original positive earth system was operated via a circuit made only when the dash mounted starter button was depressed.

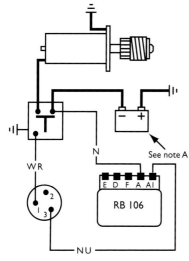

Circuit 2

Sprite III, IV, Midget Mk II, III
all positive earth and early negative earth cars
from GAN3 25788 to GAN4 74885
and from HAN8 38829 to HAN9 85286.
USA cars up to GAN4 74885 and HAN9 72041 on

An improved circuit used the ignition switch to connect the starter circuit via a starter relay, effectively isolating the user from the potentially high current flow required to start the engine.

Note A: Circuit covers positive and negative earth models. Positive earth shown.

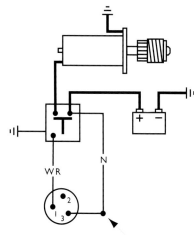

Circuit 3

Sprite IV, Midget Mk III and 1500
GAN5 74886 on, GAN6 and HAN10 85287 on
USA GAN5 74886 on
(also GAN4 74901 to 74947 and 75701 to 75735)

See note B

The circuit remained mostly unchanged throughout the rest of Sprite and Midget production with the exception of some US cars (see circuit 4 below). The wiring loom changed and thus cabling and connector block changes must be expected, though the colours remained unaltered.

Note B: On models fitted with the RB340 control box, the relay to ignition switch cable often stopped off at Terminal B of the box.

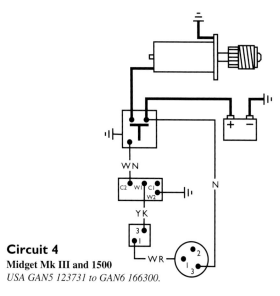

Circuit 4

Midget Mk III and 1500
USA GAN5 123731 to GAN6 166300.

Not popular, this safety circuit stopped drivers from starting their cars until the seat belts were connected. The circuit was discarded for 1976 model year cars.

Meanwhile in the UK cars could usually only be started after a mandatory call out of the AA or RAC.

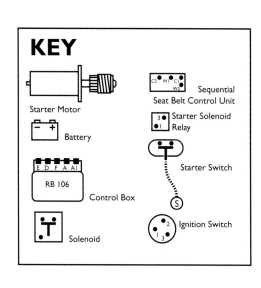

KEY

Starter Motor

Battery

RB 106 — Control Box

Solenoid

Sequential Seat Belt Control Unit

Starter Solenoid Relay

Starter Switch

Ignition Switch

Dizzy Spells

There is a particularly bumpy stretch of the A40, between Monmouth and Abergavenny, which culminates in a long, slow drag uphill. I always remember this place in particular because between that point and Ross on Wye (a few miles back towards London) more bits fell off my Midget than at any other place in the country.

On one occasion the problem was one of ignition leads. Not just any ignition leads, these were the super-wound, slinky-silicone, mega-suppressed, really-flexy, take out a bank loan type with Lycra® that are available from all good accessory shops. Trouble was, they were an appaling fit. Every time I went over a bump one of the caps just popped off. It would happen every half hour or so until I came to THE hill. The stretch of road concerned is only about two and a half miles long, but by the time I had reached the top (it took me about an hour to cover the distance), all four caps were held in place with a piece of string, wrapped around the spark plug and cap rather like the bandaged head of a patient in the dentists waiting room. After that I went back to the old green Unipart leads that cost peanuts and lasted forever.

I can't think of any one single item on a car that has caused me any more trouble than the ignition system, apart from the door of my old Rover, which fell off as a protest after I had just fixed the ignition system. Whatever car or motorbike I have owned I have spent more time trying to get points to work and spark plugs to spark, than almost any other jobs put together, and I have gradually come to the conclusion that I am one of those breed of human beings surrounded by a mystical aura which has an unsettling effect on anything electrical. Give me a candle or a tilley lamp, but not a lead lamp any time!

Despite qualifying in electrical engineering I still end up slumped in confusion and defeat over the side of a car whenever I tackle ignition faults. Make mine a diesel any day. Amongst the many things that I have learned, the most useful lessons have been the following:-

(1) Stick with Unipart leads or make up your own using standard cables and NGK spark plug caps. The expensive leads that you get from your local parts shop never seem to fit into the distributor head or clip onto the spark plugs securely. (2) Champion spark plugs are no better or worse than NGK whatever you hear said in the local pub. (3) Contact breakers will never give the same reading against a feeler gauge more than twice in a row no matter how many times you spin the engine. (4) The little carbon thrust never pops out from the distributor cap unless you check it for security. (5) The rotor arm, once installed, is there for life. (6) It is the crimp connector which fails first, never the electronic ignition system. (7) If the rev counter lurches across the dial looking as if its suffering from St. Vitas dance then the contact breakers are totally worn down and probably need replacing. (8) Finally, after hours of fiddling, the ignition system will run faultlessly until after you have had a bath and its time for you to go anywhere at all.

Distributors and the Ignition Circuit

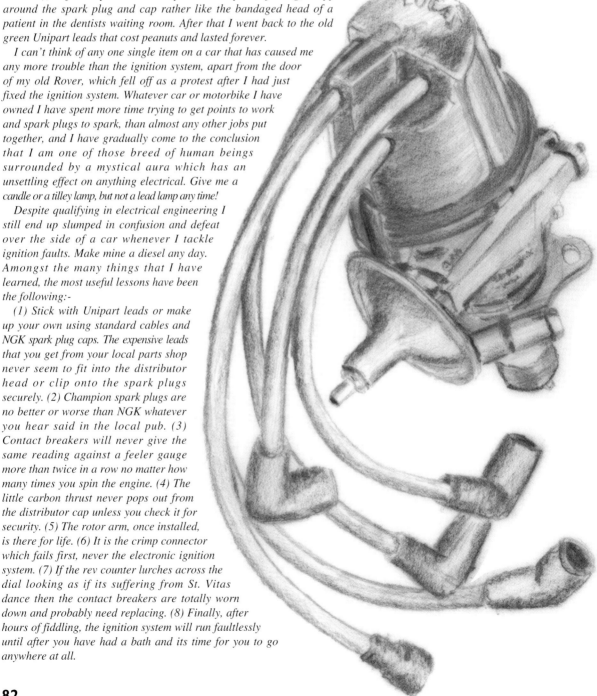

Why Fit Electronic Ignition

Electronic ignition does two things. Firstly it provides a stronger spark and works more effectively at high revs, where formerly unstoppable points bounce might make the red line sensibly unattainable.

Do you need a stronger spark? Well for general use I suspect its open to debate, but probably not. And do you need to hit the red line? It depends on whether you've just brought the car or whether you've just rebuilt the engine.

In my case I got fed up with endlessly having to buy and fit new contact breakers. More to the point I became increasingly cheesed off with trying to set the points gap. Finally, because the distributor bush appeared to be worn out and the rotor arm swayed around like a beech tree in a gale, it was practically impossible to get a regular points setting that worked throughout the rev range.

By replacing contact breakers with an optically triggered system I achieved the triple. No more buying new points. No more unpleasant bending. Instant red line.

The optical trigger in the system shown below, does not touch the armature. With no weight against the armature, variations to the points gap are less likely to occur, a real advantage on a worn distributor.

The only points it won't help you with are the concours type, but as long as you're happy driving the car, who cares what the judge thinks.

Disadvantages

Electronic ignition systems sometimes go "pop" for no apparent reason, leaving you stranded at the side of the road with no hope of furthering or completing a journey without the assistance of a tow truck.

One answer is to keep the old base plate made up with points and condenser fitted. If you ever get caught out, just replace the whole assembly. Easy.

An optically triggered system

Some History: The Ignition System

The distributor fitted to all 948cc engines was the Lucas DM2P4 type. Revised at the introduction of the 1098 cars, a 25D4 type was fitted (with the exception of some 1275 engines, being given a 23D4 distributor) and used until the introduction of the 1500.

1500 UK specification cars were given a 45D4 distributor, while European and US counterparts benefited from the electronic ignition distributor as denoted by the letter E in the type registration of 45DE4. Why are we always last to get these things?

The coil, originally strapped to the dynamo until 9C/U/H11889, was Lucas type LA12 - fitted to all 948 and 1098 engines. It looks like they couldn't make up their minds (though there was probably a good reason), but 1275 cars with the 23D4 distributor fitted were given a Lucas 11C12 coil, all other 1275 cars with the 25D4 distributor (up to 12V588F/H101) were fitted with an HA12 coil, whereupon the 11C12 coil was again fitted. All 1500 units were supplied with the 15C6 coil.

Spark plugs changed little, starting with Champion N5 plugs for 948 and 1098 models. 1275 and UK 1500 models (up to 1978) received the Champion N9Y plugs, while all European and US cars (also UK 1978 on) got N12Y plugs.

Plug leads prove to vary considerably due to local conditions or requirements and rather than list them here I would recommend sniffing out a parts manual which gives copious detail on lead lengths for a variety of circumstances and model years. (It's not that I'm lazy, there just isn't a page big enough to fit all the information on).

In France, the introduction of 10CG engines saw the fitment of the suppression screen box which encased the distributor, while Canadian markets were given a rubber waterproof cover to guard against water ingress.

According to the parts manuals, Danish and Canadian cars were introduced to the delights of suppressed leads when the 12CC engines were fitted. With 12CD engines, the suppressed net widened to engulf Germany and Newfoundland.

1500 distributors were fitted with top entry distributor caps, being better positioned to clear the steering column without fouling while at an unspecified point on the 1275cc cars a plastic pipe replaced the screw fit brass vacuum pipe. In 1979, a friend of mine carefully torqued down a cylinder head to discover that he'd sandwiched the vacuum pipe between that and the block. It is sad, true, and not in the least bit surprising to know that after a short display of pique he chopped off the offending pipe and fitted a new one. What can I say, the car still worked.

All 1500 models had their circuits revised to incorporate a resistive wire in the circuit (as shown in the following circuit diagrams). A new solenoid fitted at the same time offered a 12-volt supply to reach the coil during cranking, after which the resistive circuit was opened to allow a lower charge to operate the circuit.

Static Timing

If you've busily been pulling the engine apart, or feel that the car does not run as well as it should, then it may be as well to check the ignition timing. In theory, once set, the timing should not change - after all the cam is attached by a big chain, and the distributor fits into a slot and is held in place by a big clamp and two bolts. Yet apparently these things are always going wrong, or so I'm told.

If the timing is slipping, then either the cam chain is so worn that it is slipping on the sprockets (you may also notice some grizzly engine noise) or the distributor has come lose. Alternatively the distributor is worn, though this is likely to show up under strobe timing conditions where, under test, the timing marks jump around like a flea on speed!

1. Remove the rocker cover and spark plugs.
2. Adjust and set the points.
3. Rotate the engine until piston 1 (closest the pulley wheel) is at the top of its stroke. *The exhaust valve of piston 4 will be just closing and the inlet valve just opening.*
4. Turn the crankshaft until the timing mark on the crankshaft pulley is in line with the TDC pointer on the timing cover case. The books tell you to do this by putting a spanner over the pulley wheel, impossible unless the engine is out, because you can't get a spanner onto the nut with that large section of chassis and the radiator in the way.
   I normally do this by turning the water pump and generator pulleys together, keeping the fan belt under tension. Note: if you crimp your fingers with the fan belt don't come crying to me!
   If the engine is out and the timing cover removed then align the timing marks stamped into the camshaft and crankshaft pulley wheels. *At this point both pistons no. 1 & 4 should be at TDC. If not, then maybe you have put your engine back together wrong.*
5. Slacken the distributor pinch bolts and rotate the body anti-clockwise until the points are closed.
6. With the LT lead connected to the distributor, turn on the ignition. Connect a 12-volt lamp in parallel with the points. While the points are closed, the lamp will remain off.
7. Rotate the distributor clockwise until the lamp lights, whereupon the points will have just opened.
8. Secure the clamp and pinch bolt.
9. Check that the rotor arm is opposite the terminal in the distributor cap which goes to spark plug no. 1. *If not, you will need to keep turning the distributor around until this is the case and recheck using the lamp again.*
10. Reconnect the advance pipe, refit the distributor cap, rocker cover and spark plugs.

Why The Lamp Lights

When timing the ignition, a lamp can be attached between the CB (-) connection of the coil and earth. While the points remain closed, the lamp is switched off. When the points open, the lamp comes on because electricity follows the line of least resistance in any circuit.

The light bulb element acts like a resistor; when the points are closed the current will flow through the points to earth, because that part of the circuit offers no resistance. Once the points open, the only effective way to earth is via the lamp.

Fine Tuning

Where fitted, a vernier adjuster allows tiny changes to be made to the ignition timing, providing hours of endless entertainment to owners who drive up and down country lanes, lifting the bonnet and making these minute changes to the timing to improve the running - all of which make no apparent difference to bored and indifferent partners who still complain (somewhat unreasonably) that the hood leaks.

The knurled adjuster will advance or retard the ignition in "clicks". 11 clicks = 1°, 55 clicks = 5°. Turning the adjuster moves the vacuum unit back and forth. Marks on the body below the conical unit represent 5° of advance or retard. Click away...

Strobe Timing

1. Follow the strobe gun instructions.
2. Disconnect the vacuum advance pipe where fitted.
3. Set the engine revs as required by adjusting the idle speed screw on the carburetters, and alter the timing either using the vernier adjuster or by twisting the distributor while in position.

Note: Strobe timing the engine ends at the exact same moment as the generator pulley wheel eats its way through the strobe gun power cable.

Unleaded Fuel

Do not run your Midget or Sprite on unleaded fuel unless the cylinder head has been adapted to run on it. Do not assume that the inclusion of a lump of lead or old fishing weights slung into the tank will suffice as an additive allowing the use of cheaper lead free petrol.

The conversion of an "A" series engine to run on unleaded fuel is described in the engine section elsewhere in this book.

How A Coil Operates

A coil is made up of two coils, one inside the other and not connected in any way. Power is transferred from the outer to the inner coil by the force of magnetism.

As the contact breakers close, the outer coil is energised rapidly, allowing a strong magnetic force to build up before the points open and the current stops flowing. Instantly, the magnetic force collapses on itself, and in so doing, induces a current to flow like a shock wave, through the secondary coil. The faster the oscillation, the greater the magnetic force, and also, the greater the amount of electricity generated in the inner coil.

The windings play a contributory role in the process. If the primary coil has 100 windings and the secondary coil 1000 windings, then the voltage will be (for example) perhaps ten times larger.

The proportional difference between the windings of a coil are so great that a 12-volt supply running through the primary coil will induce between 2 and 3 kilovolts in the secondary coil. Combined with the high current being produced as the magnetic field oscillates on and off, you have the recipe for one heck of an electric shock!

Distributors (exploded views)

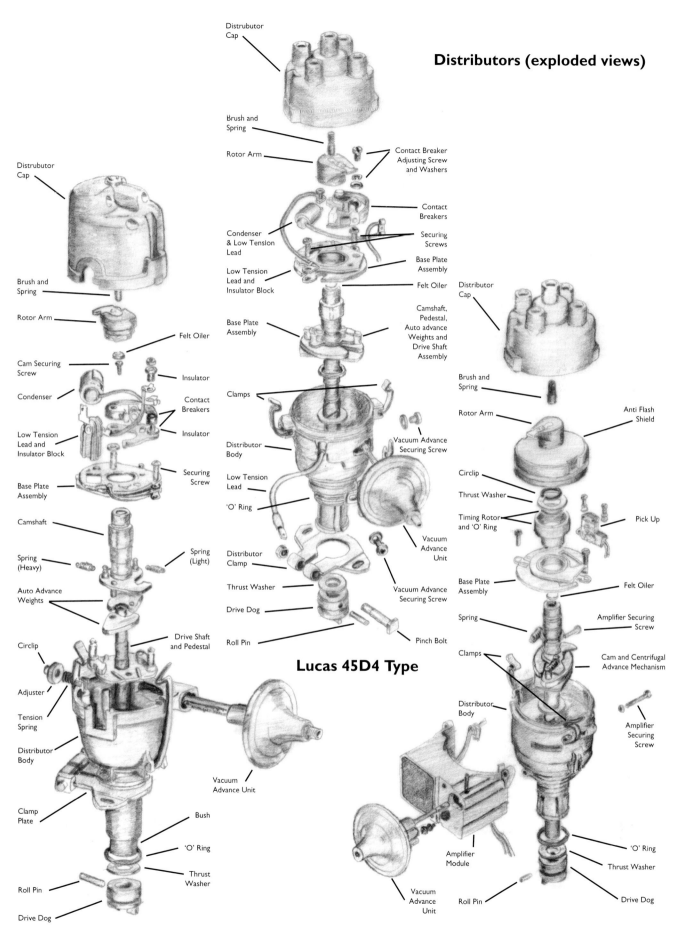

Distrubutor Cap

Brush and Spring

Rotor Arm

Contact Breaker Adjusting Screw and Washers

Contact Breakers

Condenser & Low Tension Lead

Securing Screws

Low Tension Lead and Insulator Block

Base Plate Assembly

Felt Oiler

Base Plate Assembly

Camshaft, Pedestal, Auto advance Weights and Drive Shaft Assembly

Clamps

Vacuum Advance Securing Screw

Distributor Body

Low Tension Lead

'O' Ring

Vacuum Advance Unit

Distributor Clamp

Thrust Washer

Drive Dog

Vacuum Advance Securing Screw

Roll Pin

Pinch Bolt

Lucas 45D4 Type

Distrubutor Cap

Brush and Spring

Rotor Arm

Felt Oiler

Cam Securing Screw

Condenser

Contact Breakers

Insulator

Insulator

Low Tension Lead and Insulator Block

Base Plate Assembly

Securing Screw

Camshaft

Spring (Heavy)

Spring (Light)

Auto Advance Weights

Circlip

Drive Shaft and Pedestal

Adjuster

Tension Spring

Distributor Body

Vacuum Advance Unit

Clamp Plate

Bush

'O' Ring

Thrust Washer

Roll Pin

Drive Dog

Lucas 25D4 Type

Distributor Cap

Brush and Spring

Rotor Arm

Anti Flash Shield

Circlip

Thrust Washer

Timing Rotor and 'O' Ring

Pick Up

Base Plate Assembly

Felt Oiler

Spring

Amplifier Securing Screw

Clamps

Cam and Centrifugal Advance Mechanism

Distributor Body

Amplifier Securing Screw

Amplifier Module

Vacuum Advance Unit

Roll Pin

'O' Ring

Thrust Washer

Drive Dog

Lucas 45DE4 Type

85

circlip

spring

Case Study: 25D4 Distributor

For examination purposes the distributor can be released from the engine casing by undoing the two bolts which keep it in place and withdrawing the assembly and clamp plate. Without undoing the clamp pinch bolts the unit can be replaced without needing to adjust the timing.

The box in the lower left of the picture (1) is the electronic ignition control box that had been fitted as an accessory.

1. The base plate (2) is held in position with two screws, easily seen once the distributor cap has been removed.

   Note: during removal the vacuum advance unit connects onto the base plate by means of a pin.

1. Remove the vacuum advance unit by unscrewing the knurled nut (3).

   On the end of the threaded rod is a small wire circlip (3). It stops the vernier adjuster being completely undone by mistake. Remove carefully to allow removal.

   Also, hidden away inside the body is a small spring (4) which could fly out as the vacuum unit is released. Take care not to lose it, indeed for safety put the spring, knurled nut and circlip back on the assembly to avoid losing the parts.

5. The distributor cap securing clamps can be pulled from their mountings for cleaning (5).

6. The cam and shaft can be separated by removing a screw located under the rotor arm normally hidden by a felt oiling pad (6).

   Take a careful note of how the springs and weights are fitted as the cam is removed (7). *Otherwise, during reassembly, the weights could be fitted incorrectly, jamming into the distributor body when the engine starts up. Pay particular attention to the fact that one spring is heavier and stronger than the other.*

7. Remove the shaft, by drifting out the pin securing the drive dog (9). The shaft can now be lifted out. Note the nylon washer fitted under the drive dog. Don't lose it.

The base plate

1. The base plate is of two part construction. During examination ensure that the earth wire is not frayed or damaged. The two halves simply twist and lock together (11).

Separate, clean and reassemble, lubricating with petroleum jelly.

2. Fit a new condenser and contacts, holding lightly in place with a screw and lock washer. *The adjuster screw and condenser screw are both readily available. Replace if damaged. There's nothing worse than being at the side of the road, trying to tighten damaged screws when it's dark or raining.*

3. Connect the low tension and condenser cables loosely, then temporarily secure the earth strap screw into the ring with tape (12).

Vacuum Advance Unit

The vacuum advance unit is connected by a pipe to the inlet manifold. As a vacuum is created in the manifold the diaphragm within the vacuum unit is pulled tight and rotates the base plate, thereby advancing or retarding the ignition. Replace if damaged.

Reassembly

Clean and examine the components for signs of wear or damage. In particular check the fit of the drive shaft in the bush, as wear here will be the most likely cause of problems. Replace if worn.

1. Reassemble the shaft and cam, with the springs and weights in situ before refitting into the distributor body. Refit the drive dog, nylon washer and new 'O' ring .

2. Fit the base plate and vacuum unit, ensuring that the peg on the end of the vacuum arm hooks into the socket of the base plate. Set the adjuster to the middle of its range (13).

3. Fit and adjust the contact breakers, having lightly lubricated the cam with petroleum jelly. Fit a new felt washer, oiled (14). Lubricate the cam head and refit rotor arm(15).

4. Refit the cap clamps and cap, with new leads if necessary. Refit the clamp plate to the distributor body.

Ignition Data

Model	948	1098
Firing Order	1342	1342
Spark Plugs	Champion N5	Champion N5
Plug Gap	0.24" to 0.26"	0.24" to 0.26"
	(0.625 to 0.66 mm)	(0.625 to 0.66 mm)
Lucas Coil type	LA12	LA12
Lucas Distributor	DM2P4	25D4
Points Gap	0.014" to 0.016"	0.014" to 0.016"
	(0.36 to 0.40mm)	(0.36 to 0.40mm)
Static Timing		
High comp.	4° BTDC	5° BTDC
Low comp.	1° BTDC	3° - 5° BTDC
Strobe Timing	6° BTDC	8° BTDC
	at 600 rpm	at 600 rpm

Model	1275 23D4 distributor	1275 25D4 distributor	1275 12V engine to 588F/H101	1275 12V engine from 778F/101 on
Firing Order	1342	1342	1342	1342
Spark Plugs	Champion N9Y	Champion N9Y	Champion N9Y	Champion N9Y
Plug Gap	0.24" to 0.26"	0.24" to 0.26"	0.24" to 0.26"	0.24" to 0.26"
	(0.625 to 0.66 mm)	(0.625 to 0.66 mm)	(0.625 to 0.66 mm)	(0.625 to 0.66 mm)
Lucas Coil type	11C12	HA12*	HA12	11C12
Lucas Distributor	23D4	25D4	25D4	25D4
Points Gap	0.014" to 0.016"	0.014" to 0.016"	0.014" to 0.016"	0.014" to 0.016"
	(0.36 to 0.40mm)	(0.36 to 0.40mm)	(0.36 to 0.40mm)	(0.36 to 0.40mm)
Static Timing				
High comp.	7° BTDC	7° BTDC	7° BTDC	7° BTDC
Low comp.	7° BTDC	7° BTDC	N/A	N/A
Strobe Timing	22° BTDC	13° BTDC	16° BTDC	16° BTDC
	at 1200 rpm	at 1000 rpm	at 1000 rpm	at 1000 rpm

Model	1500 1975 UK only	1500 1975-77 All other markets	1500 1977 on Fed. US/Canada
Firing Order	1342	1342	1342
Spark Plugs	Champion N9Y ††	Champion N12Y	Champion N12Y
Plug Gap	0.24" to 0.26"	0.24" to 0.26"	0.24" to 0.26"
	(0.625 to 0.66 mm)	(0.625 to 0.66 mm)	(0.625 to 0.660mm)
Lucas Coil type	15C6	15C6	15C6
Lucas Distributor	45D4	45DE4**	45DE4**
Points Gap	0.014" to 0.016"	0.014" to 0.016" *†	0.014" to 0.016" *†
	(0.36 to 0.40mm)	(0.36 to 0.40mm *†)	(0.36 to 0.40mm *†)
Static Timing			
High comp.	-	N/A	N/A
Low comp.	-	N/A	N/A
Strobe Timing	2° ATDC at	2° ATDC at	10° BTDC
	800 rpm ••	800 rpm	at 800 rpm

Notes

†† Champion N12Y from 1978 on

** "E" denotes electronic type of distributor

•• 10° BTDC at 800 rpm from 1978 on

* fitted from 12CE Da/H101 on

*† pick up air gap

Ignition Circuits

Sprite Mk I, II, III; Midget Mk I, II

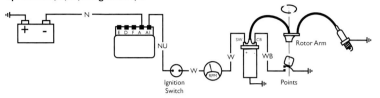

**Sprite Mk IV up to HAN9 85286;
Midget Mk III up to GAN4 74885**

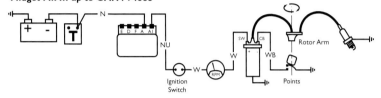

**Sprite Mk IV HAN9 85287 on
Midget Mk IV up to GAN5 128262 (UK) and GAN5 123730 (USA)**
(also GAN5 105501 to 128262 UK and GAN5 74886 to 105500 USA)

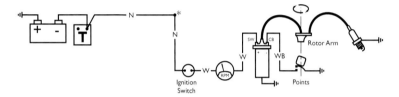

Midget up to last 1275cc models (UK and USA)

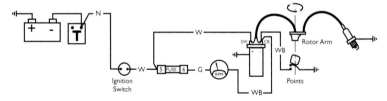

Midget 1500 (UK)

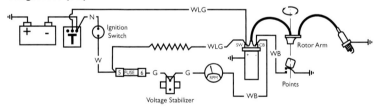

Midget 1500 (USA)

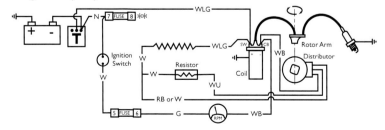

Travels by night

The dynamo shown in bits on these few pages, like many other parts on my car, has a story all of its own. It comes from a little garage in Lampeter, a market town in Dyfed, Wales. The town, small and friendly, boasts an ancient college of which I had the pleasure to be a student.

Always on the look out for spare cash, I took on a research job for one of our geography masters during the Easter holiday. The task was simple and soon over, consisting of nothing more than residing for one week, expenses paid, at the seaside town of Colwyn Bay. All day long I rode the buses, counting customers on and off. I drove the Midget up from Lampeter to the resort with a friend, one maniac by the name of John Davis. About six of us went up there in all, having a high old time throughout the week. Having no need of the car during the ensuing days, it lay idle while we went about our business, both during the day and in the bar of an evening.

On the Sunday night John and I prepared for the long journey home. As was often the case the Midget had trouble starting, but when the battery was thought nearly dead, she fired up and away we went. Typical winter weather had closed in, heavy rain and strong winds, it would be a long journey home.

We were only twelve or thirteen miles from Colwyn when the ignition light flickered on. We stopped and I checked under the bonnet. No loose connection I could see and the fan belt was attached, but the strong smell of burning convinced me that the bearings of the dynamo had failed. There was nothing else for it, but to slacken the fan belt slightly and carry on.

Now, I don't know if you know Wales at all, but Sunday, especially to the North and Middle of that country, is a fiercely protected day of rest. Be assured there is not a garage, a pub or a shop open from Holyhead to Abergavenny. There's no telephone box either.

We went on, figuring that the best thing to do was get as close to home as possible. We drove on side lights and we drove slowly, because the other thing missing from the glorious Welsh landscape is a street lamp. The weather cleared and we were able to drive by the light of the moon, and few cars were on the road. We were overtaken twice, each time we tailgated - guided and trusting in the lights and sense of the driver in front. Both drivers turned off the road and so we were left again, on our own, miles from anywhere and driving who knows how slowly.

From Aberaeron we hitched up with a milk tanker which helped lead us home and finally, with just miles to go, we ran the last little bit of the journey through Lampeter and on to the village that had become my home, without even the side lights to guide me. Even turning on the panel lights slowed the car so much that it was better to keep them off.

When I pulled into the drive of our rented cottage, I beeped the horn in triumph. The car ground to a halt and the battery, along with the old dynamo, never worked again.

Dynamos, Alternators, Batteries and the Charging Circuit

Some History:
Wiring Looms & Fuse Boxes

The original Sprite, kitted out by Lucas, was basic to say the least. Developed with economy in mind the car was just about road legal. Power was supplied to essential components via a cloth covered loom identified by a blue trace. A Lucas SF6 fuse box carried two fuses. Not many, but two more than could be found on a Citroen 2CV6!

For the Sprite Mk II & Midget Mk I, the loom was revised and clearly marked with a yellow or white trace. Spade connectors replaced screw connections and a 4FJ fuse box, mounted at the top of the RH footwell panel replaced the earlier SF6 type.

Sprite Mk IV & Midget Mk III models used an all black cotton loom which, following the introduction of the Leylandised models, was replaced by a PVC covered version. The Leylandised cars were also fitted with a 7FJ fuse box which carried four fuses and had room for two spares. So now, you could really crank up the radio. An in-line fuse was added from HAN10 86303 / GAN5 89515 to protect heater blower and wipers.

The loom was revised to cater for under bonnet changes following installation of the 1500cc engine - yet still no fuse box was fitted to a 2CV6.

Batteries

The original battery was a BT7A type giving 43 amp hours of life. Fitted behind where the heater would be (assuming you could afford that option), it sat on a black bakelite spill tray, secured by a black painted clamp and threaded rods hooked to the chassis.

There were a few changes, but none that ever made it easier to check the electrolyte level.

A new spill tray was fitted from HAN6 7960 / GAN1 3734. A Lucas N9 battery (40 amp hour), with revised clamps and bar, was fitted from HAN7 27756 / GAN2 18220 to cater for the new shape battery.

Negative earthing was introduced from HAN9 72041 / GAN4 60460 (HAN9 72034 / GAN4 60441 in North America). A Lucas A9 (40 amp hour) or A11 (50 amp hour) battery was used with reversed terminals.

Negative earthing led to other changes as well because the battery strap, rods and tray needed changing. A negative earth tacho was fitted. A "Negative Earth" warning sticker was affixed to warn people against possible incorrect connection or fitment of unsuitable accessories, you may remember all the new radios came with polarity switches. **TIP - never rub two old cars of opposite polarity together!** From engine 12V 778 FH a Lucas A98 battery was fitted.

The new Midget 1500 engine had carburation and electrical components on opposite sides from before. The loom was revised to accommodate the under bonnet changes and so too was the battery (the earth lead ran to the right hand of the bulkhead instead of the left as with all previous models). North American

cars were fitted with a battery cut-off relay from GAN6 166304.

WARNING: The information supplied here tends to oversimplify things a bit. In fact, there were over twenty four different looms fitted catering for a number of electrical changes as well as the differing legal requirements of North America (and Californian legislation), Germany, France, Sweden and so on. **Check your requirements against your chassis and engine numbers and the workshop manuals.** Wiring loom information listed here relates specifically to the charging circuit. For more comprehensive information see elsewhere in this volume.

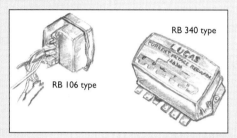

Dynamos, Control Boxes & Alternators

The Sprite charging system, like everything else on the new Sprite, was a pretty straightforward affair, with one exception. Lucas and Smiths worked together to produce a special drive which, running from the back of the C39 type dynamo, provided the take off for a mechanically driven tachometer. To regulate dynamo output a voltage control unit (RB106/1 or RB106/2) was fitted to the right hand mud shield.

The Sprite II & Midget I saw the dynamo and control box (RB106/2) revised intermittently from HAN6 7499 / GAN1 3491 onwards and permanently from HAN6 10118 / GAN1 7520. The control unit was now fitted to the bulkhead with the dynamo adjusting link improved from 9 CG 1154 onwards.

With the introduction of 10CG engine a more powerful C40-1 dynamo was fitted. A new tachometer was electrically driven. The new dynamo was updated at 10CG DA 2571 with the link pillar and top securing bolts being revised again at 10 CG 2572.

Big changes started happening when the Sprite Mk IV & Midget Mk III were introduced. Australian cars saw the dynamo replaced by an alternator and external control box (YGN4-1000 onwards). Elsewhere, Leylandised cars (GAN5 / HAN10 models) were fitted with an RB340 control box and kept the dynamo.

When the round wheel arch models were introduced North American cars were fitted with a 16ACR alternator. From GAN5 128263 on the rest of the world also got alternators. A more powerful 17ACR unit came into use from engine number 12V588 FH 2551 (N. Am 12V 671 ZL 9570 on) and to improve output a smaller diameter alternator pulley was added from engine 12V588FH 3193 (Home markets only) and 12V 671 ZL 9570 (N. America).

Take Charge Now...

The charging circuit is the heart of any car electrical system. Once the battery has got your car going, the dynamo or alternator takes over and recharges it for the next attempt. Well that's the theory. By way of background, early cars (up to the mid-70s) incorporated a dynamo and control box (diagrams 1 and 2) with later cars using an alternator (diagram 3). The big difference is that a dynamo provides direct current (DC) while an alternator generates alternating current (AC), converted internally to DC via an integral control box. For its size, weight and cost, alternators produce a lot more power, and just remember, the seventies was the time of the 8 track.

Depending upon which control box was fitted, the dynamo charging circuit was wired differently, but still achieved the same result - sometimes. The control box controls the flow of electricity between the battery and the generator. When discharged, the control box gives the battery a boost from the generator while the engine is running. Meanwhile, the generator provides sufficient power to run the lights, ignition, horn, wipers, etc.

Once the battery is charged up the control box reduces the flow of electricity to a trickle, which keeps the battery charged. Without that automatic adjustment, the battery would "cook" itself, leading to failure.

While at low engine revs, the generator produces insufficient power to run everything. At this point the control box feeds power back into the circuit from the battery. You'll know when that's happening because the ignition warning light flickers on (just like when the fan belt breaks and the generator stops working).

Finally, a cut-out relay is fitted which disconnects the battery from the charging circuit when necessary (i.e. when the ignition is turned off). This simple device stops the battery from discharging itself overnight.

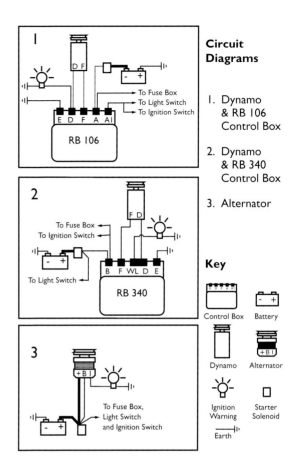

Circuit Diagrams

1. Dynamo & RB 106 Control Box

2. Dynamo & RB 340 Control Box

3. Alternator

Key

Control Box   Battery

Dynamo   Alternator

Ignition Warning   Starter Solenoid

Earth

Bad Earthing

The engine, gearbox, rear axle and suspension are mounted on rubber bushes, straps or pads. Even the exhaust boasts rubber mountings to guard against vibration. Nuts and bolts are pretty tenuous as a means to supply an earth circuit, so something is needed to guarantee a good earthing circuit, allowing electricity to flow around the car.

The only guaranteed earth return circuit is via the earthing strap, bolted between the engine and car body. It carries a lot of current. If it's not working, frayed or worn (and this is not unusual on older cars), or otherwise incapable of allowing current flow, the power will attempt to get back to the battery or down to earth using some other method. For example, fuel pipes, dual gauge tubes, braided brake hoses or by any other undesirable means.

Ensure there are good earthing connections from the engine to the body, and from the body to the battery by examining the earth strap.

Jump Starting Positive Earth Cars

If you are running an early car with positive earthing, don't let it come into physical contact with a negative earthed vehicle. Electrical failure of components or of the battery can ensue. It can also lead to an explosion. If you have a flat battery then there are three methods to use in an attempt to start the car.

1. Find someone else with a positive earth car. Connect positive to positive first, then negative (your car) to negative (donor car).

2. Using a negative earth car, disconnect the donor car battery and use it as a "slave battery" to start your own car. Extra points are always awarded to anyone who does this, fails to start their own car and disables the slave battery, making it impossible to start either car.

3. Push start the car. Select second gear, not first, because it's easier to push start the car using a gear that operates well at a slow running pace. Pushers soon get tired of the effort of trying to push a car in first gear and flop to the floor in an untidy heap - and then what would the neighbours think!

Case Study: Control Boxes

The RB106/1 or /2 control boxes consisted of a single regulator and cut out switch. The RB304 box included voltage and current regulators and a cut-out switch.

Except in Australia the external control box was removed with the introduction of alternators.

The instructions shown for checking are based on those found in the official workshop manuals.

RB106 Control Box Settings

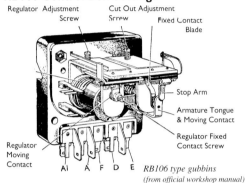

RB106 type gubbins
(from official workshop manual)

Open Circuit Setting
- Disconnect "A1" and "A" cables and join together.
- Connect volt meter between earth and D terminal.
- Gradually increase engine speed until the volt meter needle flickers and then steadies.
- At 20°C (68°F) the reading should be between 16.0 and 16.6 volts. Adjust the circuit using regulator adjusting screw.

Note:- For every increase of temperature by 10°C (18°F) - subtract 0·1°V. For every decrease of temperature by 10°C (18°F) - add 0·1°V

Cut Out Setting
- Connect volt meter between D & E terminals.
- Start engine and slowly increase speed until the cut-out contacts can be seen to close. Note voltage.

Voltage should read between 12.7 and 13.3 volts. Adjust the cut out adjusting screw as necessary.

RB340 Control Box Settings

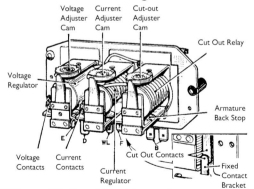

RB340 type gubbins (from official workshop manual)

Voltage Regulator Settings
- Disconnect "B" cables and join together.
- Remove cable from WL, connect a voltmeter between the terminal blade and earth.

- With the engine running at 3000rpm the following voltages should register (depending upon the ambient temperature).

At 10°C (50°F) 14.5 to 15.8 volts
At 20°C (68°F) 14.4 to 15.6 volts
At 30°C (86°F) 14.3 to 15.3 volts

Note: At temperatures greater than this you should be in the shade or in a swimming pool somewhere and not working on a car.

Current Regulator Settings
- With the voltage regulator contacts shorted out, the "B" cables disconnected and joined together, and with an ammeter between terminal "B" and the cables, make sure that every circuit is switched off.
- Start the engine, turn on the headlamps and run the engine at 4500rpm.
- The current output should equal maximum rated output stamped on the dynamo.
- If the current fluctuates by more than one amp then clean the control box terminals.
- If the current is steady but incorrect twiddle the current adjustment cam as necessary.

Cut Out Relay - contacts closing
Cut In Voltage
- Disconnect the WL cables, connect a volt meter between the terminal blade and earth.
- Switch on the headlamps, start the engine and increase the revs.
- Watch the meter as the voltage increases steadily, before dropping back as the contacts close.

At the highest point before the volt meter drops the meter should read between 12.7 and 13.3 volts. Adjust the cut-out relay as necessary.

Cut-Out Relay - contacts opening
There are two ways of checking if the contacts are opening correctly; drop-off voltage and reverse current flow. The choice is yours.

- To check drop-off voltage: Remove the B cables, connect together, then connect a volt meter between the B terminal and an earth.
- Start the engine, run at 3000rpm and slowly reduce engine speed.
- Between 9.5 and 11.0 volts the contacts should open and the voltage should drop to zero.

If not, turn off the engine, and bend the contact arm gently. Reduce gap to raise drop-off voltage, increase gap to lower it.

- To check the reverse current: Remove the "B" cables, join together and connect an ammeter between the cables and the "B" terminals.
- Start the engine and increase engine speed until the ammeter registers current flow.
- Watch the ammeter, slowly reduce the engine speed until the ammeter needle falls for a moment. *Adjust as for drop-off voltage.*

Dynamo (exploded view)

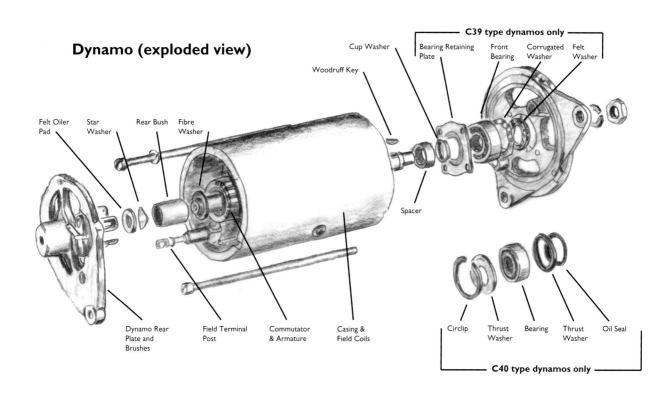

Cup Washer

Woodruff Key

C39 type dynamos only

Bearing Retaining Plate

Front Bearing

Corrugated Washer

Felt Washer

Felt Oiler Pad

Star Washer

Rear Bush

Fibre Washer

Spacer

Dynamo Rear Plate and Brushes

Field Terminal Post

Commutator & Armature

Casing & Field Coils

Circlip

Thrust Washer

Bearing

Thrust Washer

Oil Seal

C40 type dynamos only

Alternator (exploded view)

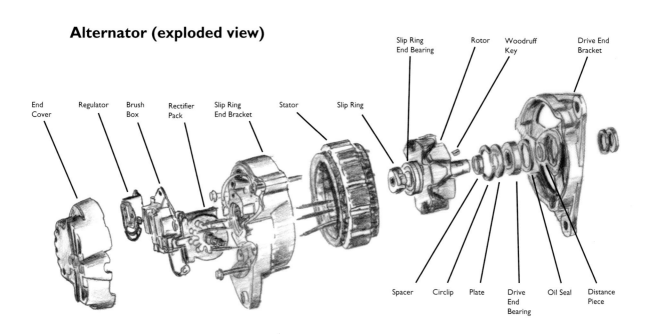

Slip Ring End Bearing

Rotor

Woodruff Key

Drive End Bracket

End Cover

Regulator

Brush Box

Rectifier Pack

Slip Ring End Bracket

Stator

Slip Ring

Spacer

Circlip

Plate

Drive End Bearing

Oil Seal

Distance Piece

Case Study: Dynamo
Removing The Fan

It's always the simple jobs. Only one big nut holds the fan and pulley in place, but try as you might you can't stop the pulley spinning. A lever wedged amongst the fan blades soon makes a bad job worse. So here's a tip for you.

Wrap sisal around the pulley and then tie it off before undoing that nut (1). The sisal fibres grip the pulley wheel; the more you apply pressure to the nut, the greater the grip becomes.

Note carefully the collar and woodruff key which are visible once the pulley and fan blades have been removed (2). The key levers out using a screwdriver blade. The collar simply slides out.

Dismantling the Dynamo

Having removed the fan, the body can be dismantled. This should be the easy bit.

1. Undo the retaining screws to release the rear plate (3) and remove carefully. Note the insulator pads (4) which prevent any earthing problems.

2. The body lifts away from the armature and front plate assembly, which can be separated using a hub puller (5).

Removing The Front Bearing

1. Remove the circlip and thrust washer (6) and then press out the bearing.

   The collar, a suitable socket and some wood blocks (7) can be used in conjunction with a vice to press the bearing out. The alternative is cautious use of a hammer and drift.

2. Remove inner thrust washer and oil seal (8).

3. Clean parts and prepare for reassembly. Examine the roller bearing for signs of wear and replace if necessary.

Removing The Rear Bearing

The rear bush is made of phosphor bronze. From what I can see, the only way to remove it is by breaking it up in situ with a flat bladed screwdriver or other such pointy tool. Be careful not to damage the casing.

Along with the broken bush will come a star washer and grubby piece of material which should resemble a felt washer. It's supposed to have oil on it, but that might be expecting too much.

Take care not to damage the bearing seat or crack the rear plate for that matter.

Rear Bearing & Brushes

1. Clean the rear plate, fit a new felt oiler and put the star washer back into position (9). *A little grease on both items helps to secure them. A point which becomes important later.*

2. Press the bush into position (10) using a suitable drift. Ensure that it does not go in at an angle. Gently tap in with a hammer or press it home using a vice or cramp (as shown).

The star washer and felt oiler are held in position by the bush which locks the four corners of the washer in place. If you get it wrong, you'll be digging out the bush and starting all over again with a new one.

3. Examine the old brushes and replace if necessary (11). These wear out as a matter of course. Picture 11 shows a new brush installed so that you can see how long it ought to be.

Front Bearing

1. Careful appliance of a vice to push the bearing home will ensure easier, positive location. *Make sure that pressure is applied to the outer bearing race during fitting, otherwise you might separate the inner race.*

2. Lock the circlip into position. It fits into the grooved wall of the bearing housing (12) - and should not be balanced above it. *Fitting may prove tiresome, but with time, patience and effort you should be able to get that wayward circlip flying to all four corners of the garage with ease and confidence.*

Fitting It All Together

Slide the armature into the front plate, fit the body over the armature and refit the back plate. Sounds simple, but here are some tips to help do the job.

Dynamo Mountings

The dynamo mounts between the water pump and an engine mounting bracket. A sliding rod (shown right) allows adjustment to take place.

Fan Belt Tension

Slacken A and B and also the adjusting rod C. The dynamo will move up and down by hand and once the adjustment is correct simply lock the adjusting rod C into place before retightening the other bolts.

The tension is correct when, at the centre of the longest run, the fan belt can move in and out over 1in (2.54 cm) and not be so loose as to slip.

You'll know if the fan belt is too loose (the lights go dim and the battery won't charge up), or if its too tight (the dynamo bearings wear out, the lights go dim and the battery won't charge up).

1. Be careful when fitting the armature back into the bearing. Some packing washers will direct the strain back onto the body while a suitable hollow drift (13) allows the armature to be pressed home correctly without fouling anything. *Ensure that the armature does not extend too far through the bearing. It is important that, when located, the woodruff key (14) locks both the fan and pulley wheel into position.*

2. Fit the body, replacing any insulating pads (15), before refitting the rear plate.

3. Fit the rear plate. The brushes are spring loaded and need to be carefully pushed away from the commutator (16) to avoid damaging the brushes or commutator surface.

4. Check that the unit spins properly, if not it may be that the armature is rubbing against one of the end plates. Re-align it if necessary.

5. Ensure the long screws locate under the insulating pads to stop any short circuit, then refit the collar, spacer and woodruff key before sliding the fan and pulley home. *Use the sisal trick to lock the armature and pulley into position before refitting the pulley nut securely.*

Finally, remember to occasionally put a few drops of oil into the aperture at the rear of the dynamo (17). This keeps the 'oilite' bush lubricated and the dynamo running longer.

Polarising a Dynamo

Always polarise a generator before installation to ensure correct operation.

Connect a strong electrical cable between the live terminal of the battery and the dynamo body.

Connect another cable to the earth terminal and "flick" the other end against the small terminal of the dynamo (normally marked with the letter "F") four or five times.

Oh, one last thing. Following the fitting of a new unit you should check the charge rate to make sure everything is okay.

Positive (+) Earth cars

Negative (-) Earth cars

'Oilite' Bushes

The press fit bush that fits into the rear plate was always known in the trade as an 'Oilite' bush. Once impregnated with oil the bush needed little further attention. What a romantic notion!

These bushes turn up in all sorts of places where it is difficult to get an oil can to (for example, inside the wiper motor or where the crankshaft meets the gearbox input shaft).

Usually, if you go to a parts shop, somebody just slings the bush across the counter at you without telling you what to do with it (probably because they don't know themselves). In fact, some preparation is necessary before installation of the bush.

Find an old jar, fill it with motor oil (preferably the green stuff) and drop the bush into it. Leave it in there for at least 24 hours allowing the oil to seep into the very porous metal of the bush. Then it will last for ages. Otherwise, just leave it for a few months and replace it again. The choice, as they say, is yours.

Travels by night 2

I used to love driving by night, and still do, except my eyes are a little more easily worn to a frazzle by the intensity of all these halogen lamps. I am guilty too however...

When I first got the Midget I fitted a set of Lucas H4s so that I could see better in the dark. They give vastly improved road coverage over the originals, and they are so easy to fit. To even assume that they might be needed anywhere within a 50 mile radius of London is perhaps stretching the imagination, but when I lived in Wales they came into their own. On a good night you could light up half of Cardigan Bay!

Lights

There's not a street lamp between Monmouth and Lampeter except for a few straggling examples scattered about the roads of Brecon and Abergavenny. Of the two located at Sennybridge I only ever saw one working. With few cars on the road it was main beam all the way, wherever you went, dipping only for the stray motorist heading out of Cardiganshire on a Sunday night looking for the nearest open pub.

Then one night one of the lights stopped working. Well, having no torch and no street lamps handy I had to drive home like Cyclops before being able to look into the problem. On closer inspection, instead of the blown bulb that I had anticipated, I actually discovered that the connector block (which plugs into the halogen unit) had melted from the heat of the bulb.

If you're going to fit Halogen units fit the bakelite connector blocks they don't melt. Alternatively, fit some decent spot lamps.

Many years ago, and after a wildly enthusiastic night out drinking at a pub in Egham - famed for the signing of the Magna Carta (Egham I mean, not the pub), three friends and I all piled into our mate's Mum's Austin 1100.

Blearily peering through the screen as my sober friend drove us slowly home I pointed out that it might be a good idea if he turned the lights on.

"They are!" came his agitated retort. Everyone strained their eyes for a few moments as they gazed drunkenly forward, before falling about laughing while I, seriously humbled, apologised profusely for causing any embarrassment. In my defence I have since heard that they call Lucas the "Prince of Darkness".

Some History: Lights

Headlamps

From the original Sprite the headlamp assemblies changed little except to account for local variations - right or left hand drive, right, left or vertical dip, etc.

Probably the most significant change came when, with the introduction of the Midget 1500 UK models, a pilot bulb was included in the headlamp. The rubber bumper contained the indicator units only.

UK and non-European LHD bulbs: 50W main, 40W dipped. European LHD and Sweden RHD bulbs: 45W main, 40W dipped.

A foot operated switch controlled the dip and main beam until the introduction of GAN5, HAN10 models.

Front sidelamps

For the sake of simplicity and economy, the front sidelamp and indicators, using twin filament bulbs, shared single, bullet-shaped, white lenses.

From the introduction of the Sprite II & Midget I new style sidelamp and indicator assemblies were specified. Two single filament bulbs were fitted with an amber shroud fitted over the indicator bulb. The clear lenses were handed for many markets (see page 101) though in some instances single, twin filament bulbs were fitted under white lenses.

Side lamps in the West German Sprite III & Midget II models (from HAN8 50192and GAN3 38970 on) were installed in the headlamps, the indicators now being given amber coloured lenses (not handed).

To cater for the introduction of the Midget 1500 rubber bumper models the sidelamps were incorporated into the headlamp assemblies. The indicators, with single amber lenses, were fitted into cut-outs within the front bumpers.

Rear Lamps

Starting with the original Sprite the tail / stop lamp assembly, as fitted to many other cars of the same period, incorporated a twin filament bulb; this time under a red lens. The rear indicators were of the same design as the front side lamp / indicator assemblies using a single filament bulb with amber lens.

The Sprite II and Midget I models were given new rear lamp assemblies that incorporated the indicators. In some instances local requirements demanded red lenses, rather than amber, for the indicator part of the assembly.

West German Sprite III and Midget II models (from HAN8 50192and GAN3 38970 on) replaced the red indicator lenses with an amber equivalent.

With the introduction of the Leylandised Sprite Mk IV and Midget Mk III models the shape of the rear lenses changed to a flatter, more squared off design. Red over amber lenses prevailed in the US and amber over red lenses in the UK - again other local variations would have been a consideration).

From GAN5 129951 US rear lamp assemblies were altered, though from the parts book information available I am unable to say what that change was, the component parts (including the lenses) indicate no obvious changes.

Number Plate Lamps

Originally a single number plate lamp was located centrally above the number plate. From AN5 36194 the assembly incorporated a second bulb.

Things stayed pretty quiet until the Leylandised Sprite Mk IV & Midget Mk III models were introduced. The new quarter bumpers saw the fitment of a new rectangular number plate and, hidden behind the bumpers, were new bubble shaped lamp units.

US markets saw the introduction of a pair chromed conical lamps from GAN5 143355. With the introduction of the Midget 1500 models the chrome part was replaced with a black casing.

In the UK and elsewhere the rubber bumpers saw the introduction of a pair of lamp assemblies similar to the original type (but with a different part number, suggesting some modification or variation) in chrome. From GAN6 169644 on the chrome covers were changed to black.

UK 1500 models had the whole number plate assembly mounted below the black bumper, US models had the assembly mounted above it. Perhaps the kerbs are higher out there.

Reversing Lamps

Twin reversing lights, operated by a remote sensing switch in the gearbox housing were installed from HAN9 70268 / GAN4 58112 on. In France the assemblies incorporated amber filters.

In North America the reversing lights were revised from GAN5 113617 and again from GAN5 129951.

Courtesy Lamps

Courtesy lights were fitted in cockpit and boot from HAN10 86303 and GAN5 89515. The interior courtesy lamp is operated by switches in the A posts or by a switch on the lamp assembly The boot lamp being operated by a switch under the boot lid.

Marker Lamps

At some time during the production run of GAN4 and HAN9 models US laws demanded the introduction of reflectors to the front and rear wings as a way of improving night time visibility and safety. The actual point of fitment is not listed in the parts book.

From GAN5 74886 onwards the reflectors were replaced with marker lamp assemblies.

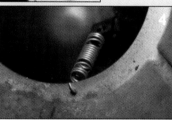

CASE STUDY: HEADLAMPS

1. Remove the grille and disconnect the headlamp cables from the loom.

2. Remove outer chrome bezel and inner chrome ring which locks the bulb in position. As you turn away the bulb will fall out of the shell. Disconnect the now broken remains! *Examine reflector for damage to the glass and silvered surface (which peels) and ensure that the lens is not cloudy or cracked.*

3. Unscrew headlamp bowl from the wing (1). *Shells were secured with machine screws, or screws and nuts, or rivets. If the bowls have been removed before they may be attached using a combination of the above.*

   The inner bowl is held in place with two screws and a spring which allow the light beam to be aligned. To the rear of the outer bowl there should be a rubber seal (2), sandwiched between the bowl and the wing.

Reassembly

If using new headlamp bowls ensure that the plastic adjuster nuts, screws and outer chrome ring fit. Use new plastic adjuster nuts (the old ones become hardened and broken).

3. Fit the adjuster screws (3), having brushed the threads with anti-seize lubricant (necessary for future adjustment). Hook the inner rim into place, locating it onto the adjuster screws. Fit the spring (4).

4. Install the wiring harness. *It's a tight fit, whether you fit the wiring into the grommet first and then put the grommet into the shell, or if you fit the grommet into position first. Some petroleum jelly might help.*

5. Fit a new rubber seal over the rear of the headlamp assembly (5). Then connect the bulb to the loom and lock it into position using the inner chrome ring (6). *Note the lugs on the lens face. The bulb and rim will only fit together in one position.*

9. Finally attach the outer rim and secure it with the correct retaining screw (7).

Which lens, where?

From the Sprite Mk II / Midget Mk I until the introduction of rubber bumpers, the sidelamp / indicator lens consisted of a single lens. When fitted, the indicator lamp should be at the outer edge, allowing the flashing lamp to be visible from the side of the car. LH and RH lens can be mistakenly fitted the wrong way round.

Unscrupulous dealers have a tendency to sell you whatever hand they have in stock and, in some instances, will swear blind that its "the correct one squire"!

The lenses display patterns of concentric rings, of which the more dominant rings fits over the amber indicator filter (shown below).

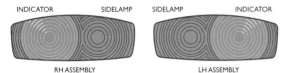

INDICATOR SIDELAMP SIDELAMP INDICATOR

RH ASSEMBLY LH ASSEMBLY

UK SIDELAMP ASSEMBLIES
(as viewed from front of vehicle)

Amber Filters

If the inner amber lens requires replacement, note that the colour tends to vary a bit between manufactured batches. Sometimes a replacement lens will be quite dark, at other times it will be pale. Sadly, when you order a pair, the average parts man will send you one of each, so take your original sample to the parts shop or order three to save time, effort and disappointment.

Halogen Headlamps & Driving Lamps

Throughout production, headlamps fitted to Sprites and Midgets consisted of fairly typical sealed beam or tungsten bulb assemblies. Reasonable power output and just about right for the kind of conditions encountered. If more lighting power was required then the answer was to fit auxiliary driving lamps. A modern trend is to fit halogen headlamps. Be warned, these are much hotter and can melt the wiring loom behind them (see above).

Owners of later cars with alternators should not worry about more powerful lamps, but owners of earlier, dynamo-driven vehicles will begin to find that the extra lighting is a bit of a drain on resources. The BMC Competitions Department, based at the MG factory in Abingdon, would have suggested fitting a C40L dynamo which, with its longer armature, extra wire and bigger magnets, packed more of a punch. Imagine being able to turn on all the lights and the heater, or being able to turn left without the headlamps going dimmer, brighter, dimmer, brighter, dimmer, brighter, dimmer....
See page 207 for fog / driving lamp fitting.

Case Study: Side Lamps

Due to the internationally agreed and approved standard regarding bumper height, the Sprite and Midget sidelights are normally wiped out during other people's standard parking procedures.

If your side lights or indicators don't work (and nobody has parked anywhere near you recently) then suspect an earthing fault, broken or corroded wire. Again, like the headlamp assemblies, these units suffer badly from salt corrosion due to a lack of reasonable protection.

Always try to save the chrome bezels since replicas often prove to be of an inferior quality.

Disassembly

1. Disconnect wiring and unscrew nuts from inside the wing which secures the assembly (1). *The backplate studs break and frequently end up being replaced by a screw and nut. Hours of endless fun in the years to come.*

2. Unscrew and remove chrome bezel, lens and rubber seal to gain access to the lamps. The orange filter (where fitted) simply pulls free having been held in place by spring clips (2).

4. Remove bulbs to reveal mica plates, springs and wires (3). Earthing is achieved via the bulb body and backplate back to the chassis.

Renovate as practicable!

Left: At a recent MG Car Club show at Silverstone I spotted this early 1275 Midget.
Below: At the same show I spotted this Leylandised model - again with an incorrect wing, this time the right one.

HiLo!

Some Sprites and Midget tend to look, well, a bit uneven and the apparent cause is not always very obvious. Is it the grille or the bonnet at fault, perhaps the bumper is twisted. The truth is that many owners get sold incorrect wings.

In the picture above you'll notice that one sidelamp is higher than the other. The left hand wing is for later cars with narrower bumper blades. This sort of mistake is not that easy to spot at the parts counter, and many people don't notice or assume that the wing has not been built correctly.

Dealers can spot the difference and, frankly, there's no confusing the early and late part numbers. Some Sprite and Midget "experts" seem more interested in making quick sales than building a reputable business. Watch out...

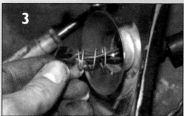

Case Study: Rear Lamps

Rear lamp assemblies on the 1098/1275/1500 Sprites and Midgets are very simple to dismantle and examine, though renovation may prove difficult especially if the chrome work is damaged. Replacement parts are readily available.

1. Notice that the wiring is held in position with a "P" clip (1) and that speed nuts with matching rubber washers (2) are used to secure the units. These nuts are irreplaceable, so try not to lose them if possible.

2. Clean the assembly thoroughly - chrome polish and wire wool works wonders - and ensure that the spring loaded terminals are clean (3).

3. Finally, ensure that the gaskets (one fits under the lens and another fits at the rear of the unit) are in good condition. (4) These are readily available from specialists.

4. Damaged lenses can be replaced, but may be worth replacing in sets since batches of the plastic used sometimes seem to be of varying shades.

Case Study:
Number Plate Lamps

The lamp assembly sits on a platform and consists of a base, gasket, lens and cover held together by the two screws.

Hidden behind the split rear bumpers, the screws of the number plate lamp often prove impossible to undo. If penetrating fluid fails to help, drilling the screws out may be the only option of gaining access for cleaning or bulb replacement.

This is worse than it sounds because you can't get a drill to the screws without risk to the surrounding chrome work. To remove the whole assembly means:-

> Disconnecting the wiring (from inside the boot (1), and unbolting the entire quarter bumper (2) just to gain access to the number plate lamp bracket (3). (The nuts here are also usually seized solid as well.)

During reassembly use plenty of anti-seize lubricant on the screws to enable easier removal when the next bulb blows. Replace the rubber gasket, if worn, to stop water ingress and subsequent failure of the unit.

Case Study:
Reversing Lamps

The simple two piece assembly is affixed to the rear panel with machine screws and captive nuts. The lens design appears to have modified slightly over the years so replacement of damaged or discoloured lenses should be undertaken in pairs.

If using a new bodyshell you will notice that the captive nuts are missing from the shell and either appropriate nuts or speed nuts will be required.

The lens and body will only fit one way round - note the length of the locating projections of the body and lens (2).

TIP: During storage, fit the screws into position and nip a "flag" of tape around the threads (3), this stops them from being lost.

Headlamp Circuits

See page 207 for fog / driving lamp fitting.

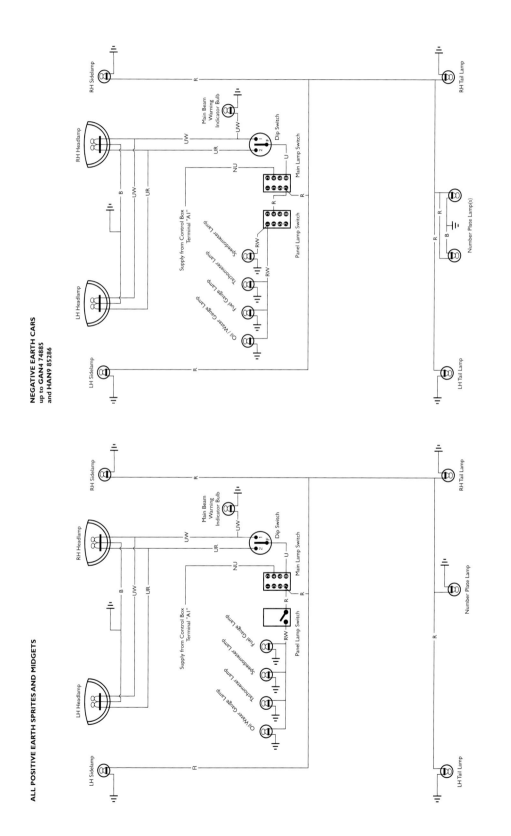

NEGATIVE EARTH CARS
up to **GAN4 74885**
and **HAN9 85286**

ALL POSITIVE EARTH SPRITES AND MIDGETS

Wire Colours							
N	Brown	P	Purple	W	White	K	Pink	U	Blue	G	Green
Y	Yellow	O	Orange	R	Red	B	Black	LG	Lt. Green		

Headlamp Circuits

See page 207 for fog / driving lamp fitting.

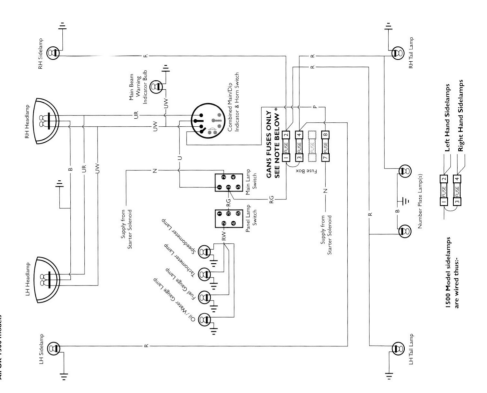

NEGATIVE EARTH CARS
from **GAN5 128263** onwards
All UK 1500 models

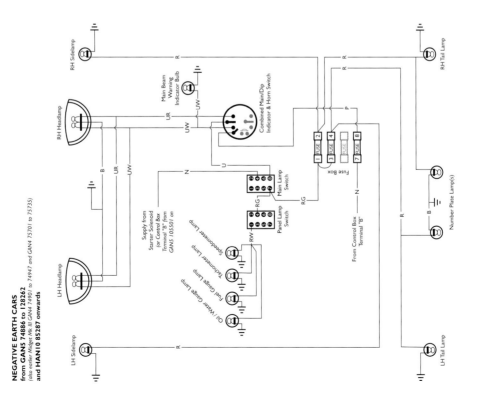

NEGATIVE EARTH CARS
from **GAN5 74886 to 128262**
(also earlier Midget Mk III GAN4 74901 to 74947 and GAN4 75701 to 75735)
and HAN10 85287 onwards

Headlamp Circuits

See page 207 for fog / driving lamp fitting.

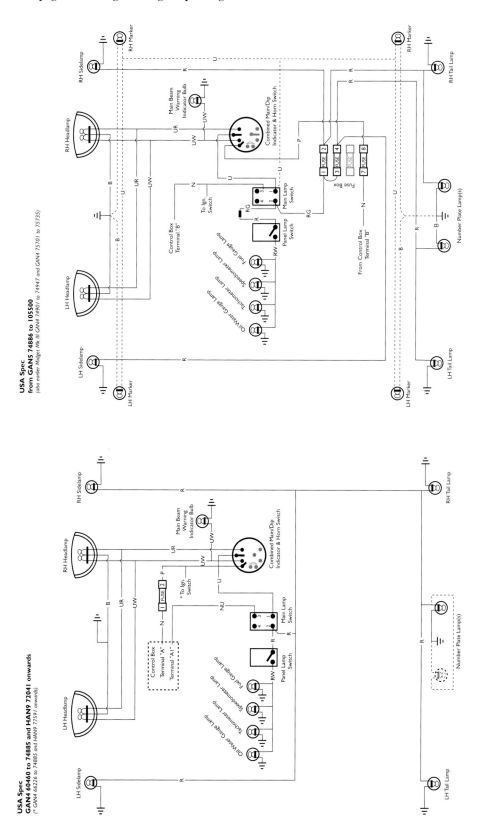

USA Spec
from GAN5 74886 to 105500
(also earlier Midget Mk III GAN4 74901 to 74947 and GAN4 75701 to 75735)

USA Spec
GAN4 60460 to 74885 and HAN9 72041 onwards
(GAN4 66226 to 74885 and HAN9 77591 onwards)*

Wire Colours

N	Brown	P	Purple	K	Pink	U	Blue	G	Green
Y	Yellow	O	Orange	B	Black	LG	Lt. Green		
		W	White						
		R	Red						

Headlamp Circuits

See page 207 for fog / driving lamp fitting.

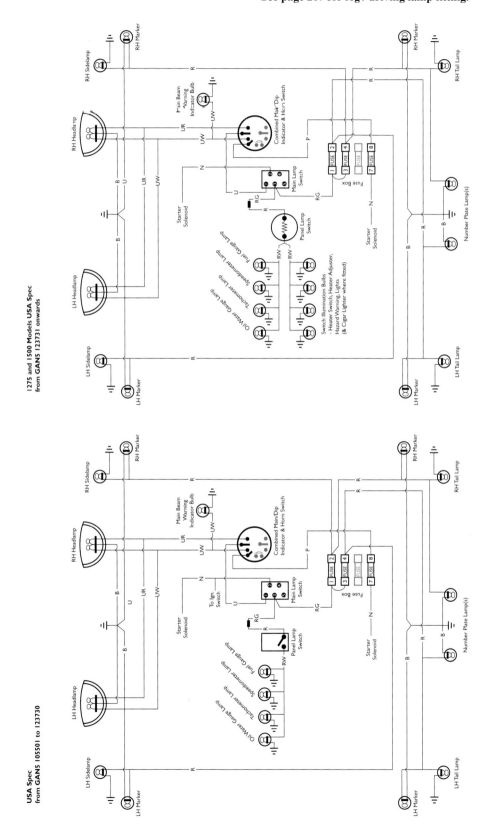

1275 and 1500 Models USA Spec
from GAN5 123731 onwards

USA Spec
from GAN5 105501 to 123730

Indicators and the Hazard Warning Circuit

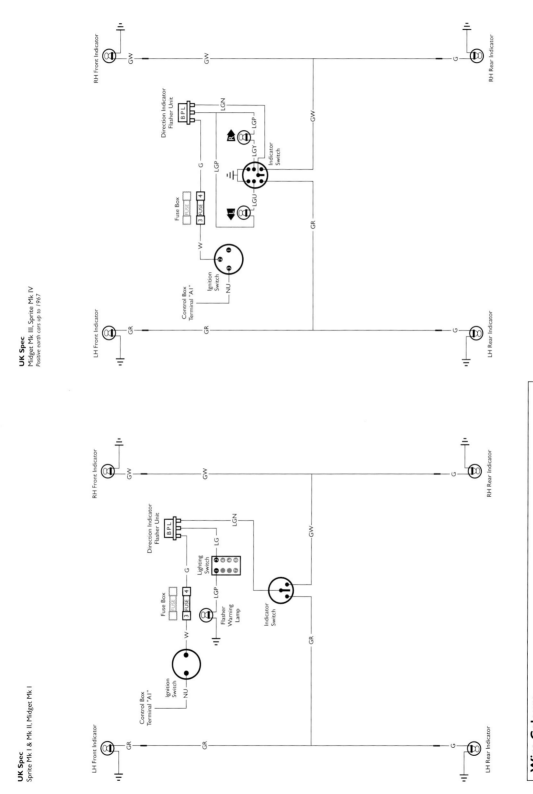

UK Spec
Midget Mk III, Sprite Mk IV
Positive earth cars up to 1967

UK Spec
Sprite Mk I & Mk II, Midget Mk I

Wire Colours

N	Brown	P	Purple	W	White	K	Pink	U	Blue	G	Green
Y	Yellow	O	Orange	R	Red	B	Black	LG	Lt. Green		

Indicators and the Hazard Warning Circuit

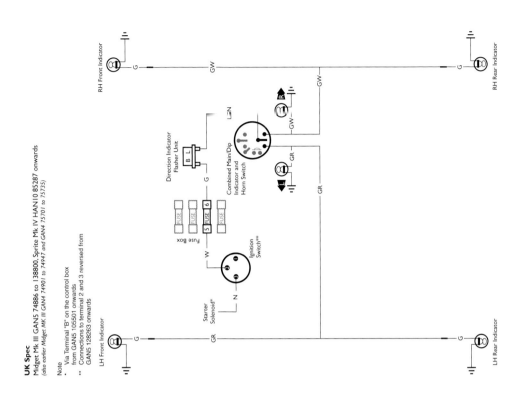

UK Spec
Midget Mk III GAN5 74886 to 138800, Sprite Mk IV HAN10 85287 onwards
(also earlier Midget MK III GAN4 74901 to 74947 and GAN4 75701 to 75735)

Note
* Via Terminal "B" on the control box
  from GAN5 105501 onwards
** Connections to terminal 2 and 3 reversed from
  GAN5 128263 onwards

UK Spec
Midget Mk III GAN4 60460 to 74885, Sprite Mk IV HAN 9 72041 to 85286
The first negative earth models

Indicators and the Hazard Warning Circuit

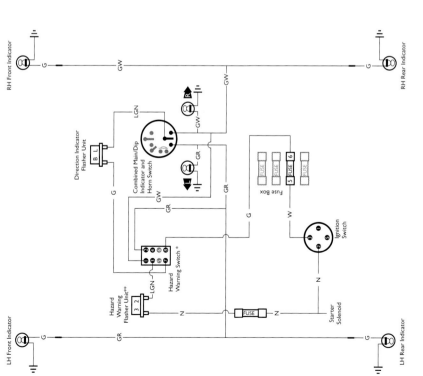

USA Spec Midget Mk III and Sprite Mk IV
GAN4 60460 to 74885 and HAN9 72041 onwards

Notes
* Up to GAN5 66225 and HAN9 77590 the colour codes for the direction indicator bulb wires were LGU (later GR) and LGY (later GW).

RH Front Indicator

RH Rear Indicator

Direction Indicator Flasher Unit

Combined Main/Dip Indicator and Horn Switch

Fuse Box

Ignition Switch

Control Box "A" "A1"

Starter Solenoid

Hazard Warning Indicator

Hazard Warning Flasher Unit

Hazard Warning Switch

LH Front Indicator

LH Rear Indicator

UK Spec
GAN5 138801 onwards, All GAN6 models

Note
* The wires to 7 and 8 were, up to 1975 model year, connected to positions 5 and 6.

RH Front Indicator

RH Rear Indicator

Direction Indicator Flasher Unit

Combined Main/Dip Indicator and Horn Switch

Fuse Box

Ignition Switch

Starter Solenoid

Hazard Warning Flasher Unit**

Hazard Warning Switch *

LH Front Indicator

LH Rear Indicator

Wire Colours

N	Brown	P	Purple	W	White	K	Pink	U	Blue	G	Green
Y	Yellow	O	Orange	R	Red	B	Black	LG	Lt. Green		

Indicators and the Hazard Warning Circuit

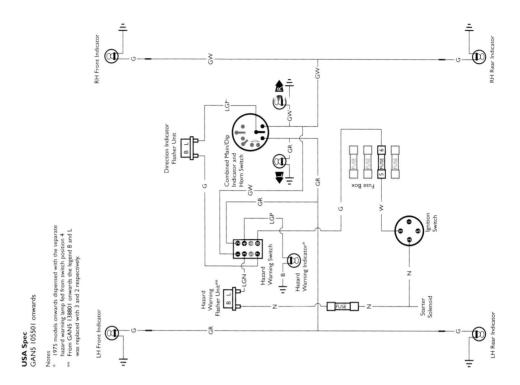

USA Spec
GAN5 105501 onwards

Notes
* 1975 models onwards dispensed with the separate hazard warning lamp fed from switch position 4
** From GAN5 138801 onwards the legend B and L was replaced with 3 and 2 respectively.

USA Spec
GAN5 74886 to 105500
(also earlier Midget Mk III GAN4 74901 to 74947 and GAN4 75701 to 75735)

Brake and Reversing Lamp Circuits

All UK Sprites and Midgets, USA models up to GAN5 89514

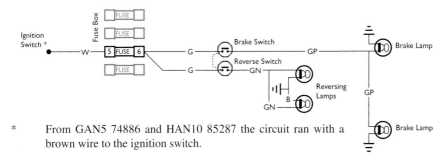

*   From GAN5 74886 and HAN10 85287 the circuit ran with a brown wire to the ignition switch.

From GAN5 105501 (UK) and GAN5 74886 (USA) the circuit went via Terminal "B" of the control box (where fitted) before going on to the fuse box.

------   All UK cars from GAN5 74886 up to GAN5 138801 and HAN10 85287 on, the wiring circuit was altered so that the feed for the reverse lamp circuit went directly from the brake lamp switch.

From GAN5 123731 the UK circuits reverted to being separated at the fuse box.

Early car wiring (up to GAN4 74885 and HAN9 85286) differed slightly from later cars and is shown right.

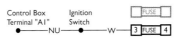

USA models from GAN5 89515 onwards

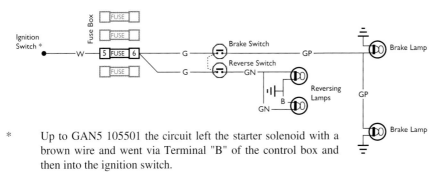

*   Up to GAN5 105501 the circuit left the starter solenoid with a brown wire and went via Terminal "B" of the control box and then into the ignition switch.

**   Between GAN5 89515 and GAN5 138800 the green wire left the fuse box and went to the back of the tacho before going on to Brake Switch.

------   For the USA 1975 model year only, the wiring circuit was altered so that the feed for the reverse lamp circuit went directly from the brake lamp switch.

†   For all USA and Canada cars from 1976 model year onwards the brown wire, having left the starter solenoid went onto fuse terminal 7 and then on again to the ignition switch.

Wire Colours												
N	Brown	P	Purple	W	White	K	Pink	U	Blue	G	Green
Y	Yellow	O	Orange	R	Red	B	Black	LG	Lt. Green		

Some History: Wiring Looms

Original Sprite wiring was basic to say the least and though it altered through the years to meet new and tougher legislation both in Britain and overseas, it never evolved much beyond the wiring equivalent of Homo Erectus. Extras consisted of optional heater, twin horns, cigar lighter and (following the introduction of the 10CG engines) an impulse tachometer.

The Midget Mk III / Sprite Mk IV (up to 1967) incorporated significant safety changes including an electrically operated starter solenoid powered via the ignition switch, revised wiper wiring and direction indicators with left and right warning lamps. Despite these advances the tragic inclusion of an electric fuel pump rendered the car inoperable on many occasions.

Negative earth cars saw a split between UK/European cars and their US counterparts. Across the Atlantic the electrical system developed rapidly.

UK Cars

From GAN4 60460 and HAN9 72041 (the first negative earth cars), major circuits were revised, notably the wiper motor circuit. Reversing lamps were added.

From GAN5 74886 and HAN10 85287 (and prior to this from GAN4 74901 to 74947 and 75701 to 75735), indicators / headlamp dip and horn switches moved to the steering column. The charging circuit was revised to include a new control box and four-way fuse box.

From GAN5 89515 and HAN10 86303 the horn moved to the centre of the steering wheel and could therefore be applied using the hand. Interior courtesy and boot lamps were fitted.

From GAN5 105501 rocker switches were fitted and the wiring loom was revised so that the optional radio ran from a connector off the heater circuit, rather than directly off the back of the wiper switch. In an effort to save lives, the cigar lighter option appears to have been deleted. They continued to fit the ash tray however, strange logic but there you go!

GAN5 128263 saw fitment of an alternator. At GAN5 138801 a hazard warning circuit was fitted in response to the electric fuel pump.

1500 models had re-routed engine bay wiring, resistive ignition wire, new coil and starter solenoid. Connector blocks abounded while the hazard warning lamps had become redundant due to the cunning inclusion of a mechanical fuel pump.

An oil pressure light and sensor was fitted from GAN6 200001. The oil pressure gauge was too scary!

From GAN6 212001 a handbrake warning lamp was fitted, the cigar lighter came back as standard and a brake pressure failure circuit was installed.

US Cars

Negative earth (GAN4 60460 and HAN9 72041) US Sprites and Midgets were given an electric washer pump, hazard warning lamps, brake pressure failure switch and two speed wipers. At GAN4 66226 / HAN9 77591 the brake pressure test circuit was revised.

From GAN5 89515 a new control box, four-gang fuse box and ignition switch were fitted, the brake circuit was again revised and the horn moved to the steering wheel. Courtesy lamps for the cockpit and trunk were installed incorporating an audible buzzer to remind drivers where they had left the keys. Marker lamps made the cars a more visible target for Jeeps.

At GAN5 105501 the hazard warning circuit was revised thanks to alternator fitment. For safety reasons, seat belt warning switches were introduced. The panel lamp switch was replaced with a rheostat. The heater switch was illuminated from GAN5 123731 (how did they ever manage before), though more importantly the distributor wiring was altered.

From GAN5 138801 a sequential seat belt control unit was fitted. Complex and aggravating it was short lived, being deleted on the Midget 1500, having proved as popular as VW door mounted seat belts.

The 1500 model wiring made allowances for service interval counter, running-on valve, catalytic converter service counter and lamp. An electronic distributor was accompanied by a resistive wire in the loom.

At GAN6 166301 a time delay buzzer was incorporated to make short journeys more arduous, while a resistor was added into the ignition circuit.

Californian cars (GAN6 182001 on) remained unchanged, but Federal cars dispensed with much of the emission control equipment. From GAN6 200001 on an electrical temperature transmitter replaced the original ether filled bulb while an oil pressure switch replaced the useful gauge formally fitted to the fascia.

Wire Colours

N	Brown	P	Purple	W	White	K	Pink
U	Blue	G	Green	Y	Yellow	O	Orange
R	Red	B	Black		LG Lt. Green		

Where a wire has two colours the first letter indicates the main colour while the second is the thin "trace" line. E.g. WB is a white wire with black trace, PB is purple with a black trace and UR is blue with a red trace.

Under a street lamp this may appear as YB, PP and GRB (where GR = Grey). Connecting them together under these circumstances results in a loss of ignition, one working headlamp and a high pitched burbling horn sound which continues to operate until the cable coloured R (or B in the darkness) melts through, leading to a call out of the recovery service.

Major Colour Coded Circuits

Brown	Battery & charging circuit	White	Ignition Circuit
Red	Side Lights	Blue	Main Lights
Purple	Horns	Black	Earth
Green	Stop Lights, Wipers and Indicators		

Trace colours on the wires identify left (red) and right (white), main (white) or dip (red) or earthing (horn wire - purple with black trace)

Some History: Horns

A single horn warned the world of the presence of a Sprite, and though not detailed fully here, it was modified twice for performance and quality. High and low note "Windtone" horns were offered as an optional extra. The steering wheel mounted horn push depicted a "Lightening Bolt".

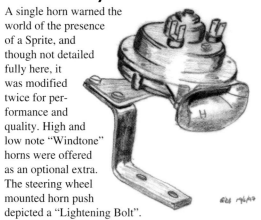

The Sprite Mk II / Midget Mk I models saw the economy horn upgraded to a high note Windtone. Optional twin Windtone horns were also upgraded and improved, in particular the low note horn was superseded three times, there was a problem there.

The Sprite horn push continued to have a Lightning Bolt centrepiece; the Midget was given the MG logo.

When wire spoked wheels were fitted, the pushes were changed to show the Austin Coat of Arms or a bolder, bigger MG logo.

Swedish vehicles (HAN9 69049 and GAN4 56715 on were given different specification Windtone horns. History does not record why.

US Models HAN9 72034 and GAN4 60441 on had the horn push attached to the combined headlamp flash/direction indicator/horn switch mounted on the left hand side of the steering column. Canadian models were altered in the same way (at the same time) but unfortunately no change points are listed.

As for the rest of us, the horn push moved to the steering column switch from HAN10 85287 and GAN5 74886, (when the new square ended indicator switch was fitted). Maybe this wasn't popular because at HAN10 86302 and GAN5 89514 the horn push went back to being in the centre of the steering wheel. A moulded rubber push was fitted with plain centrepiece (Sprite) and raised MG logo for the Midget, so you could really let rip without injury.

The rubber horn push was revised at GAN5 105501 (with red painted background), again at GAN6 154101 (white detailing to badge) and finally at GAN6 157173 (more white detailing).

From GAN6 200001, the horn push once again became part of the combined headlamp flasher and indicator switch assembly.

A Popular Fault

The horns are fitted in the valance recess and suffer the worst of the winter weather.

Watch out for broken lugs, often the cause of a failed horn.

Construction

The horns, marked with an H or L in the sound hole to denote high or low pitch, are a three part sandwich. The upper section is a steel pressing, the two lower sections are aluminium castings - together forming a spiral tube and sound hole. Triangular mountings and handed brackets are used to secure the horns in place.

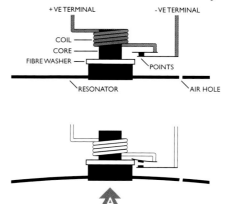

How it Works

The resonator is part of a solenoid operating on a cyclic principle. Power goes on, the resonator lifts (A) and the points are separated by the fibre washer sitting on the pedestal. The power cuts off and the resonator falls back to its original position, allowing the points to reconnect.

The resonator cycles in this fashion causing an air disturbance. The air modulates in the spiral winding being amplified as it goes, finally expelling the sound in the time honoured fashion.

The performance continues until the participant removes finger or hand from the horn button.

The big screw and locking nut controls volume, the smaller screw with a hexagonal or Phillips head (with a left hand thread) controls pitch (by adjusting the points gap). They'll both be seized.

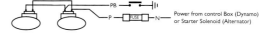

The circuit remained consistent throughout the life of the cars (shown above). The switch shown would be either the horn pencil located inside the steering wheel boss or the horn push on the column assembly.

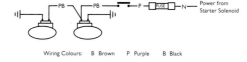

In the last year of manufacture however, the whole circuit was turned on its head, with the horns being earthed and not the switch.

TIP: A quick fix for a non-operating horn is to hit it with a block of wood. Sometimes the resonator jams in the Windtone horns. I'm not saying this always works, but it has worked for me.

Resonator

Fibre Washer

Case Study: Twin Horns

1. To separate assembly, drill out six rivets around the rim (1). The resonator is held in place by two bitumen coated gaskets (2).

3. The electrical windings, points and terminal posts can now be examined (2). Look for points burn and clean if necessary.

Note the fibre washer (2) which sits on the resonator - this isolates it and cuts off power to the points.

5. The bitumen on the cases and resonator can be removed easily using a solvent cleaner.

The main problem with the horn is caused by corroded terminals. Replacements are available from radio / electrical spares shops or from an old coil or scrap electrical unit. I made up new terminals (3 and 4) from a broken unit.

6. The terminals are held in position with copper rivets (5), and should be replaced with the same. If it proves impossible to find any small screws and nuts will achieve the same effect. Lock them in place with solder (6).

7. Clean and grit blast the surface of the shells (7). *The manufacturing date stamped on the steel case will be revealed during this process - a nice finishing touch.*

Cut new gaskets from a sheet of gasket material and coat with bitumen during reassembly.

8. During reassembly ensure that the fibre washer is replaced correctly. Assemble using steel rivets rather than pop rivets if possible. Then bench test the units prior to painting, adjust as necessary and repaint. *Parts of the shell are made of aluminium or steel so use a base primer that works on both materials since many paints do not work well on both aluminium and steel.*

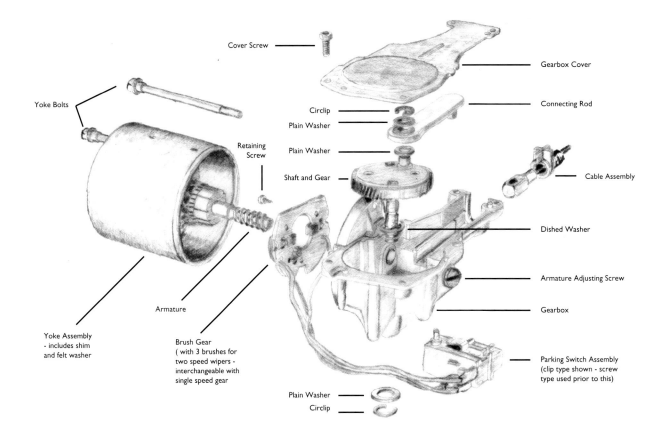

Cover Screw

Yoke Bolts

Gearbox Cover

Connecting Rod

Circlip

Plain Washer

Retaining
Screw

Plain Washer

Cable Assembly

Shaft and Gear

Dished Washer

Armature Adjusting Screw

Gearbox

Armature

Yoke Assembly
- includes shim
and felt washer

Brush Gear
(with 3 brushes for
two speed wipers -
interchangeable with
single speed gear

Parking Switch Assembly
(clip type shown - screw
type used prior to this)

Plain Washer

Circlip

Wiper Motors, Racks & Washers

Some History: Wipers

Originally fitted with a DR2 type single speed wiper motor with a square body and domed gearbox lid, the Sprite motor was revised from HAN5 5477, visually the gearbox cover now had a flat lid. A DR3A motor was fitted from HAN6 6276 / GAN1 3007.

Wheelboxes were revised from HAN5 26824, and again with the introduction of the 14W type round bodied wiper motor. Wiper arms were revised to fit.

Those wiper arms were then changed at GAN5 123751 - replacing the "spoon" with "straight" ends - making it impossible to get the old blades off. There's progress for you. *The arms and corresponding blades should always be bright finished (except LHD 1500 models from GAN6 183592).*

From GAN4 60460 and HAN9 72041 onwards US cars got two speed wipers with an electric washer pump. We all had to wait until long after the arrival of the 1500 models (GAN6 212001 onwards).

The US electric pump was revised from GAN5 139307 allowing Californian drivers the opportunity to fill the washer bottles with denser sun tan lotion.

The washer system initially offered a choice of a single jet, glass bottled Trafalgar system or the twin jet plastic Tudor alternative. The Trafalgar option ceased at HAN5 50116.

From HAN5 26724 the Tudor kit was offered with a larger filler cap (for easier filling, though you still couldn't get the kettle spout any closer).

The system was revised again at HAN6 20105 to include a new pump with one outlet rather than two the early pump supplying water separately to both jets. The new single outlet led to a 'T' piece and then to both jets (though not necessarily at the same time).

The cross-flow radiators of late 1275 models led to the water bottle being moved (the space was needed by the expansion tank) and replaced by a smaller version. This little bottle, after some toing and froing, ended up mounted to the footwell, remaining there even in the early days of the 1500. It was superseded by a rectangular container of no fixed abode from GAN6 154101.

The only variation here being that Swedish Sprite IV and Midget III cars used a flexible bag suspended from a hook (as per the Hillman Imp). No, I don't know why, everything else on the Imp was pretty good.

Sprite Mk I, II & III, Midget Mk I & II

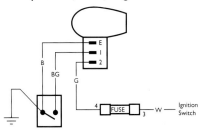

Sprite Mk IV & Midget Mk III
from introduction of rocker switches onwards

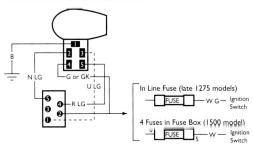

- - - - - - - - - Indicates connection for 2 speed wipers (where applicable)

Sprite Mk IV & Midget Mk III
to end of positive earth (1967)

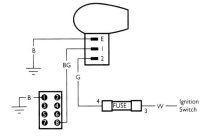

Sprite Mk IV & Midget Mk III
from introduction of coloumn mounted switch (USA Spec)

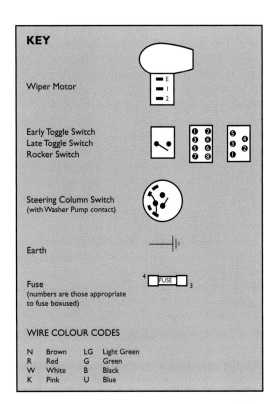

Sprite Mk IV & Midget Mk III
negative earth cars up to introduction of rocker switches

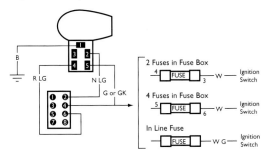

Wiper Circuit

The basic principle of the wiring circuit changed little, though improvements to the motor continued throughout the life of the cars. Early motors were earthed through the switch itself, which may have led to some safety problems. The circuit was revised with the introduction of Sprite Mk IV/Midget Mk III.

Negative earth circuits ran through a twin fuse fuse box, later a 7FJ box and finally the wiper circuit had its own in-line fuse.

Rocker switches replaced toggle switches. 1500 models dispensed with the in-line fuse, the circuit reverting again to the fuse box.

The dotted line is the feed for the slow speed part of the two-speed wiper circuit.

The round bodied wiper motor was wired either for single or two speeds. The two-speed version having three brushes. An extra wire runs between the park switch and the wiper switch, so by fitting the two-speed rocker switch, a new brush plate and the missing wire you should be able to get two speeds. I haven't tried it, so I will not comment further.

Later US spec. models incorporated a column mounted switch, had two-speed wipers from day one and an electric washer pump. Early US systems were exactly as European spec.

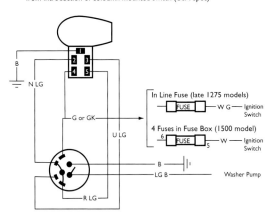

KEY

Wiper Motor

Early Toggle Switch
Late Toggle Switch
Rocker Switch

Steering Column Switch
(with Washer Pump contact)

Earth

Fuse
(numbers are those appropriate to fuse boxused)

WIRE COLOUR CODES

N	Brown	LG	Light Green
R	Red	G	Green
W	White	B	Black
K	Pink	U	Blue

117

Case Study:
Wiper Motor and Rack
Rebuilding The Motor

1. Remove the gearbox cover. Withdraw circlip, washer and connecting rod (1), beneath which is another washer with larger hole. The rack cable can now be released.

2. Release the power connector. Unclamp wiper motor from footwell. *The bolts are not held in place with captive nuts, so you need to have a spanner in the footwell and by the bulkhead. You can do this on your own only if you have arms like a gorilla, or if the doors have been removed.*

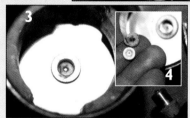

3. Turn the motor upside down to remove the circlip and withdraw the gear wheel (2). Unscrew (early) or unclip (late models) the parking switch. If faulty this is not easily repaired. Replace if necessary. *Typically a faulty parking switch can be detected by a failure of the wipers to return to the park position. When the wipers are switched off they just stop where they are.*

4. The yoke assembly can be separated from the gearbox by undoing two long bolts which run through the yoke. The yoke, gearbox and armature can be separated. *Note: The armature incorporates a ball bearing which rests against a felt oiling washer and a shim plate in the yoke (3 and 4). DO NOT LOSE THEM - REPLACEMENTS ARE NOT EASILY AVAILABLE.*

Clean component parts. Examine brushes and bushes - replace if necessary.

5. Refit the armature ensuring correct location of the shim and felt bush.

6. Refit the yoke assembly to the gearbox matching up the groove and triangle shown (5). *A screw in the side of the wiper body stops forward and aft movement of the armature. Check to ensure that the armature can turn freely and that there is not too much fore and aft movement.*

9. Refit the shaft, gear and connecting rod, greasing liberally during reassembly. Be sure to fit washers and shims correctly (6 and 7).

10. Reassemble onto base, preferably using a new rubber pad and clamp to ensure freedom from vibration (8).

above: the wiper rack in situ under the dashboard

Removing The Rack

1. Withdraw the rack inner cable (1). Undo the nuts holding the wheel box back plates in position (2) and reveal the drive gears. Release the wiper rack outer tubes (3).

4 Undo wheel box nuts to release wheel box and bezel. Gosh, that sounds easy. *These often seize but can be replaced. Don't do like I did years ago when, in a fit of despair, I sawed through the wheel boxes in order to get them out. Bezel kits, which include the nuts, are a far cheaper alternative to wheel-boxes.*

5 Examine the wheel boxes and wiper rack mechanism for signs of wear and replace if necessary.

Windscreen Washer System

Washer jets can be adjusted with a small screwdriver. The jet itself can be removed for cleaning if necessary (either blow through or clean with a piece of wire).

Use screen wash in the system. Not only does it aid cleaning but good brands contain anti-freeze. DON'T use washing up liquid - it contains salt.

The bottle incorporates a non-return valve (on the end of the tube). If it is missing or worn the water will always drain back down the tubes so that every time you need to clean the screen the system needs priming. The valve also includes a filter which should be cleaned on a regular basis.

A dash mounted pump sucks the fluid from the bottle, through a valve and into the pump body, before forcing fluid through an exit pipe and up to the screen. The pump inlet is marked with "supply" or "S" with the outlet labelled "jet" or "J".

TIP: If you connect it up the wrong way, you'll never get your windscreen clean but hey, you'll get great bubbles coming up from under the bonnet.

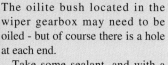

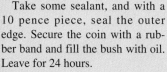

Soaking That Bush!

The oilite bush located in the wiper gearbox may need to be oiled - but of course there is a hole at each end.

Take some sealant, and with a 10 pence piece, seal the outer edge. Secure the coin with a rubber band and fill the bush with oil. Leave for 24 hours.

Finally, remove the rubber band, the coin and sealant releases quite easily and you end up with a neat puddle of oil on your workbench / foot*.

* delete as appropriate

Fuel Get Me Not...

Why do SU carburetters have such a bad name for themselves. I've never understood it really. They are easy to set up, need virtually no maintenance, last the life time of the car and, as long as you don't over-tighten the air filters, don't break easily. You can, if so inclined, adjust them at the road-side (as opposed to Webers which need a rolling road and a walletful of cash to adjust) which allows you infinite tinkering possibilities.

Of course, my carbs did have the obligatory split lug where someone had over-tightened the filters, though it never caused any problems really, the other three bolts held the filters in place. The big problem tends to be that the linkages eventually wear out and air gets sucked in to cause uneven idling. This is eventually what happened to mine. It can be repaired though, so I chopped mine in for a reconditioned pair - gleaming, clean and without broken lugs!

To stop the lugs getting broken again I dispensed with the old saucepan filters. I fitted a neat (but noisy) set of chromed pancake filters which lasted as far as the A316 fly-over near Hanworth. One of the chromed covers came loose, fell out of the bottom of the engine, got picked up by the back wheels and flung into the windscreen of the car behind me. Well, the 'saucepan' filters were quieter and stayed on!

Fuel pumps, now that's another matter. Who, just who, thought of sticking an electric fuel pump above the back axle. I must have replaced more fuel pumps on the Midget than any other component and what a place to work in. Why not fit it in the engine bay?

One can, allegedly, fit a Morris Minor pump into the engine bay. The Midget pump won't work because it is designed to 'push' the fuel to the front of the car, rather than the Minor pump which 'pulls' it from the rear. I am bound to say, however, that I have never seen this put to the test. All I can say is that 1500 Midget owners don't know the meaning of the word suffering.

The exhaust system bears a mention here as well. The day I bought the Midget I drove it home and went to park it in the garage. The garage was at the end of a long hardcore track and to get into it, meant driving up over a hump onto the garage floor. On my first attempt into the garage, the exhaust grounded and the flange at the base of the manifold gave way somewhat noisily. Upon inspection I discovered it had been previously broken and bodged together. Never mind, a quick trip to the shop and a sharp intake of breath ,followed by a deflation of the wallet by £30.00, and I had a new manifold.

Three months later it mysteriously shattered. Six months went by and another one broke in the same way, always around the flange where it met the downpipe. Huh?

Some months later, the single pipe exhaust system gave way while on holiday and so I had to order a replacement system post haste. An MG specialist in London sent me a bright shiny new one in stainless steel by courier. Unfortunately they sent a twin box system, and single box fittings. Still, a few coat hangers soon got me going and it was then that I discovered why the manifolds had been shattering. The silencer had been bolted straight to the boot floor instead of being suspended from rubber bushes, the vibration from the engine kept shattering the manifold, attached as it was to a rigidly mounted downpipe. All that expense for the cost a few pence!

The Fuel and Exhaust Systems

Some History: The Fuel System

The original Sprite fuel tank incorporated a long filler pipe which reached up almost to the filler point and incorporated a "screw secured" sender unit. A single fuel line connected the tank with the mechanical fuel pump affixed to the left hand side of the engine block. The pipe was coiled near the fuel pump to allow for engine vibration. A further fuel line took fuel to the front carburetter float chamber. A short braided hose then took fuel to the rear carburetter float chamber.

With the introduction of the Sprite Mk II and Midget Mk I, the fuel tank was revised. The filler pipe was shortened and linked to the filler cap via a long hose. The sender unit was also revised at the same time.

Electric fuel pumps by S.U. were fitted from the first Sprite IV (HAN9 64735) and Midget III (GAN4 52390) models, necessitating a change in the fuel pipe layout to allow for its fitment under the right hand wheel arch.

Due to its position, the fuel pump could suffer from problems caused by the low pressure found under the car at speed. To cure this, breather tubes were fitted to the boot floor under the carpet.

The fuel sender unit was again revised at HAN9 72041 (Sprite), continuing to be fitted to the end of its production run, and from GAN5 74886 (Midget) until 105500, where it was replaced along with the fuel tank now secured by a locking ring rather than screws.

At the same time and only listed for the MG Midget (GAN5 74886) US specification cars began to be fitted with the first evaporative loss systems requiring a raft of additions and changes to the fuel supply system. The systems were modified with increasing frequency from this time on, changing yearly towards the end of the car's life. I haven't included information here because I have no experience of these systems. There must be many more competent people in America who could produce a definitive version of its history and I leave it to their skill and knowledge to tackle the job - hats off to them, whoever they are!

The 1500 Midget sported a mechanical fuel pump (not before time) and once again required alterations in the fuel line layout to accommodate the change of position (now mounted on the right hand side of the engine block). To cure vibration problems the pipe was connected to the pump via a length of flexible hose. A revised pump was fitted for 1977 model year and then again from engine number FP50968 on.

In the US the Midget 1500 pump was revised at engine number FP311392E and revised again for the 1978 model year.

The UK tank was finally revised on the later 1500 Midget cars at GAN6 182001 but otherwise remained unchanged until the end of production.

Throughout production fuel tanks incorporated internal fuel filters and drain plugs.

Carburetters

There were many changes made to the carburetters over the years, not least due to changes in legislation in the USA.

To make it easier to see, and understand the history, please look at the chart on page 118.

Air Cleaners

The original air cleaners were of a wire mesh "pancake" type of filter and were fitted until HAN5 50116.

From this point "saucepan" type filters were fitted consisting of a pair of saucepan shaped filter covers and replaceable paper air filters. Great care had to be taken over installation as the filter assemblies were bolted directly onto the carburetter mouths which, being made of alloy, tended to fracture easily.

The early saucepan filters were vented to to the rocker cover to allow recirculation of crankcase gases.

The assemblies were revised with the introduction of Sprite II and Midget I models to allow fitment of the HS2 carburetters.

The assemblies were revised again with the introduction of the 1275cc engines. These later units no longer incorporated a breather pipe (UK and Europe only).

1500 models in the UK tactlessly used the Rover / Triumph badged air filter assembly. In late 1978 this was replaced by an assembly incorporating the 'BL cars' legend.

US spec Midget 1500 models used a sandwich box design which was revised for the 1976 model year and fitted until the end of production.

Heat Shields

Revised at 9CU/H101/17364 with the addition of a folded section. Revised again at 9CU/H101/49201 along with the fitment of HS2 carburetters.

The heatshield was revised again for the 10CC engined Sprite III and Midget II models. This later design incorporated brackets to help limit vibration. The design was lightly modified twice over subsequent years before giving way to the onslaught of the Triumph 1500 engine which incorporated heatshields to accommodate the UK HS4 carburetters or the US market Zenith Stromberg.

Fuel Lines: 948, 1098

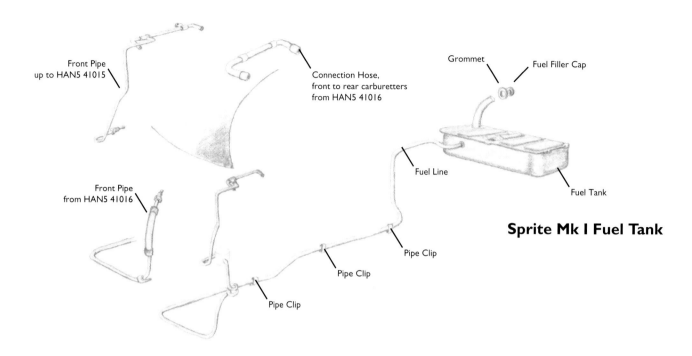

Front Pipe
up to HAN5 41015

Connection Hose,
front to rear carburetters
from HAN5 41016

Grommet

Fuel Filler Cap

Fuel Line

Fuel Tank

Front Pipe
from HAN5 41016

Sprite Mk I Fuel Tank

Pipe Clip

Pipe Clip

Pipe Clip

Fuel Lines: 1275

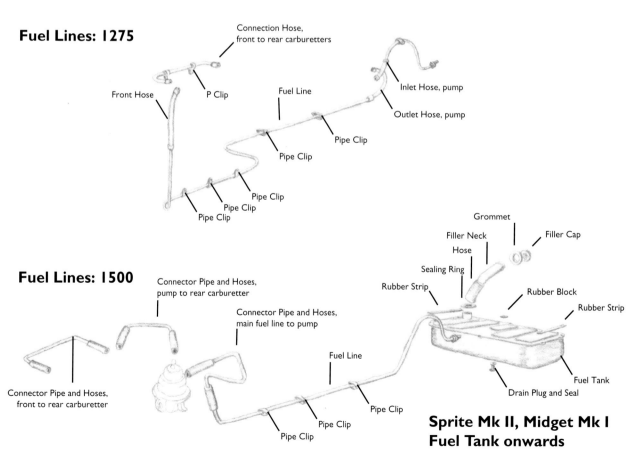

Connection Hose,
front to rear carburetters

Front Hose

P Clip

Fuel Line

Inlet Hose, pump

Outlet Hose, pump

Pipe Clip

Pipe Clip

Pipe Clip

Pipe Clip

Pipe Clip

Fuel Lines: 1500

Connector Pipe and Hoses,
pump to rear carburetter

Connector Pipe and Hoses,
main fuel line to pump

Grommet

Filler Neck

Filler Cap

Hose

Sealing Ring

Rubber Strip

Rubber Block

Rubber Strip

Fuel Line

Fuel Tank

Connector Pipe and Hoses,
front to rear carburetter

Pipe Clip

Drain Plug and Seal

Pipe Clip

Pipe Clip

**Sprite Mk II, Midget Mk I
Fuel Tank onwards**

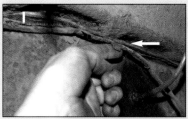

What can you do to restore a rotten fuel tank...

There is not much you can do to restore a fuel tank. Either it's solid and serviceable, or it leaks. It cannot be repaired and, if corroded, should be discarded for safety reasons. Never try welding or patching the damaged areas.

When refitting the tank, use a new seal around the filler cap (4) and fit new protective strips as shown in the illustration left. There should be three of them, two long and one small square.

Never use slushing compounds in the tank if a fuel filter is fitted (all original tanks incorporate one). The compounds merely block up the filter rendering an otherwise serviceable tank useless, as I discovered to my cost.

With regard to the sender unit, checking it with a ohm meter will determine whether it works. If not, replace it and also the rubber seal. If you don't replace it now, you'll only have to drop the tank again later.

Finally, replace the fuel pipe which may have become damaged during dismantling.

Case Study: Fuel Tank

By their very nature, fuel tanks won't rust out from the inside because they are always being washed over with fuel. The gauge steel used is usually heavy enough to stop the tank warping due to pressure build up; again this tends to limit serious corrosion problems.

In the case of the Sprites and Midget, the fact that the tank is suspended under the car is the real cause of corrosion. Most notably, the fuel lines may corrode and snap or, more commonly, the top of the tank rusts out due to water getting trapped between the top of the tank and the boot floor.

Be warned that many replacement tanks use lighter gauge steel, are more prone to damage and don't include the necessary drain plugs. Pick one up and compare it to your original and you'll see what I mean. So, if your tank is okay, look after it.

1　Before removing the tank, ensure that the battery is disconnected and then drain any residual fuel from the car. Not easy if it is a replacement tank without a drain plug.

2　Note that the sender unit and fuel pump wiring is secured to the lip around the top edge of the tank by clips (1 arrowed). Remove the clips, noting that the fuel pump cable runs along a sheaf along the fuel line.

3　Unscrew the fuel line, taking care not to damage the threads in the tank. The fuel line will likely need replacing, if not initially, it will after you try unscrewing it.

4　From inside the boot, disconnect the fuel filler pipe by undoing the clamps and pulling the pipe away from the tank.

   Early Sprites had a solid tube from the tank to the filler cap - in this case care will be needed, when "dropping" the tank, that the fuel filler pipe and grommet (as seen in 3) are carefully released to avoid damage.

5　Unbolt and lower the tank, remembering to disconnect the wire from the fuel sender unit.

6　Examine for corrosion, particularly around the filler hole (4) where the foam seal soaks up and traps water eventually causing a leak.

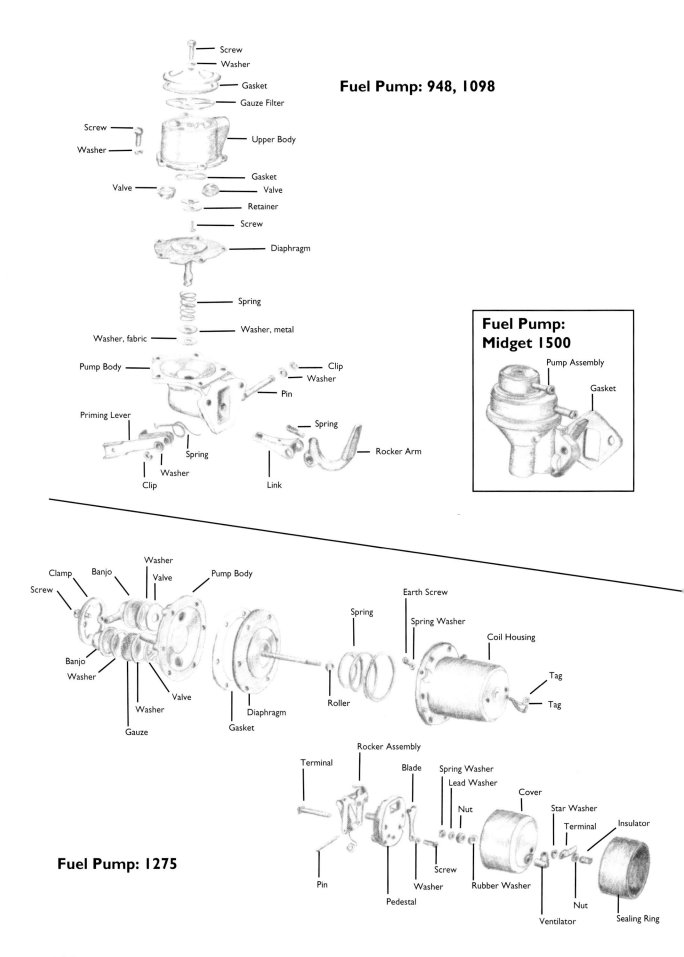

Fuel Pump: 948, 1098

Screw
Washer
Gasket
Gauze Filter
Screw
Washer
Upper Body
Gasket
Valve
Valve
Retainer
Screw
Diaphragm
Spring
Washer, metal
Washer, fabric
Pump Body
Clip
Washer
Pin
Priming Lever
Spring
Spring
Washer
Rocker Arm
Clip
Link

**Fuel Pump:
Midget 1500**

Pump Assembly
Gasket

Clamp
Banjo
Washer
Valve
Pump Body
Screw
Spring
Earth Screw
Spring Washer
Coil Housing
Banjo
Washer
Valve
Washer
Gauze
Diaphragm
Gasket
Roller
Tag
Tag

Terminal
Rocker Assembly
Blade
Spring Washer
Lead Washer
Nut
Cover
Star Washer
Terminal
Insulator
Pin
Pedestal
Washer
Screw
Rubber Washer
Ventilator
Nut
Sealing Ring

Fuel Pump: 1275

Case Study: Restoring the S.U. Electric Fuel Pump

Early Sprites and Midgets were fitted with a mechanical fuel pump. 1500 Midgets were fitted with a mechanical fuel pump. Somebody bring me the head of the luminary who decided to fit an electric fuel pump to the 1275 cars.

Just who decided to stick it above the rear axle? Tell me, I really want to know.

The main problems with the electric fuel pumps are worn points (frequent), split pump diaphragm (rare) and dirty or damaged filter or valves (what have you been putting in your tank!). The easiest form of renovation is by exchange with a rebuilt or new unit. But if you really feel up to it...

Dismantling

1 Note the positions of the pump inlet and out-let in relation to the pump head. Original SU pumps include the words "POSITION OUT-LET AT TOP" (1)

2 Clean the pump (2) carefully to remove dirt prior to disassembly. Remove the vent pipes.

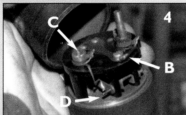

3 Having removed the bracket and the rubber sleeve, you should find a weatherproof sleeve itself covered with sealing tape. Remove the tape and the sleeve (2A).

4 Remove the rubber terminal sheath and unscrew the nut holding the terminal in place (3). Remove the points/rocker cover to reveal the contact blade and points rocker in its pedestal (4). Note the live connections to the contact blade (B) and earthing screw (C).

Note also the pin (D) which holds the points rocker assembly in position. Once this is pulled clear, the pedestal can be unscrewed and lifted away from the main pump housing, leaving the points/rocker assembly (5) behind.

5 The points/rocker assembly is held in situ by the diaphragm, accessed by removing the six screws securing the pump head (6).

6 Once the head is pulled free, the diaphragm can be removed by unscrewing it from the points (7). A return spring and roller (E) are then revealed.

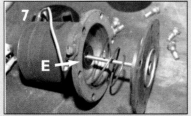

The main pump body is a powerful electro-magnet. When the power goes on, the diaphragm is sucked down drawing in fuel and opening the points. This cuts the power and the magnet switches off allowing the spring to force the diaphragm back to its rest position, expelling fuel through the outlet valve. The operation starts all over again until there is sufficient pressure in the fuel pipe to stop the pump from operating.

7 The pump head is easily examined by removing the clamping plate which secures the two banjo unions.

   Below each banjo is a valve (8) and, under the inlet banjo, a gauze filter (F). The filter may require cleaning, but treat that and the valves with care, taking careful note of the way they are fitted.

   Note also the 'O' rings (G), two for the inlet valve, one for the outlet.

Examine each component for wear and replace faulty components as necessary.

Reassembly
Reassembly is pretty much the reverse of the above procedure except for the installation of the points rocker assembly.

8 Hold rocker assembly steady (9) and, turning the unit upside down, refit the spring, roller and diaphragm. Screw the diaphragm clock-wise until it locates and secures the points rocker assembly.

9 Lightly screw the pedestal into position, ensuring that the earthing terminal is attached. Fit the contact blade with its terminal and then fit the pin through pedestal and rocker (10).

   Note that the lead from the rocker assembly is sandwiched between the lock washer and the screw head (11H). Two leads come from the main body of the pump, the larger fits over the spring washer and under the lead washer and lock nut, over which is placed the rubber washer (11I). The smaller tag fits above the contact blade, not below (as shown in 11J) and is held in place by the screw and spring washer.

10 With the pump at rest, the contact blade should be in contact with the rocker points. Indeed it will be bent slightly upwards (12).

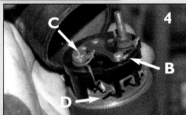

Case Study: Restoring the S.U. Electric Fuel Pump

Early Sprites and Midgets were fitted with a mechanical fuel pump. 1500 Midgets were fitted with a mechanical fuel pump. Somebody bring me the head of the luminary who decided to fit an electric fuel pump to the 1275 cars.

Just who decided to stick it above the rear axle? Tell me, I really want to know.

The main problems with the electric fuel pumps are worn points (frequent), split pump diaphragm (rare) and dirty or damaged filter or valves (what have you been putting in your tank!). The easiest form of renovation is by exchange with a rebuilt or new unit. But if you really feel up to it...

Dismantling

1 Note the positions of the pump inlet and outlet in relation to the pump head. Original SU pumps include the words "POSITION OUTLET AT TOP" (1)

2 Clean the pump (2) carefully to remove dirt prior to disassembly. Remove the vent pipes.

3 Having removed the bracket and the rubber sleeve, you should find a weatherproof sleeve itself covered with sealing tape. Remove the tape and the sleeve (2A).

4 Remove the rubber terminal sheath and unscrew the nut holding the terminal in place (3). Remove the points/rocker cover to reveal the contact blade and points rocker in its pedestal (4). Note the live connections to the contact blade (B) and earthing screw (C).

Note also the pin (D) which holds the points rocker assembly in position. Once this is pulled clear, the pedestal can be unscrewed and lifted away from the main pump housing, leaving the points/rocker assembly (5) behind.

5 The points/rocker assembly is held in situ by the diaphragm, accessed by removing the six screws securing the pump head (6).

6 Once the head is pulled free, the diaphragm can be removed by unscrewing it from the points (7). A return spring and roller (E) are then revealed.

The main pump body is a powerful electro-magnet. When the power goes on, the diaphragm is sucked down drawing in fuel and opening the points. This cuts the power and the magnet switches off allowing the spring to force the diaphragm back to its rest position, expelling fuel through the outlet valve. The operation starts all over again until there is sufficient pressure in the fuel pipe to stop the pump from operating.

7   The pump head is easily examined by removing the clamping plate which secures the two banjo unions.

Below each banjo is a valve (8) and, under the inlet banjo, a gauze filter (F). The filter may require cleaning, but treat that and the valves with care, taking careful note of the way they are fitted.

Note also the 'O' rings (G), two for the inlet valve, one for the outlet.

Examine each component for wear and replace faulty components as necessary.

Reassembly
Reassembly is pretty much the reverse of the above procedure except for the installation of the points rocker assembly.

8   Hold rocker assembly steady (9) and, turning the unit upside down, refit the spring, roller and diaphragm. Screw the diaphragm clockwise until it locates and secures the points rocker assembly.

9   Lightly screw the pedestal into position, ensuring that the earthing terminal is attached. Fit the contact blade with its terminal and then fit the pin through pedestal and rocker (10).

Note that the lead from the rocker assembly is sandwiched between the lock washer and the screw head (11H). Two leads come from the main body of the pump, the larger fits over the spring washer and under the lead washer and lock nut, over which is placed the rubber washer (11I). The smaller tag fits above the contact blade, not below (as shown in 11J) and is held in place by the screw and spring washer.

10 With the pump at rest, the contact blade should be in contact with the rocker points. Indeed it will be bent slightly upwards (12).

11 Make sure that the contact blade points meet squarely with those of the rocker assembly. If not, loosen the contact blade and adjust its position.

12 As the diaphragm moves upwards into the rocker, it lifts up the arm (into which it is screwed). This arm is spring loaded and when it reaches a certain height, the spring twists enough to force the points to separate.

The points are set correctly when, with the contact blade held gently over the little ridge in the pedestal, the points have just come into contact with the contact blade. (If not, turn the diaphragm until this is achieved.)

At this point, a 0.030in feeler gauge should fit under the arm of the points rocker assembly (again see 12). Fine adjustments can be made to the rocker arm to set it correctly.

On early models the arm may not be provided, in which case, check that the same 0.030in gap exists under the rocker roller and then bend the contact blade to ensure that the points are just meeting.

13 Adjust and tighten down the contacts and ensure that the gap remains at 0.030in.

14 Finally, screw the diaphragm in until the rocker will no longer click over. Then, using the pump head securing screw holes as a guide, turn the diaphragm back through four holes.

15 Using a new gasket, re-attach the pump head to the body casing, carefully tightening down the six screws diagonally

16 Fit the points cover, terminal and rubber sheath (which stops damage to the terminal post thread). Fit the protective rubber band over the points cover and secure it using insulation tape (13).

17 Fit the mounting rubber and earthing strap (14).

18 Test on a battery to ensure it pumps.

19 Fit new vent tubes to the head and points cover, securing with the appropriate clamps.

SU Fuel Pump Connections and Fittings

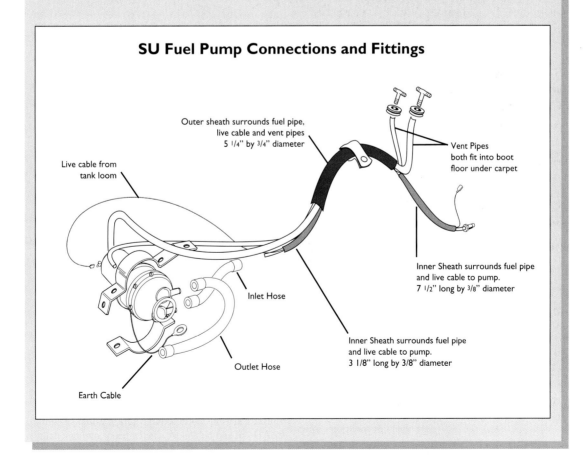

Outer sheath surrounds fuel pipe, live cable and vent pipes 5 1/4" by 3/4" diameter

Vent Pipes both fit into boot floor under carpet

Live cable from tank loom

Inlet Hose

Inner Sheath surrounds fuel pipe and live cable to pump. 7 1/2" long by 3/8" diameter

Inner Sheath surrounds fuel pipe and live cable to pump. 3 1/8" long by 3/8" diameter

Outlet Hose

Earth Cable

Carburetter Reference Chart

The carburetters listed here are identified by the numbers stamped onto the tags normally found under one of the dashpot screws.

Part No.	Model	Type	Engine No.	Other Information
Universal Fitment				
AUC863	Sprite	SU H1	9C/U/101 to 49201	948cc
AUC990	Sprite II & Midget I	SU HS2	9CG/Da/H101 to 36711	948cc
AUD73	Sprite II & Midget I	SU HS2	10CG/Da/H101 to 21048	1098cc
AUD136	Sprite III/IV & Midget II/III	SU HS2	12CC/Da/H101 to 16300	1275cc non vented
UK and European Specific				
AUD327	Sprite IV & Midget III	SU HS2	all 12CE, 12V586F and 12V588F engines	1275cc vented
AUD662T	Sprite IV & Midget III	SU HS2	all 12V778F engines	1275cc vented

From this point the information provided is a little bit sketchy. It is worth pointing out that the same engine and ancillaries (including carburetters) were fitted as a 'lump' into both the Triumph Spitfire 1500 and the MG Midget 1500. While researching this I found that both the BL Parts book and subsequent microfiche suggests that only one carburetter pair was fitted (AUD665). The SU Parts books also mention a pair of FZX1122 carburetters from 1978 onwards.

Turn to the Triumph Spitfire parts books and you get a more complex story. I don't know what the truth is, so I'm listing all four sets shown in the Triumph Spitfire Parts book which I think is more likely to be correct.

Part No.	Model	Type	Engine No.	Other Information
AUD665	Midget 1500	SU HS4	1974 to 1976	
FZX1258	Midget 1500	SU HS4	1976 to 1977	
FZX1122	Midget 1500	SU HS4	1978 to 1979	
FZX1327	Midget 1500	SU HS4	1979 to 1980	
USA & Canada				
AUD266	Sprite IV & Midget III	SU HS2	12CD/Da/H101 to 8700	1275cc non vented
AUD328	Sprite IV & Midget III	SU HS2	12CD/Da/H8701 on 12CF, 12CG and 12CH engines	1275cc vented
AUD404	Midget III	SU HS2	12CJ/Da/H21201 on	1275cc vented
AUD502	Midget III	SU HS2	12V587Z/101 on and 12V671Z/101 on	1275cc vented
CHA327	Midget 1500	150CD4*	USA / Canada 1974 to 1976.	
CHA511	Midget 1500	150CD4T*	USA / Canada 1975 to 1976.	
RKC3933	Midget 1500	150CD4T*	USA 1977	
RKC3169	Midget 1500	150CD4T*	Federal from 1977 to 1978.	
RKC3896	Midget 1500	150CD4T*	Federal cars 1978	
RKC3170	Midget 1500	150CD4T*	California cars 1977.	
RKC3897	Midget 1500	150CD4T*	California cars 1978.	

* Single Zenith Stromberg Carburetter

What SU stands for...

It's funny, but a lot of automotive manufacturers have an unusual history. William Morris was a bicycle manufacturer, Wolseley cars came out of a sheep shearing company and the SU Carburetter Company was started by two brothers who worked in the family shoe business.

George H Skinner patented the first SU carburetter in 1905. He and brother Thomas started the company (SU stood for Skinners Union) setting up shop in Euston Road, London to manufacture carburetters for the fledgling motor industry.

During the 1st World War they, like many other manufacturing companies, produced armaments - machine gun parts. After the war they went on to make radio parts and other engineering products to survive. In 1926 the company was purchased by Morris Motors and the company grew and grew as it supplied Morris, Wolseley, MG and Riley parts, and then Austin, Jaguar, Rover and Triumph as well before declining into the quagmire of corporate silliness which prevailed throughout the BMC/BL/Austin Rover years. Despite this however, they made a lot of MGs run very well.

The SU name is still with us (at the time of writing), thanks to their safe retrieval from ruin by the Hoburn Eaton Group, and then thanks to the US cavalry now known as the Echlin Corporation.

SU Automotive still supplies parts for our valuable MG carburetters. Bless 'em!

About SUs.

SUs are really great carburetters. They work forever (even if worn out). You can set them up yourself, getting it right very quickly, and even if minor adjustments are required they can be done quickly and easily at the roadside. So stick with them. They are also easy(ish) to recondition.

SUs have gained a poor reputation which is unwarranted. Many people might recommend chopping them in for DCOE carbs claiming that they offer more power, are easier to set up and require no adjustment. My personal experience, and the experience of many tuners in the trade, is that the reverse is largely true. Comparable sized units offer remarkably similar power outputs, with the DCOEs offering marginal improvement in mid-range power but sometimes less power than equivalent SUs at the top end.

For me, the proof came during rolling road tests that I had undertaken for research purposes. Some embarrassment ensued so I mention no names. The car in question was fitted with a DCOE carb and took to the rolling road for setting up and a dyno power test. Power was up on this particular car from around 87bhp to 106bhp. The DCOE was removed and SUs were fitted, balanced and tested. The output graph was a shadow of the DCOE until the top end - where the power just kept coming, peaking at 5300rpm at 110bhp. I rest my case, I'll stick with SUs thanks.

For efficiency DCOE carbs need to be set on a rolling road. They are prone to going out of tune leading to excessive fuel consumption. But give them their due, they do look great under the bonnet!

Throttle Cable Problems

Early Sprites and Midgets were fitted with the hair drier heaters which did not interfere with the throttle cable. Later 1275cc cars had a new heater blower assembly with a re-routed trunking. The trunking passed directly over the top of the outlet for the throttle cable on RHD cars. The throttle cables twist and break and the accelerator pedal often becomes sticky, with the frayed cables jamming.

British Leyland couldn't be bothered to do anything about this problem. However, if you hunt around you may be able to find a longer cable (outer length 28in, inner length remains the same) which will route around the back of the offending trunking.

I fitted one successfully to my Midget many years ago and it is still as good as new. Be warned, however, that the longer cable will rub against the bonnet. To avoid damage therefore some protective means will be required to stop the paint work being rubbed off. If, like me, you don't care then just don't worry about it, but enjoy the pleasure of trouble free acceleration.

H1 Carburetter

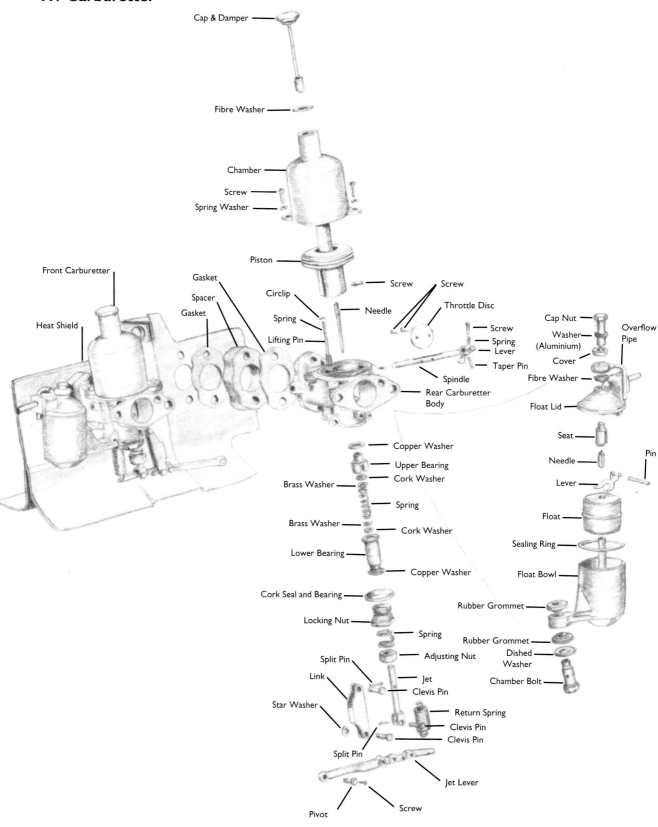

Cap & Damper

Fibre Washer

Chamber

Screw

Spring Washer

Piston

Front Carburetter

Gasket

Spacer

Gasket

Heat Shield

Circlip

Spring

Lifting Pin

Screw

Needle

Screw

Screw

Throttle Disc

Screw

Spring
Lever

Taper Pin

Spindle

Rear Carburetter
Body

Cap Nut

Washer
(Aluminium)

Overflow
Pipe

Cover

Fibre Washer

Float Lid

Seat

Needle

Pin

Lever

Float

Sealing Ring

Float Bowl

Copper Washer

Upper Bearing

Cork Washer

Brass Washer

Spring

Brass Washer

Cork Washer

Lower Bearing

Copper Washer

Rubber Grommet

Cork Seal and Bearing

Locking Nut

Spring

Split Pin

Adjusting Nut

Link

Jet

Clevis Pin

Star Washer

Return Spring

Clevis Pin

Clevis Pin

Split Pin

Jet Lever

Pivot

Screw

Rubber Grommet

Dished
Washer

Chamber Bolt

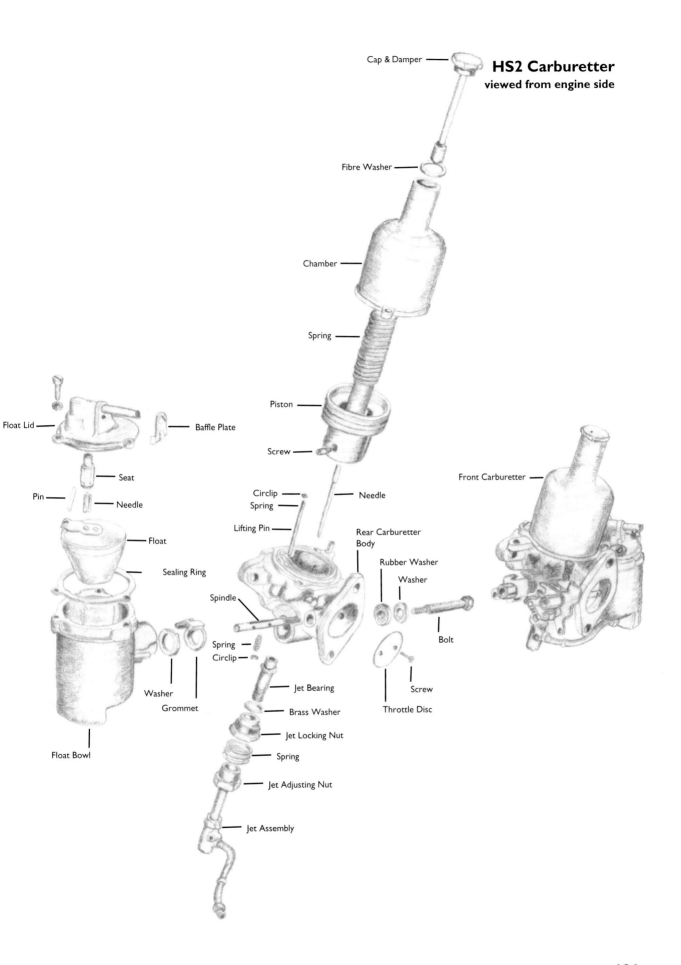

Cap & Damper

HS2 Carburetter
viewed from engine side

Fibre Washer

Chamber

Spring

Piston

Screw

Float Lid

Baffle Plate

Seat

Pin

Needle

Float

Sealing Ring

Circlip

Spring

Needle

Lifting Pin

Rear Carburetter
Body

Front Carburetter

Rubber Washer

Washer

Spindle

Spring

Circlip

Bolt

Washer

Grommet

Jet Bearing

Brass Washer

Screw

Throttle Disc

Jet Locking Nut

Float Bowl

Spring

Jet Adjusting Nut

Jet Assembly

HS4 Carburetter

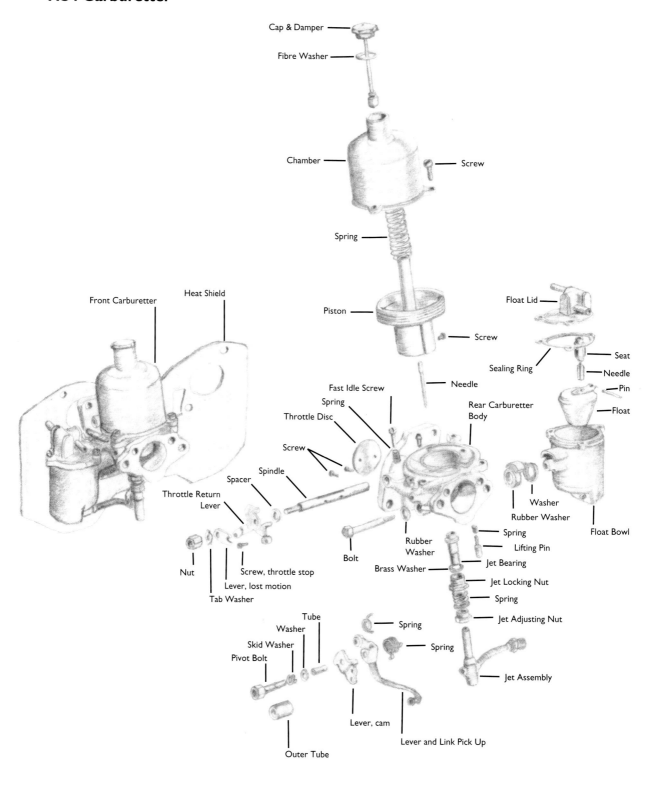

Cap & Damper

Fibre Washer

Chamber — Screw

Spring

Float Lid

Front Carburetter   Heat Shield

Piston — Seat

Screw — Sealing Ring — Needle

Fast Idle Screw — Pin

Spring — Float

Throttle Disc — Rear Carburetter Body

Needle

Screw — Washer

Spacer   Spindle — Rubber Washer

Throttle Return Lever — Spring

Bolt — Float Bowl

Rubber Washer — Lifting Pin

Nut — Brass Washer — Jet Bearing

Screw, throttle stop — Jet Locking Nut

Lever, lost motion — Spring

Tab Washer — Jet Adjusting Nut

Tube — Spring

Washer — Spring

Skid Washer

Pivot Bolt — Jet Assembly

Lever, cam

Lever and Link Pick Up

Outer Tube

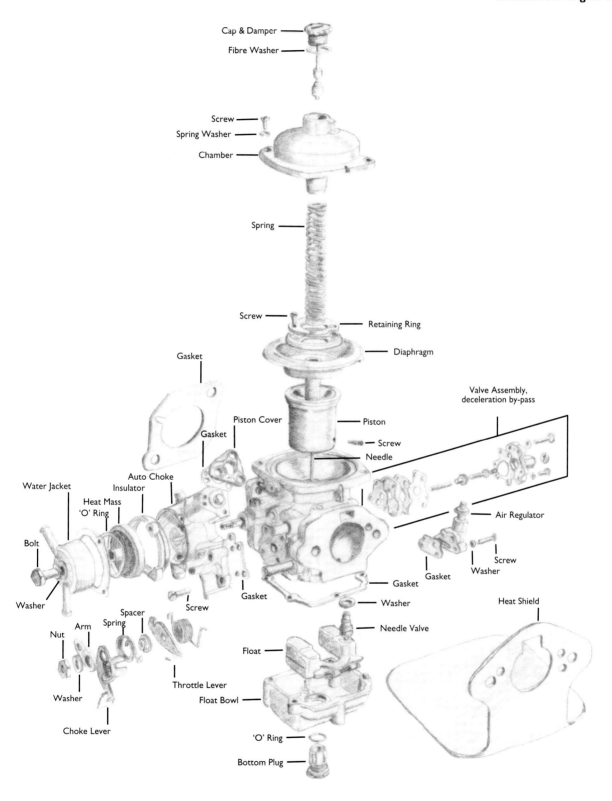

Cap & Damper

Fibre Washer

Screw

Spring Washer

Chamber

Spring

Screw

Retaining Ring

Diaphragm

Gasket

Valve Assembly,
deceleration by-pass

Piston Cover

Piston

Gasket

Screw

Needle

Auto Choke
Insulator

Water Jacket

Heat Mass
'O' Ring

Air Regulator

Bolt

Screw

Washer

Washer

Gasket

Gasket

Washer

Gasket

Screw

Heat Shield

Spacer

Needle Valve

Nut

Arm

Spring

Float

Washer

Throttle Lever

Choke Lever

Float Bowl

'O' Ring

Bottom Plug

Case Study:
HS2 Carburetters

Note: Arguments abound over the spelling of the these fuel flow devices. Some people call them carburettors, other's opt for carburetters. I have read English mechanical books dating back to the 1940s with the latter spelling and I'm going to stick with that. Somehow it also sounds more British. If you disagree strongly, please feel free to go through the next few pages and use a ballpoint pen as necessary. I really don't mind, just don't write to me about it.

1 Remove the air filters (1), noting the gaskets that fit between the filter bases and the carburetter mouths.

2 Disconnect the air pipes to the crankcase circulation system (2), throttle and choke cables and the fuel hose.

3 The entire carburetter / heat shield / inlet manifold assembly can be removed in one lump (3) by undoing the six brass manifold nuts, though this is a bit tricky.

Take care since fuel is likely to still be found in the float chambers. Tipping the carburetters over will allow fuel to escape.

During removal note the two inlet manifold sleeves which are pushed into the engine block (4). These simply pull out and should be stored safely (otherwise they will end up lost on the garage floor).

4 Clean down the external parts of the carburetters prior to disassembly. Ensure that any grit and dirt has been removed before disassembly commences.

What to look for...
Generally three problems tend to arise after high mileages.

A The needles and jets wear out.

Needles and jets must be replaced as a pair to make any improvement in fuel flow

B Float needles stick or won't seat properly when worn.

Buy new float needle and seat sets or, as an 'up market' alternative, fit Grose Jets - precision valves which use ball bearings in place of the traditional valves.

C Either the throttle butterfly spindles wear at the point of contact with the carburetter body, or worse the carburetter body wears. In either case this wear is sufficient to allow air to be sucked into the carburetter making it difficult to set them up.

This problem typically causes uneven idling.

Carburetter specialists will take your old unit, bore out the guide holes by 0.010in and fit larger diameter rods.

Well, actually, they'll just sell you an exchange pair of carburetters if you want!

Back to work...

5 Take note of the fuel hoses. These should be braided and have rubber end fittings. If the hoses appear worn, or the rubber ends are damaged in any way, these should be discarded and replaced with new ones.

6 The spacers (fitted between the carburetters and heat shield) are prone to cracking. Examine carefully and replace if damaged.

The spacers keep the carburetters away from the inlet manifold. Heat is transferred into the inlet manifold from the cylinder head and will heat carburetters to an alarming degree, making the fuel boil up. Fuel will evaporate away leaving a very poorly running car.

Watch out for conversion kits to bigger SUs where the spacers are often replaced by a few thin gaskets, making for a very lumpy ride in traffic.

Carburetter Disassembly

Note: All photos in this section refer to the front carburetter body.

TIP: Only strip and rebuild one carb at a time. If in difficulty, the other is there for reference.

7 Remove the damper cap (5).

8 Unscrew dash pot top (6) and then remove the spring, piston and needle assembly (7).

9 Unscrew retaining clamp (8), pipe and float nut (9) before withdrawing the entire jet assembly (10).

Unscrew the float cap, noting the tag (in this case, AUD327 is the model type and "E" means exchange). Remove the float lid (11).

Note: The overflow outlet from the float chamber is covered by a clip to stop the ingress of dirt (12). People can be fooled into thinking that petrol is pouring from the fuel lines themselves, not from the float chamber.

11 Using pliers, withdraw the steel pin (arrowed 13) to separate the float from the lid. The needle simply drops out.

12 If needs be, the float body can be separated from the carburetter by undoing the bolt (14) and withdrawing the entire body.

Note the arrangement of the washers, etc.

13 Unscrew and remove the butterfly valve.

Note that the screws are split (15) to lock them and the butterfly in position. To remove them, they will require pinching together. Never use them twice - buy new screws!

14 The butterfly (16) can be withdrawn from the slot in the operating arm.

The operating arm can be removed from the body (17). Examine it for wear. If worn the body may require machining to allow fitment of a larger operating arm. This is tricky, I'd leave it to somebody else.

Carburetter Reassembly
Just one thing before we start here. Dash pot tops are not supposed to be polished, and look sadly unoriginal when they are. Avoid polishing them since there are better things to do with life and, let's face it, if you want girls to take you seriously you need to spend a little less time under the bonnet with the chrome polish.

Most Important Note: Any rubber seals, gaskets and sealing washers should not be re-used. Ensure that prior to rebuilding all perishable components are purchased and are ready to be used.

15 Refit the spindle and butterfly, using new split screws (not forgetting to turn the threads over to lock them. Then refit the float bowl to the carb body.

16 Fit jet (green for front carb, pink for rear) into body, and reattach the lever.

Note the bush (18) which fits between the jet and operating lever. The bush allows the jet to be opened and closed without jamming.

Note also how twisting the throttle lever (19) causes the jet to raise and lower (20).

17 Fit new needles, using a steel rule to ensure that the waist of the needle is square with the piston body. (21) Secure loosely.

18 Fit the piston into the carburetter body (22). Hold it firmly in position (23) while screwing the jet clockwise as far in as it will go.

Carefully remove the piston assembly and tighten the needle. The jet and needle should now be centred correctly.

To test, refit the piston, spring and cover. Gently raise and lower the piston at the carburetter mouth. It should rise and fall cleanly. If not, go over the process again.

Finally unscrew the jet by seven flats. This setting will be roughly correct to start the car.

Setting The Float Level
Note: I fitted a pair of precision Grose jets (24), shown here with a standard needle and jet.

19 Find a bar between 1/8in and 3/16in diameter.

20 Fit the jet and float into the float lid. With it upside down, the float will press onto the jet.

21 Insert the bar between the float and the lid. It should just allow the float to rest upon it. (25) If not, remove the jet and fit shims supplied until the float is able to just rest on the bar. That should then be correct.

Note: Float designs changed over the years along with needle valve. To adjust the height of the plastic float, the securing hinge may require some manipulation.

22 Fit new gaskets (26) under the lids. Don't forget the identification tags!

Reassembly onto the manifold
Before you start it is worth noting that really the exhaust and inlet manifolds should be attached first to the engine block prior to fitting the carbs. The manifolds should be torqued down to stop leaks and you can't do this with the carburetters and heatshield in the way.

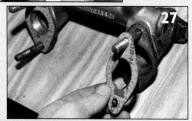

Practically however, you probably want to rebuild the carbs and mount them to the manifold prior to storage for the sake of simplicity.

Simply mount them, springs and all, and just hand tighten the nuts that secure them to the manifold studs. When the time comes, carefully remove the carbs as an assembly and leave them on the table, while fitting the manifolds to the engine.

23 Use new gaskets (27) when mounting the carbs and heatshield onto the manifold.

24 Fit the heat shield (28), a pair of gaskets, the spacers and the second pair of gaskets.

25 Assemble both carburetters with linkages between, and lift the assembly carefully onto the manifold (29).

26 Ensure that the linkages fit properly, by testing them with your finger. Do they feel like they are turning properly?

27 Remember to fit the petrol pipe 'P' clips (30) at the top under the nuts.

28 Fit a new fuel hose and secure it.

Note: Don't forget, when fitting the hose, to install the protective sheaths. A small amount of lubricating oil will help.

29 Fit the air filters, with new gaskets, (31) ensuring that the base plates are the correct way up. Don't overtighten them as this breaks the lugs off of the carburetter body.

30 The final finishing touch is to apply the Coopers transfers.

Soak the transfers in warm water. They will curl up in the water and then uncurl. When this happens, remove the transfer, position carefully and then, maintaining their position with your finger (using the gentlest of pressure) slide the backing sheet out from beneath. Easy does it. Leave to dry (32).

Some History:
Manifolds and the Exhaust System

Inlet and Exhaust Manifolds

The original inlet and exhaust manifolds were revised with the introduction of the 9CG engines. The inlet manifold was again revised at 9CG/Da/H3170 and was also fitted to the 10CG engines until 10CG/Da/H18628. The inlet manifold and cylinder head were then modified to allow fitment of ferrules to help guard against air leaks.

This same inlet manifold was fitted then all the way through to the first 12CD (1275cc) engines where it was revised. This revised version was also fitted from 12CE/Da/H3401 (with a small group of these manifolds being supplied between 12CE/Da/H3201 and H3300). This inlet manifold was fitted until the end of 1275cc production.

10CC engines had a revised exhaust manifold which continued to be used until the end of 1275cc cars (with the exception of US vehicles). In the US, from 12CD engines onward (HAN9 72034 / GAN4 60441, the manifold was modified to allow a 'bolt' fit to the exhaust system.

With the introduction of the 1500 models in the UK, with its HS4 carburetters, a new inlet manifold was used, continuing to be fitted until the end of production. Correspondingly, a new exhaust manifold was provided and continued to be fitted until the end of production.

In the US, use of the single Zenith Stromberg carburetters led to the fitment of a specific manifold, replaced in 1977 by Federal and Californian variants due to the demands of emission controls. In the same year, the exhaust manifold was also adapted for the new legislative requirements.

Exhaust Systems

Originally, the exhaust system varied only between UK and European markets, presumably with US cars having the same system as the British. Both the pipe and single silencers varied between the two markets.

With the introduction of the Sprite III/Midget II models the 'can' shaped silencer was replaced with a 'bomb' type, while in the US (from HAN9 72034 / GAN3 60441), the down pipe flange was revised so that the pipe could be bolted to the manifold.

European models were fitted with the twin silencer systems from HAN8 38829 / GAN3 25788, while us Brits continued to let the world know that we were coming from at least a mile away (or even further on a good night).

Somebody evidently complained to *The Times* about us because, from HAN10 85287 / GAN5 74886, we got a twin silencer system as well. This new system was supplied to both UK and European markets.

Meanwhile, back in North America, the cars had been fitted with an all-in-one downpipe and silencer system from HAN8 38829 / GAN3 25788. Now, thanks to tighter legislation and due to "some kind of bad karma man", the Californian cars were given revised systems from engine 12CJ/Da/H21201 and again at 12V/671Z/401. That clearly wasn't enough because the cars were revised again from GAN5 139773.

1500 models were given a whole new system due to the installation of the Triumph engine. That system was revised from GAN6 172237 when the fitment of a separate downpipe allowed catalysts to be added to Californian cars. Elsewhere the catalyst was replaced by a simple pipe.

In the UK the system was revised again from GAN6 200001 and revised in North America again from GAN6 213312, by which time one could hardly hear anything.

Exhaust Systems

The exhaust systems varied across markets due to local requirements for peace and quiet. The letters relate to the type of
exhaust fittings used (see opposite page for illustrations).

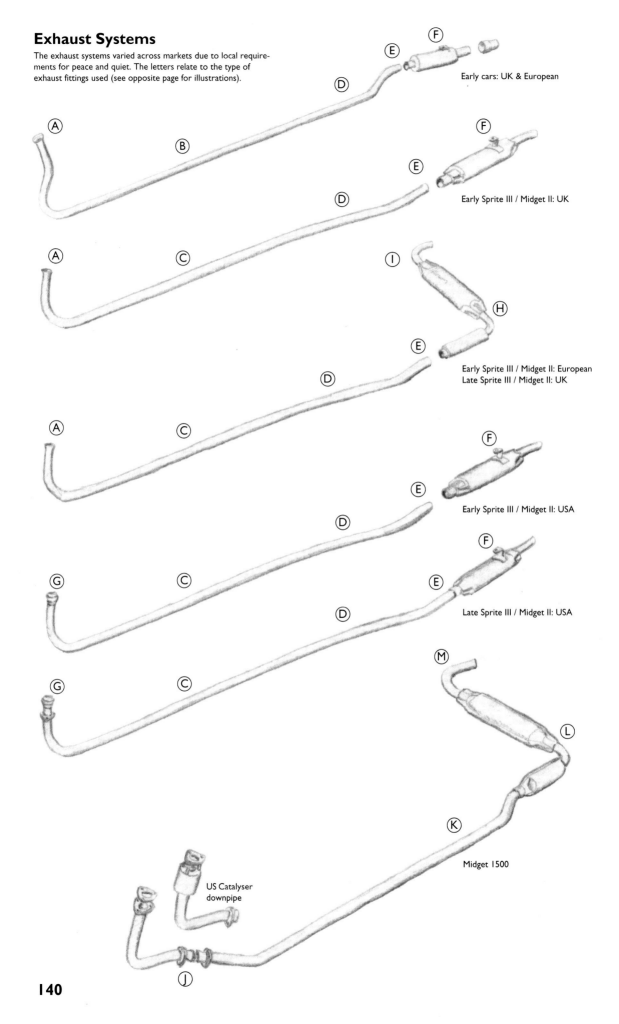

Early cars: UK & European

Early Sprite III / Midget II: UK

Early Sprite III / Midget II: European
Late Sprite III / Midget II: UK

Early Sprite III / Midget II: USA

Late Sprite III / Midget II: USA

Midget 1500

US Catalyser
downpipe

Exhaust Fittings

The exhaust systems are pretty straightforward to fit and in many cases utilised very similar brackets and clamps to support them.

The various systems are shown left, and on this page the fittings applicable to each part of the system are shown.

Never replace just one part of an exhaust system. Always replace the whole thing. When you do, always replace the rubber mountings as well. It's not unusual to see a vehicle dragging its new pipework behind it after an old mounting has failed.

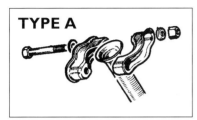

TYPE A

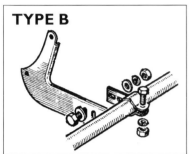

TYPE B

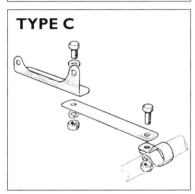

TYPE C

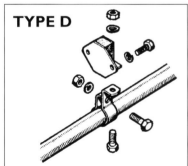

TYPE D

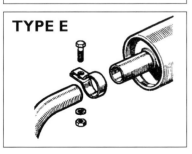

TYPE E

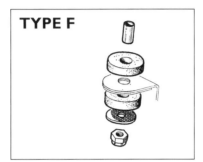

TYPE F

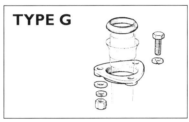

TYPE G

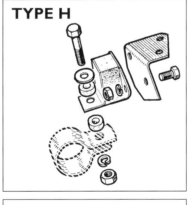

TYPE H

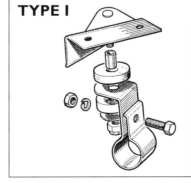

TYPE I

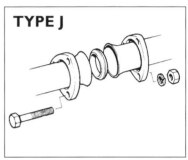

TYPE J

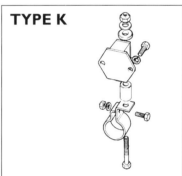

TYPE K

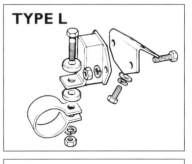

TYPE L

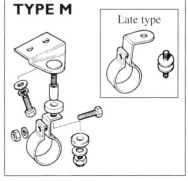

TYPE M

Late type

"Does this sound funny to you?"

My Midget used a lot of oil. It sounded alright but, along with a recurring nightmare of exploding head gaskets, this oil thing was a bit of a problem. To combat this I got a good deal from my local parts shop for some straight 50 grade oil. It wasn't like this runny multigrade stuff, oh no, this came out of the can like treacle. It didn't do any good though, the oil stayed in for only as long as it took to warm up and then it exited the engine even faster than multigrade oil. When I was down to my last can of 50 grade I arranged for an engine "specialist" to take the engine away for rebuilding.

The result was a neatly painted engine with a skimmed head and, as I later discovered, all of the original components. The only other difference being that if I shouted loud enough, my wallet echoed back at me. Still, the engine lost its appetite for oil, much to the appreciation of anyone who drove behind me to work.

A few years later I got my hands on an MGB GT. The previous owner had fitted a newly rebuilt engine following an incident of chronic oil loss. I'd never owned a car with a new engine, so I decided early on that I would look after it. This meant buying oil and an oil filter, which I fitted one sunny afternoon. Imagine my horror when, after servicing the car, I reversed out of the parking bay to find oil all over the tarmac.

There was a lot of oil there and it hadn't dripped out while I had been servicing the B, so where had it come from? The oil filter screw (fitted in the filter head) was cross threaded and the old filter had been carefully applied to make use of what was left of the original thread. Suddenly the whole ridiculous history of the new engine clicked into place. It must have happened something like this...

One day, somebody tried fitting a new oil filter and cross threaded the screw fitting. Rather than replace the damaged part they left it and, with a bit wiggling about, got the filter to fit on what was left of the thread. The oil filter must have worked loose - pumping all of the oil out of the engine and into the road. The driver, failing to notice the sudden drop in pressure probably carried on hurtling down the road until the engine "ate itself for lunch" as we say.

The hapless owner then went to the expense of fitting a new engine, not realising the cause, while the mechanic who installed it failed (?) to notice the damaged thread on the filter head and bolted it (probably still dripping with oil) onto the new engine. Was this the same mechanic that serviced the car originally, and did the same mechanic fail to spot that oil had pumped itself out all over the engine bay from somewhere low down...

I got a second hand screwed insert from the local breakers yard for fifty pence and fixed the problem. My budget wouldn't allow me the cost of another engine.

Engine, Clutch & Gearbox

Some History:
Engine, clutch and gearbox

The engine chosen for the Sprite was the same as fitted to the A35. Under Eddie Maher, the engine was modified at the Morris Engines plant in Coventry where stronger valve springs and improved (stellite faced) exhaust valves were fitted. Otherwise there was little difference but, coupled to a sports exhaust and having the advantages of a pair of SU H1 carburetters, the engine gave quite acceptable performance. The gearbox, like the suspension among other components, came straight from the A35.

For the Sprite II/Midget I models the crankshaft was strengthened and a re-profiled camshaft was fitted, along with HS2 carburetters.

By increasing the bore size and fitting a longer stroking crankshaft, the engine was raised from 948cc to 1098cc (HAN7/GAN2 models on). A larger clutch was fitted to cater for the extra power output and the gearbox ratios were revised to make better use of the increased power output.

The 1098cc unit proved not to be as strong as required so, with the introduction of the Sprite III/Midget II models, the engine was given a stronger crank with larger main bearings. The cylinder head ports were altered and improved to improve fuel and exhaust flow.

The Sprite IV/Midget III models were fitted with a Cooper engine, though with a de-tuned head. The crankshaft was modified soon after its introduction to incorporate a "tuftrided" finish, making it last longer.

US legislation caused many problems for the UK motor industry, not least those caused by the fitting of environmental controls and safety legislation. The 1275 engine gradually sank under a morass of changes and badly needed upgrading by the mid-1970s. British Leyland's finances dictated the limits to which engine development could be carried out and in the end, due to various constraints, Triumph's small engine was chosen over the A series equivalent for improvement. Consequently, virtually the entire engine, with all of its ancillaries and gearbox were taken from the Triumph Spitfire and shoe horned into the Midget engine bay. Indeed for some years, the engine even retained its Triumph badge on the rocker box, to the justifiable annoyance of MG owners.

However, this engine alone had a very long and proud history. Developed for use in the late 1940s and early 1950s, the engine first saw action in the Standard Eight, at only 803cc. Over the years it was heavily modified and appeared in the Herald, Spitfire, Vitesse (known as the GT in the US) and then, with some extensive modification work and some extra pistons, saw its way into the Triumph GT6, among other cars.

The gearbox came from the Spitfire, also having been redeveloped extensively over many years, going on to be fitted to a diverse range on cars such as the Marina, Herald, GT6 and Rover SD1. I have to say though, the inclusion of synchromesh on first gear took all of the fun out of driving round town.

Model	Capacity cc	Comp Ratio	BHP Rating	Torque lb/ft	Clutch	Gearbox Ratios				
						1	2	3	4	Rev
HAN5: Sprite I	948	8.3:1 (9.0:1)	43	52 (3,300)	6 1/4in sdp	3.627:1	2.374:1	1.412:1	1.0:1	4.664
HAN6: Sprite II GANI: Midget I	948	9.0:1 (8.3:1)	46	52.8 (3,000)	6 1/4in sdp	3.2:1	1.916:1	1.357:1	1.0:1	4.114:1
HAN7: Sprite II GANII: Midget I	1098	8.9:1 (8.1:1)	56	62 (3,250)	7 1/4in sdp	3.2:1	1.916:1	1.357:1	1.0:1	4.120:1
HAN8: Sprite III GAN3: Midget II	1098	8.9:1 (9.1:1)	59	65 (3,500)	7 1/4in sdp	3.2:1	1.916:1	1.357:1	1.0:1	4.120:1
HAN9: Sprite IV HAN10, AAN10 GAN4: Midget III GAN5	1275	8.8:1 (8.0:1)	65	72 (3,000)	6 1/2in ds	3.2:1	1.916:1	1.357:1	1.0:1	4.120:1
Midget 1500	1493	9.0:1	66	77 (3,000)	7 1/4in ds	3.41:1	2.11:1	1.43:1	1.0:1	3.75:1

Notes: Compression Ratio. Compression ratio in brackets was an optional extra.
Torque lb/ft. Beneath each figure is a number in brackets. This is the RPM figure for maximum torque.
Clutch. sdp = single dry plate type clutch; ds = diaphragm spring type clutch.

'A' Series Engine, typical

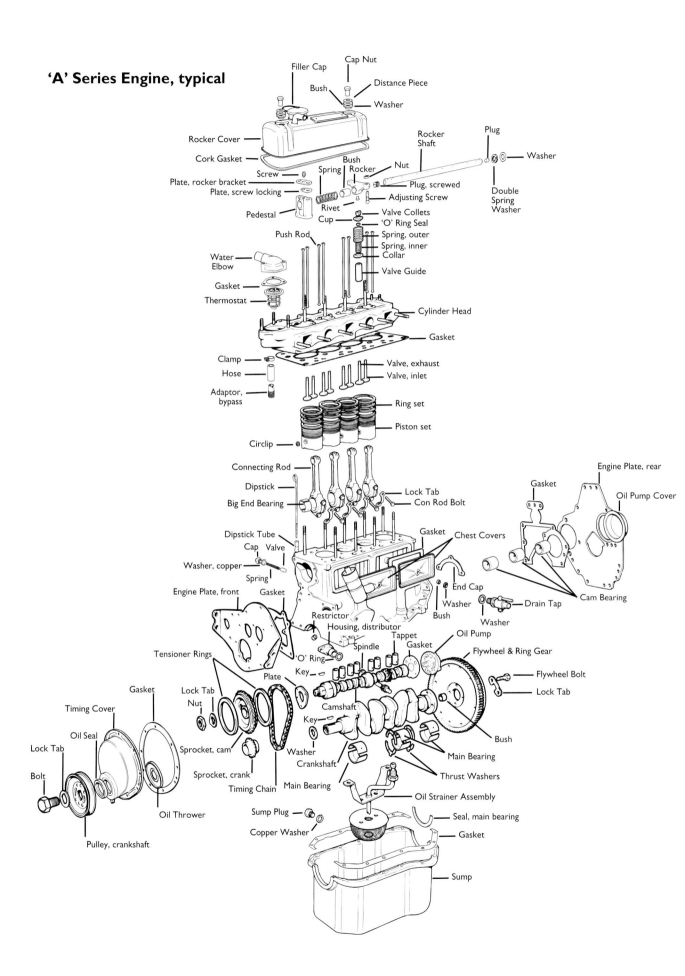

Filler Cap

Cap Nut

Bush

Distance Piece

Washer

Rocker Cover

Cork Gasket

Rocker Shaft

Plug

Washer

Screw

Bush

Rocker

Nut

Spring

Plate, rocker bracket

Plate, screw locking

Plug, screwed

Double Spring Washer

Pedestal

Rivet

Adjusting Screw

Cup

Valve Collets

'O' Ring Seal

Push Rod

Spring, outer

Spring, inner

Collar

Water Elbow

Valve Guide

Gasket

Thermostat

Cylinder Head

Gasket

Clamp

Valve, exhaust

Hose

Valve, inlet

Adaptor, bypass

Ring set

Piston set

Circlip

Connecting Rod

Engine Plate, rear

Dipstick

Gasket

Oil Pump Cover

Lock Tab

Big End Bearing

Con Rod Bolt

Dipstick Tube

Gasket

Chest Covers

Cap

Valve

Washer, copper

End Cap

Spring

Washer

Bush

Cam Bearing

Engine Plate, front

Gasket

Washer

Drain Tap

Restrictor

Housing, distributor

Oil Pump

Tappet

Gasket

Tensioner Rings

Spindle

Flywheel & Ring Gear

'O' Ring

Key

Plate

Camshaft

Flywheel Bolt

Lock Tab

Nut

Key

Lock Tab

Sprocket, cam

Washer

Bush

Timing Cover

Gasket

Main Bearing

Oil Seal

Sprocket, crank

Washer

Thrust Washers

Lock Tab

Crankshaft

Bolt

Main Bearing

Timing Chain

Oil Strainer Assembly

Oil Thrower

Sump Plug

Seal, main bearing

Pulley, crankshaft

Copper Washer

Gasket

Sump

144

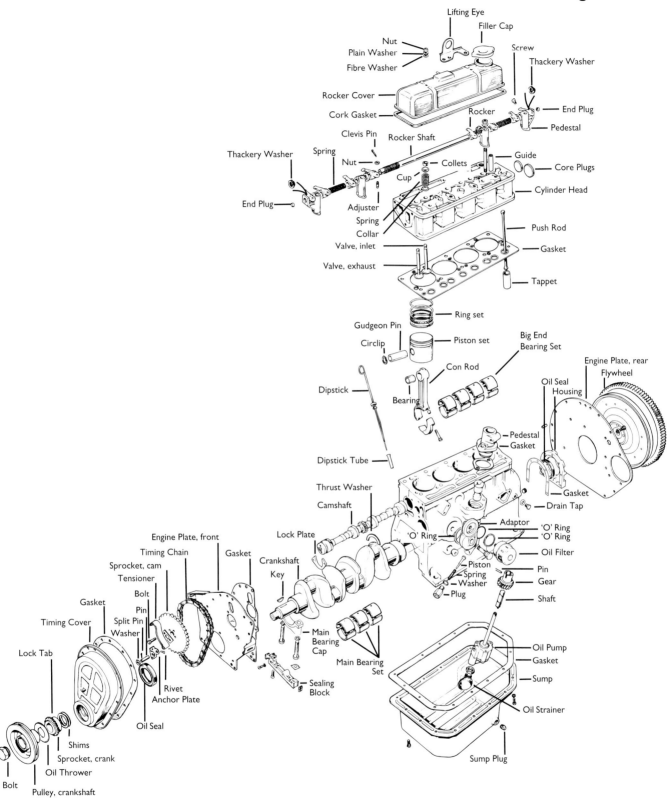

Lifting Eye
Filler Cap
Nut
Plain Washer
Screw
Fibre Washer
Thackery Washer
Rocker Cover
Cork Gasket
Rocker
End Plug
Clevis Pin
Rocker Shaft
Pedestal
Thackery Washer
Spring
Guide
Nut
Collets
Core Plugs
Cup
Cylinder Head
End Plug
Adjuster
Spring
Collar
Push Rod
Valve, inlet
Gasket
Valve, exhaust
Tappet
Ring set
Gudgeon Pin
Circlip
Piston set
Big End
Bearing Set
Engine Plate, rear
Flywheel
Con Rod
Oil Seal
Housing
Dipstick
Bearing
Pedestal
Gasket
Dipstick Tube
Gasket
Thrust Washer
Drain Tap
Camshaft
Adaptor
'O' Ring
Lock Plate
'O' Ring
Engine Plate, front
'O' Ring
Oil Filter
Timing Chain
Gasket
Piston
Pin
Sprocket, cam
Crankshaft
Spring
Gear
Tensioner
Key
Washer
Bolt
Plug
Shaft
Pin
Main
Split Pin
Bearing
Gasket
Cap
Oil Pump
Timing Cover
Main Bearing
Gasket
Washer
Set
Sump
Lock Tab
Rivet
Sealing
Anchor Plate
Block
Oil Strainer
Oil Seal
Shims
Sprocket, crank
Oil Thrower
Bolt
Sump Plug
Pulley, crankshaft

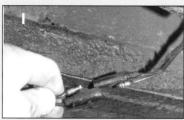

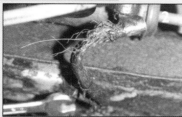

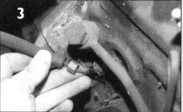

Case Study: Engine Rebuild

Before attempting to remove the engine, remove the bonnet, get the radiator out of the way and remove the steering column and steering rack.

Ensure that all of the ancillary components have been disconnected:-

> clutch pipe.
> speedo cable.
> electrical cables - inc. reverse lamp cabling (1) if removing gearbox at the same time.
> earth strap (2).
> oil cooler hoses (if fitted).
> oil pressure gauge tube (3).
> water temperature sensor and tube.
> Don't forget the gear lever!

Drain the oil from the engine (and gearbox if necessary) and then do the same with the water.

There are two ways to remove the engine:-
A. Brute strength.
B. Using a hoist.

Method A: Brute Strength

If you don't own a hoist, or are not in a position to use one, even if you could hire it, then break the engine down into manageable lumps. In other words, remove what you can while the engine is in-situ:-

carburetters	air filters
dynamo	starter motor
water pump and fan	cylinder head
distributor head	oil filter housing

Getting the front valance out of the way helps.

1 Undo the engine mounts (easiest where the mounts touch the sub frame).

2 Undo the gearbox mounting.

   Two bolts can be released from beneath the car, just where the gearbox tunnel begins (4), there is also one bolt on each side of the gearbox tunnel which must be undone from inside the car (5).

3 Put a jack under the sub-frame (a trolley jack is ideal if you've got one).

4 Lift the body up on the trolley jack high enough to place a support under the engine.

   In my case I used a car ramp with some wood blocks (6).

5 Lower the body back down so that the engine sits on the support. As the body lowers, the engine is raised higher in the engine bay.

6 Once clear of the crossmember the engine and gearbox assembly can be slid forward with relative ease (7).

If required, the gearbox and engine can be separated but I managed to pull the whole assembly forward and out onto a waiting support.

Before going any further make sure you have enough room to put the engine down, perhaps on a work bench. Make sure it is a place you can reach easily - remember you are going to have your hands full. You don't want to trip over a lead, the toolbox, or the cat and you do want to be able to put the engine down safely!

6 With the help of a fit friend lift the engine block out and pop it onto the workbench.

Method B: Using a hoist
If you don't have a hoist, you can hire one. Make sure of the following though:-

You need room to raise the hoist up high enough to get the engine out.

You need room to roll the car out of the way while the engine is slung under the hoist.

You need to be able to incline the engine (and gearbox) at a steep angle to clear the engine bay.

1 Undo the engine mounts (easiest where the mounts touch the sub frame) and the gearbox mounting.

Two bolts can be released from beneath the car, just where the gearbox tunnel begins, and one bolt on each side of the gearbox tunnel must be undone from inside the car.

3 Having securely attached the engine and gearbox to the hoist, *and* being sure that you have enough room to raise the hoist, *and* roll the car back out of the way, go ahead and make as light work as possible in removing the engine.

You'll be horrified at how steep the angle has to be in order to remove the engine and gearbox!

**USING BRUTE STRENGTH!!!
IF YOU HAVE ANY DOUBTS ABOUT USING THE BRUTE STRENGTH METHOD, DON'T! I DON'T ADVOCATE THIS METHOD EVEN THOUGH I'VE DONE IT MYSELF - AND I'M NOT PAYING OUT COMPENSATION FOR PEOPLE WHO INJURE THEMSELVES REMOVING ENGINES FROM CARS WITHOUT USING A HOIST!**

SO, IF YOU WANT TO DO IT, FINE, DON'T BLAME ME IF YOU GET HURT...

AND, COME TO THINK OF IT, THAT COUNTS FOR ANYTHING ELSE YOU DO AFTER READING THIS BOOK!

Engine Strip down and Restoration

1. Remove the clutch assembly and throw it away. Spend some cash on a new one.

   Let's face it, you don't want to get the engine out again for a while.

2. Remove the flywheel by knocking back the lock tabs and remove the securing bolts.

   Locking the flywheel is simple. You need two clutch bolts and a long bar. Fit the two clutch bolts back into the flywheel (leaving an empty hole between them).

   Leave the bolts jutting out enough to fit a lever underneath one and over the other. Now, holding the lever steady (this locks the flywheel) you can undo the the flywheel bolts (1).

3. Examine for damage to the ring gear and the flywheel face.

   If the flywheel face is scored then it will need to be machined flat. To fit a new ring gear, the old one must first be broken off. A new one must be heated until it glows cherry red and then dropped into position. As it cools down it shrinks and locks into place.

   Best to give your flywheel and a new ring gear to the nearest sensible engineer.

4. Remove the rear engine plate (2) to reveal the oil pump (3).

5. Remove the front engine mounts (4) and the fan blades (5).

Removing the Cylinder Head

1. Remove thermostat housing, thermostat and water stop cock from the cylinder head.

2. Remove the rocker cover.

3. Slacken off the rockers (6) to avoid damage while dismantling the cylinder head.

4. Undo the small rocker shaft nuts (7 arrowed).

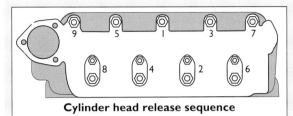

Cylinder head release sequence

5 Undo the cylinder head nuts in stages, using the sequence shown in the diagram left.

6 Lift off the rocker assembly in one easy movement and examine for wear.

7 Remove the push rods and keep in order.

Use a piece of card to mount them (8).

8 Remove the cylinder head. If stuck, drift off using a soft faced mallet or wooden block.

Don't knock the head directly with a hammer as this may damage the casting - and then you'll have a problem.

Note: Don't forget that there is a hose (9) connecting the water pump to the cylinder head. Failure to undo this impedes your chances of removing the cylinder head.

Dismantling the Cylinder Block

1 Remove the water pump (10).

2 Remove oil filter, filter head and pipe (11).

3 Lock the flywheel end of the crankshaft using a suitable bar and then undo the pulley wheel bolt.

TIP: prior to removing the bolt completely, you may find it useful to leave it half unscrewed and then use a hub puller to release the pulley wheel.

4 Remove the timing chain cover, noting that one bolt has a nut (used to secure the heat-shield bracket).

Note the oil thrower and woodruff key. Also note that the raised centre section of the oil thrower faces outwards (12).

5 Undo the camshaft sprocket nut and remove both sprockets and chain, noting that there is a right and wrong way to refit them (13).

6 Remove the front engine plate.

7 Remove the oil pump and discard it.

Note the three eared key (14) which fits on to the end of the camshaft.

149

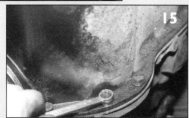

8 Once the cylinder head studs have been removed, turn the block upside down.

Note: Inevitably, there will be some oil inside. Cover the bench with paper to soak up any oil before rolling the engine over.

9 Undo and remove the sump (15), noting the special elongated washers which help to spread the load evenly around the sump lip.

10 Remove the oil strainer assembly (16).

11 Release the pistons and con rod assemblies, making a note of which piston goes where.

Mark the con rod shells prior to dismantling (though check, these may have been stamped with numbers or indentations (17).

In my case, each con rod was stamped with a number. From the front of the engine backwards, they were marked 3, 2, 1 and 4.

12 Slacken the crank main bearing journals (18) and remove the crankshaft.

Note the thrust washers mounted around the centre journal. The thrust washers, when in position, have the indented facings looking away from the journal (19).

13 The half moon shaped plate (20) can be removed from the rear end of the engine.

14 Remove the distributor drive shaft (21) - which simply lifts out once the securing plate has been removed.

15 Remove the camshaft and, finally, the tappets.

Dismantling the Cylinder Head

1 Use a valve spring compressor to compress the springs (22) and remove the collets (23).

2 Release the compressor tool to remove the upper collar, spring(s) and lower collar (24).

Note the valve stem oil seals (arrowed).

3 Withdraw the valves one at a time. Marking them and their relative positions if it is your intention to re-use them.

TIP: If rebuilding the head. Remove, grind and refit each valve at a time.

So now what are you going to do...

Examine the block, crankshaft, camshaft, and components carefully. Ask yourself what you actually want to achieve and then decide how to go about the rebuild process.

In my case I wanted to build an "as new" engine and, since it had already been bored out 0.0040in oversize, I needed some professional help...

Restoration

Various jobs needed doing on my engine which I could not do myself. The cylinders had been bored out, as mentioned above, to 0.0040in oversize and this caused a few problems with the carburation and ignition timing. In fact, it was always a bit lumpy.

The larger capacity of a bored out engine has a requirement for more fuel (the flow of which is limited by the valves) and more time is required to ignite all of the fuel in the chambers - so the timing needs advancing as well.

At +0.0040in the engine had gone from 1275cc to 1310cc. Reboring to +0.0060in would give the engine a capacity of 1330cc, by which time the carburation would be hopelessly out, requiring modification.

I could have made some modifications to the timing and carburation, maybe even fit a more aggressive camshaft - but I wanted to have the car the way it should be.

I contacted Engine Machining Services in Worksop. They fitted liners into the engine and bought the engine back to standard size. They also rebuilt my cylinder head to run on unleaded fuel, supplied a new camshaft (mine was somewhat pitted), cleaned out and re-cored the block and re-painted the entire assembly in its original black (the car was constructed in early 1971).

I then put the assembly back together again.

Engine Colour

By the way, before anybody writes to me telling me that the engine should have been green, forget it. The engine was original, with the front and rear plates oversprayed black, as was the original gearbox. Various ancillary components dated (I found from subsequent grit-blasting) from the time the car was built were also black. Also, the original BL sticker was on the black rocker cover which, when removed, revealed black paint underneath.

It was a black engine. OK! Now forget it....

Reassembly

The A series engine evolved a little over the years, mainly due to changes in the fit of ancillary components or increases in power output. See page 11 or official workshop manuals for accurate data regarding torque wrench settings. The guide written below was my way of doing the job and I accept that owners may want to refer to official guides. Well, here's my method.

1   Use camshaft lubricant liberally on all of the components as you rebuild the engine.

This will prove to be of immense value as time goes on. Most engine damage and wear occurs (or at least the seeds are sown) within the first few hundred miles of an engine's life. Leave nothing to chance.

2   Fit the tappets into position.

3   Fit the camshaft carefully into position (1).

4   Fit the crankshaft, noting that the thrust washers are fitted with the grooves facing away from the mating surfaces (2). Ensure that the end cap faces are sealed with Welseal.

5   Fit the oil pump, not forgetting to include the key (3). Take careful attention when fitting the gasket (4) that the holes correspond to those in the block (for drainage purposes).

Note: Many guides suggest that the oil pump should be primed with oil prior to fitting. This is impossible - you'll discover that the official workshop manual does not suggest this course of action. As soon as the pump is fitted, the oil just pours out everywhere making a mess. The gasket will be soaked before you've even done the bolts up, and finally, any oil remaining will come out when you turn the engine over to fit the sump.

6   Ensure that the pistons are replaced in the order in which they were removed. Remember that the con rods were numbered (5). Now, where's that piece of paper.

Note that the number on the con rods abut against the number on the end cap.

7   Use plenty of lubricant on the bearings and cylinder walls.

8   Fit the front plate, using a new gasket (6) and camshaft retaining cap.

9 Fit the distributor drive (7, 8 and 9).

10 Fit the oil strainer (10) and sump, using a new cork seal (11) around the crankshaft cutaway.

Don't forget the elongated washers for the sump bolts (12).

11 Fit a new oil pressure relief valve and spring (13).

12 Fit a new cam chain onto the camshaft and crankshaft sprockets, noting that alignment marks are visible on the sprockets (14).

The alignment marks should, when fitted, be facing each other.

13 Fit the lock tab over the cam wheel, fit the nut and fold the lock tab over to stop the nut from undoing (15).

14 Fit the timing chain cover, using a new oil seal and gasket.

15 Refit the pulley, using a new lock tab.

As with undoing the pulley, the crankshaft can be held rigid by using a bar fixed to the rear of the crankshaft.

16 Fit the rear engine plate using a new gasket.

17 Fit the flywheel, with a new ring gear if required. Note that the lock tab should be folded over to secure the bolts.

18 Fit the oil filter housing, dipstick tube and other sundry items.

By now this assembly will be getting rather heavy. I built a stand (16) on which to place the engine and then had to work outside to finish it off. The stand needed to be strong enough to take the weight of the engine and gearbox and offer enough space to fit all of the gearbox bolts.

19 Fit the cylinder head studs and torque down to the appropriate levels.

Two nuts locked together on the stud will enable you to torque the stud down. Use locking compound to keep the stud positioned.

20 Fit the water pump, using a new gasket, fan blades and connection hose (17).

21 Fit the dynamo and fan belt.

Adjust the belt to allow about 1in of lateral movement at the middle of its longest reach.

22 Refit the cylinder head, having first fitted a good quality head gasket - copper faced!

Note that the gasket has a top and bottom face (18).

Ensure that the mating surfaces are clean (19), before fitting the head onto the block. *DO NOT USE A JOINTING COMPOUND.*

23 Fit the push rods into the appropriate guide holes (20) and lightly refit the rocker shaft and rockers (21).

24 Torque down to the correct levels in stages in the sequence shown (22).

25 Adjust the tappets for correct clearance.

26 Fit the manifold studs, followed by the exhaust manifold, using a new gasket and not forgetting the inlet sleeves (23).

27 Fit the inlet manifold and torque down. Use new gaskets under and over the spacer blocks (24), followed by the heatshield and more gaskets and, finally, the carburetters, more gaskets and air filters.

28 Make sure that where a thermostat ether bulb is fitted, the appropriate spacer has also been used in the cylinder head (25).

29 Fit the distributor and sundry components, such as the water stop cock (26) and rocker cover (loosely).

Fitting a new clutch and finishing the engine / gearbox assembly
The gearbox input shaft has a number of splines which locate the clutch plate. The number of splines changed on later gearboxes. Check your new clutch plate (you are using a new clutch aren't you) to ensure that the splines match (27).

Having the wrong clutch plate fitted is the last thing you'll think of that could be stopping the engine and gearbox mating together.

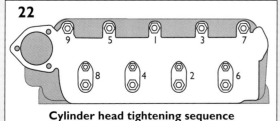

Cylinder head tightening sequence

1 Attach the clutch cover loosely. Then, using a clutch alignment tool in the prescribed manner (28), make sure the cover is properly located and tighten the bolts down a little at a time. Work diagonally to avoid warping the clutch cover.

Remove the tool and then insert it into the hole again, ensuring that the cover is correctly fitted - allowing the tool (and by inference, the input shaft) to move in and out freely.

2 Fit a new thrust bearing (29).

3 Bolt the restored or new slave cylinder to the gearbox. Fit the gearbox mounting, using new rubber mounts. Fit the gearbox to the engine. Fit the starter motor. Now go get a hoist.

Footnote: Didn't I forget something
Most engine restoration work requires skills and tools that few of us have, so professional help may be required. Apart from replacing worn parts such as cam belts and rockers, grinding valves and fitting guides, there is little you can do. Give the engine (in one piece) to a good reconditioner and let them do the tricky bits.

IMPORTANT
GEARBOX NOTE

You may notice that I haven't mentioned the gearbox. As time goes on, less and less gearboxes are available to replace irreparably damaged old units.

Reconditioners find it easier to restore complete units than boxes of bits.

My recommendation is to not dismantle your own gearbox under any circumstances. "If it ain't broke - don't fix it". If it is broken, take it to a gearbox specialist. If you dismantle it and can't fix it, you've got a problem which money is increasingly unlikely to solve.

"Rain...well, it's good for the garden, Sir!"

My hood leaked, well the old bit of rag leaked anyway. Drip, drip, drip, on to my right shoulder. Gradually, on a long journey, my right arm would get damp and then wet and then, drip drip, drip, went my elbow. Once I fitted a new 'proper' hood - the one made by the original manufacturer - the car was mostly water tight. I say mostly, because with the aid of a hose pipe I could still get some water into the car, but that was cheating. In the US, they call soft top cars "rag tops" which evokes an awful vision of wind and water whenever bad weather is likely, but in truth the weather proofing is pretty good on the Sprites and Midgets.

In using a soft top, there are two tricks to avoid. Don't fit cheap economy hoods, because they don't fit and they don't last. Secondly (if you have the later folding hood) don't be lazy when you fold it down. I've seen lots of people putting the hoods down by just undoing the header rail clamps and pushing the hood assembly back. This stretches the hood (it gets noisier once it has been stretched), rips the material where the hood is pinned to the rear cockpit and finally, if the hood is not pulled free of the frame, the material can get cut as it is caught in the scissor action of the folding frame. People who treat hoods like this are, in my experience, those who claim that the hoods are rubbish, that they leak and declare that they would never buy another British sportscar. Fine, more sports cars for the like of me then. In fairness though, many MG owners, having purchased cars second, third or forth hand, never get to see the handbook and miss out on that essential hood folding information.

Internal and External Trim

Prior to fitting a new hood I was driving down the M3 motorway one wet night in November. Kath and I were house hunting at the time and we were on our way to Fleet to experience yet another hovel in the back of beyond. My right arm had gone through the customary phases of damp / wet / sponge like and elbow dripping when I discovered a new experience. The rain was falling like stair rods and I began to feel a little uncomfortable. I shifted in my seat and realised that I was sitting in a pool of water.

The webbing under the seat had collapsed from old age and I was sitting on the floor. The split foam, soaked up the water and transferred it to my trousers. I had to endure squelching round the worst pit of a house I'd ever seen (apart from the one I live in now) and then I had to sit back in the puddle to drive home again.

Subsequently I not only didn't buy the house in Fleet but I rebuilt the seats with new webbing and seat foams - it was amazing. One doesn't realise how sad seats get. It felt as though I were sitting on a throne once I had finished, and I was so high up, my head almost poked a hole through the hood! Restoring the seats was truly a highlight of Midget ownership. Recommend to anyone under six foot tall.

Some History: Trim & Hoods

Internal Trim

The Sprite was introduced into austere times, a fact particularly obvious with regard to trim, Sprite and luxury were not words that went together, though there was enough humanitarian consideration to keep body and soul together.

The early interior trim was available in red, blue, black or green and, because there were no winding windows, door pockets and elbow room were included in the deal. The Sprite floor was luxuriously covered with pre-formed rubber mats and included (from HAN5 501) covered wheel arches and a boot liner. The boot liner was revised from HAN5 4685 due to its obvious excessive quality and fit! The fascia was a fabric, kidney shaped design and included a chromed grab handle for the nervous passenger.

The Sprite Mk II and Midget saw the introduction of a boot lid. A rear bulkhead panel separated the boot from the cockpit. Material specifications changed at the same time as material changes occurred to the seats (for information see the seats pages). A padded crash roll was fitted above the fascia from HAN6 24731.

The door pockets remained, as did the rubber floor mats, though carpet was added to the rear parcel shelf area. The carpet matched the carpet material used on the Midget seats. The Midget, on introduction, included a fleck rubber floor covering.

The dash panel of the Sprite II and Midget I was revised slightly to allow for changes to switch gear. The Sprite continued to be fitted with the grab handle whereas all the Midget got was a badge (try holding on to that on a sharp left hander).

Trim panels were revised from HAN7 24732 / GAN2 16184 with improved door liners and a padded lower fascia crash roll. Colours now included red, black, blue and hazelnut. Wall to wall carpeting had arrived (followed soon after by a curious mouldy smell of rotting carpet). Carpet colours matched the seats and trim - cardinal red, black, blue and hazelnut.

The Sprite III and Midget II were fitted with winding windows which meant that the door pockets were lost (along with any elbow room). Trim was limited to red, black or blue. In the US sun visors were fitted, not here though, but then we don't really get much sun do we. Again, carpet colours matched the trim with red, black or blue being available. A new style fascia was fitted in black crackle paint finish.

A parcel tray was added to limit leg room and stop any late night hanky-panky from HAN8 38829 / GAN3 25788 much to the annoyance of the young and agile.

In the US an instrument nacelle preceded the radio console by a short period. (The radio console was fitted from HAN9 79354 / GAN4 68305 onwards)

The US padded fascia was fitted from HAN9 72034 and GAN4 60441 on, being revised some short time later.

The Sprite IV / Midget III models saw new interior trim and seats (HAN10 / GAN5). Black and Autumn Leaf appeared with matching carpets and seats. 1972 model year cars saw black replaced with navy blue and in 1973, autumn leaf was replaced with ochre. Clearly not popular the 1974 model year saw black and autumn leaf return with a vengeance. Black continued to be used throughout production, while Autumn Leaf was replaced from 1977 onwards with beige trim and chestnut carpets.

UK / European fascia panels were revised consistently throughout this period due to changes in switch gear. Revised initially for the introduction of HAN10 / GAN 5 models it was changed at GAN5 105501 when the rocker switches were introduced, again from GAN5 138801 when hazard warning lights were fitted, and again with the introduction of the Midget 1500 models. A cigar lighter caused further ructions at GAN6 182001 and finally, at GAN6 200001, the MG badge was deleted and the panel had to be revised to fill in the holes.

Hoods and Hard Tops

The Sprite was introduced into austere times, oh, yes, I've already said that. Actually, I'm surprised they didn't just issue an umbrella with each car. The original fold away hood was available in black or white, the design being revised slightly from HAN5 5477 to stop it coming detached in the wind. A full length tonneau cover was also supplied. An optional hard top was available in ivory.

The Sprite II / Midget I hoods came in black, blue or grey, with red and hazelnut being added from HAN7 24732 / GAN2 16184. Full tonneau covers continued to be supplied along with a revised optional hard top available in old english white, blue, red and grey (or primed).

Sprite III / Midget II models had a longer cockpit, necessitating new hoods in red, grey, blue or black. Optional hard tops were primed or came in riviera blue, tartan red, black or old english white.

The Sprite IV and Midget III models were given folding hoods. To make up for this needless extravagance they were supplied in black only. The frame and hood were revised from HAN9 77591 / GAN4 66226 on (and now included velcro fittings to hold the hood sides to the 'B' posts). Full and half tonneaux were now available - full tonneau in black, blue and red for some reason. The revised hard top was available primed only. And that's pretty much the way things stayed until the end of production.

Seat Types

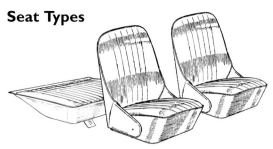

Type 1
Sprite I
Sprite II to HAN7 24731

Red with White piping   Sprite I / Sprite II (HAN6 101 to HAN6 15218*)
different grain material   *Sprite II (from HAN6 15219 to 24731**)*

Blue with Blue piping   Sprite I / Sprite II (from HAN6 101 to HAN6 6284)
different grain material   *Sprite II (from HAN6 6285 to HAN6 24731)*

Black with Yellow piping   Sprite I (HAN5 501 to HAN5 9604)

Black with White piping   Sprite I (HAN5 9605 on) / Sprite II (from HAN6 101 to HAN6 6722)
different grain material   *Sprite II (from HAN6 6723 to HAN6 24731)*

Green with Green piping   Sprite I / Sprite II (HAN6 101 to HAN6 24731)

Red with Black piping   Sprite II (HAN6 101 to HAN6 15218*)
different grain material   *Sprite II (from HAN6 15219 to 24731**)*

Black with Red piping   Sprite II (from HAN6 101 to HAN6 6722)
different grain material   *Sprite II (from HAN6 6723 to HAN6 24731)*

*   *less 14842 to 14965 and 14980 to 15211*
**   *plus 14842 to 14965 and 14980 to 15211*

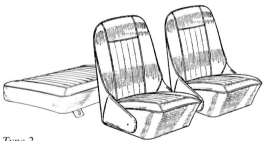

Type 2
Midget I to GAN2 16183

Black with red piping and black carpet with red flecks   GAN1 101 to 10741
Black with red piping and red carpet with black flecks   GAN1 10742 to 16183
Black with white piping and black carpet with white flecks   GAN1 101 to 16183
Red with black piping and red carpet with black flecks   GAN1 101 to 10741
Red with black piping and black carpet with red flecks   GAN1 101 to 10741
Red with black piping and red carpet with black flecks   GAN1 10742 to 16183
Red with white piping and red carpet with black flecks   GAN1 101 to 16183
Red with white piping and red carpet with white flecks   GAN1 101 to 16183
Blue with blue piping and blue carpet with black flecks   GAN1 101 to 16183
Green with green piping and black carpet with white flecks   GAN1 101 to 16183

Rear cushion shown also used in Sprite II

Type 3
Sprite II from HAN7 24732 on
Midget I from GAN2 16184 on

Red
Black
Blue
Hazelnut

Rear cushion as per type 2 seats

Type 4
Sprite III from HAN8 38829 on
Midget II from GAN3 25788 on

Red
Black
Light Blue

Rear cushion as per type 2 seats

Type 5
Sprite III from HAN8 55625 on
Midget II from GAN3 42827 on

Red
Black
Light Blue

Rear cushion as per type 2 seats

*US Market cars seats differed slightly in construction
due to safety regulations and the covers though
similar, vary slightly as well.*

Type 6
Sprite IV from HAN9 77591 on
(all markets except West Germany)

Black only

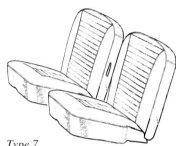

Type 7
Sprite IV from HAN9 77591 on (West Germany only)
Midget III from GAN4 66226 on

Black only

Type 8
Sprite IV from HAN10 85287 on
Midget III from GAN5 74886 on
Midget 1500 to end of production

Black	Sprite to end of production Midget to GAN5 105500 and re-introduced from GAN5 138801 on. GAN6
Navy	Midget GAN5 105501 to 138800
Autumn Leaf	Sprite to AAN10 87824 Midget GAN5 74886 to 123644 and re-introduced from GAN5 138801 to GAN6 198804
Ochre	GAN5 123731 to 138753
Chestnut	GAN6 200001 to end of production

Case Study: Seat Restoration

For some reason, the BMC engineers bolted the seat runners to the floor using a combination of captive nuts and studs making it impossible to remove the seats with ease.

The studs often rust and shear away from the runners, and the captive nuts simply rust to the bolts which also shear off when the seats are being removed. Prepare for a long job.

Over a long period of time the seat foams squash flat, the covers fade and tear, and the rubber seat webbing (or diaphragms) collapses. There's no point in simply replacing the covers if the cushions are worn because the covers will quickly become misshapen and split if there is insufficient support behind them. Replace the seat foams and rubber base.

Tip: The later, stretched rubber diaphragm is much better than the early webbing base.

Preparation
Work on a clean surface, covered by a heavy cloth, since any dirty marks will transfer to the material, and rough surfaces may scuff or tear it.

Rebuild one seat satisfactorily before starting the other. This way you always have a tactile guide to view and feel ensuring that both restored seats are comfortable and correct.

Dismantling
1 Remove the rake adjuster handle (1).

2 Pull off the rear cover clips at the base of the seat back (2).

   Carefully remove these to avoid damaging the cardboard frame

3 Withdraw the flap of seat material. Note how it was tucked up inside the side of the back-rest (3).

4 The cover is pulled tight and stapled into a wooden strip at the base of the seat backrest (4). Remove the staples and gently pull the seat cover up and away from the cushion, or, assuming you are fitting new covers, just have a great time ripping it to bits.

Note: The headrests, when fitted, are secured by a barbed clip. These can only be removed when the seat backrest cover and foam cushion have been removed.

Late Type Seat Construction

Cushion Cover

Flap

Piping

Back Board

Seat Back Foam - tape to board

Squab Cover

Flap

Piping

Squab Foam

Hessian

Diaphragm

Seat Frame

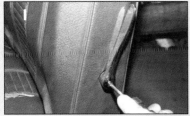

5 The cushion is glued to the cardboard frame. Tape was used to secure it while the glue set and this will be clearly visible (5).

Cut through the tape (6) and then carefully peel or slice the cushion away from the frame with a sharp knife.

6 Having separated the cushion from the frame the head restraint can now be removed.

7. Remove the clips securing the squab cushion and cover.

8 The cover and cushion lift away to reveal hessian sacking used to help stop the webbing from cutting into the cushion.

9 Examine and renovate the seat frame as required. Often this involves little more than cleaning surface rust from the frame and repainting, but ensure that the mechanisms all work correctly and render the seat safe at all times.

Reassembly: the seat back

10 Fit the seat back cushion over the cardboard frame, glue and secure with fresh masking tape (7).

Note: The bottom face of the cushion includes a flap which should be pulled down, wrapped around the back of the frame and taped into place.

11 Note that the cushion covers are handed. Fit the correct cover over the seat and carefully pull down to avoid tearing, or dislodging the foam cushion.

The piping extends below the bottom of the cover to provide the means by which the cover can be pulled down and tensioned correctly.

Note and note well:
The seat covers must be pulled tight to look their best. Work hard to ensure that they have been pulled evenly into position and that the covers are fitted squarely.

Ensure that the head restraint holes (if appropriate) are correctly located above the seat frame fixture.

12 Having pulled the cover down tight, fold the side pieces under the cardboard frame and secure with appropriate clips.

Note: Avoid damaging the cardboard and cover by gripping with a pair of (material covered) wide nose pliers and gently tapping the clips into place.

13 Push the remaining strips and piping up and under the cardboard frame.

14 A flap hangs down from the bottom of the seat facing. Pull it tight (evenly) and staple it to the wooden base.

15 As with the seat facing flap, pull the seat rear facing flap down, pull tight over the wooden base and staple into position.

Note: Staples should be used, but if you don't have a staple gun carefully secure with pins and fold them over before using a retaining strap to firmly locate the material. Though not genuine, it will prevent the fabric from tearing.

Reassembly: the Seat Base (Squab)

16 Replacing the diaphragm is straightforward, but you need real muscles to stretch the rubber material enough to locate the clips.

17 Fit some new hessian and the foam cushion onto diaphragm and lay the cover over the top.

Note: Ensure that the cushion is pushed far back towards the rear of the seat and under the back-rest.

18 Having made sure that the squab and backrest piping is aligned, begin fitting the clips from the front, by wrapping the squab material tightly around the steel frame and securing.

Note: Fit the clips carefully as they will rip the seat material. They must be hidden from view.

19 Repeat at the rear of the frame and then along both sides, ensuring that the material is kept tight and square at all times.

20 Fold the corners underneath the rear of the squab frame for neatness.

Head Restraints

Optional head restraints, where fitted, were of two types in the UK and Europe. HAN5, AAN5, GAN5 and GAN6 cars up to 1992236 had a head restraint with a D shaped profile. Later cars, from GAN6 192237 on, had a head restraint with a more oval profile.

Seat Belts

The seat belts should be in good condition, not torn, ripped or holed, and certainly not showing signs of rot. Early belts are difficult to replace, but look closely through scrap yards where particularly the early clip type will be fitted to a wide variety of older vehicles often in excellent condition. Note, however, that fittings alter between makes and models. Rootes Group cars, for example, had this really neat way of removing the seat belt entirely for cleaning, without needing to unbolt anything.

As far as Sprites and Midgets are concerned, removing the seat belts may be the first indication that more serious structural problems have developed. Sills tend to rot from the inside out, the rear section being no exception. As you try undoing the lower belt anchorage you may find the bolt has rusted to the captive nut. In more extreme cases the nut shears away making it impossible to remove the belt. In my case I resorted to pulling hard on the seat belt and ripping the anchorage from the rusted panel!

The belts can be cleaned using warm soapy water - don't use any chemicals since these might affect the strength and durability of the belt. Unless you want to unstitch the belts, damaged or worn chrome work will need to be endured rather than restored. Any surface rust or "pin spots" can be removed with chrome polish and wire wool. Again be careful not to damage the material.

If wear is present along the length of the belt it should be discarded. The only option would then be to restore the belts using new material and stitching securely. Hard work by hand or by a domestic sewing machine. Trim specialists may be able to help, but will be reluctant, so you may need to hunt around and be prepared to accept liability for any work carried out on your behalf, or try to find second hand belts. Alternatively, fit modern replacements for peace of mind.

Wheel arch fixing, static belt

Sill fixing, static belt

Tunnel fixing, static belt

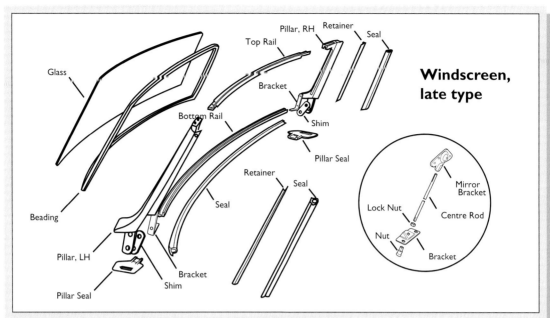

Windscreen, late type

Labels: Glass, Top Rail, Pillar, RH, Retainer, Seal, Bracket, Bottom Rail, Shim, Pillar Seal, Beading, Retainer, Seal, Seal, Pillar, LH, Bracket, Shim, Pillar Seal, Mirror Bracket, Lock Nut, Centre Rod, Nut, Bracket

Case Study: Windscreen

WARNING: replacement parts for the windscreen are not all available. Many of the frame components are now irreplaceable and are easily damaged.

Anodising

The frames were anodised, a process which coats the aluminum to protect against corrosion. It is not an awfully effective process having little resistance against salt water. Also the quality of aluminium used was variable. Aluminium becomes porous.

Many platers advise against reanodising, since getting the process to work well requires practice. As the grade of aluminium changes, so too does the process of anodising - a major problem to be aware of.

I opted to have the frame powder coated but even this proved disastrous. As windscreen castings become porous they soak up considerable grime, oil and salt deposits. When my powder coated castings were placed in the oven for curing the salt and grime deposits erupted as the castings were heated. The result was a pitted, pock marked surface which needed rubbing down and recoating for a second time.

When I fitted the screen and tensioned the hood, the powder coating just cracked looking little better.

If you do intend to have a bash at this, consider putting the frame into the oven first to expel some of the oily deposits that lurk within.

Disassembly

Disassembly is a straightforward process made almost impossible due to seized screws which hold the brackets together. Extreme caution is needed during dismantling since once the screws are damaged or threads split, you've got a problem.

Reassembly

Work on a blanket to avoid damage.

1 Mount the glass into new beading. Then assemble the top, bottom and one side piece together loosely.

2 Using Vaseline or soap fit the glass and beading into the frame and fit the remaining side piece.

   No matter how hard I tried, I couldn't pull all of the pieces close enough together to secure the brackets. I gave up and thought I'd have another go the next day. Overnight, I had a great idea...

3 Get some rope and wrap it around the frame. Use a length of wood to twist the rope tighter. As the rope tightens the frame pulls itself together.

4 Do the same again, lengthways this time to pull the sides in and then secure the brackets.

6 Fit the lower seal. There are two channels in the base of the frame. The channel towards the front is the groove for the front face of the seal. Behind is a flanged channel into which the main section of the rubber fits. Drop the front edge into the groove and then push home the rear part in using a broad bladed screwdriver. Avoid piercing the seal.

10 Refit the side channels with rivets. The side seals then (with the aid of Vaseline) simply slide into position and are rivetted to stop them pulling out.

11 Refit finishing items as necessary.

   Don't refit the windscreen until the doors have been built up and fitted to the shell.

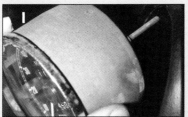

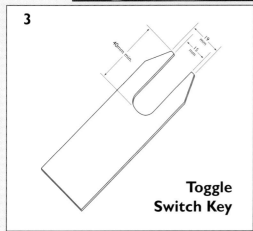

Toggle Switch Key

Case Study: Dashboard

During manufacture, bodyshells were supplied to MG painted, partially trimmed and with the dashboards fitted. Removing the dashboard is possible once the wiring has been disconnected, the speedometer cable undone and the choke cable, heater button and water temperature gauge removed.

You may have purchased a new wiring loom, but don't go nuts by cutting off the existing wires. Make a note of which wire goes where. The wiring diagrams may not prove reliable and you can't be sure that wiring changes have been adequately recorded.

Removal of Instruments and Switches

1 The instruments are secured with clamps and nuts - the larger instruments use two clamps, the smaller use single clamps.

Note that an earth cable is secured under one of the knurled nuts in each case.

2 The speedo is removed by pulling it out as far as possible and then tilting it downwards in an arc. The casing is dished, allowing it to clear the hole without damaging the trip winding handle (1).

The reason that the trip winding handle is bent is to allow easy removal of the gauge.

The trip winding handle is often broken irreparably by people as they get in and out of the car. These will need to be repaired by a specialist. The parts are not available. *Note: They do not unscrew.*

3 The heater switch knob is removed by depressing a small button hidden at the underside of the knob. A small screwdriver should do the trick (2).

4 To remove the toggle switches I made a key tool (3) which helps to tighten and release the chrome bezels (4).

5 Removing the dual gauge must be done with great care since it is easily damaged. First, the oil pressure pipe can be unscrewed and separated from the gauge. Note that a small leather washer is used to stop oil leaking out. It will require replacement.

6 Release the water temperature sensor bulb from the cylinder head (5) before carefully retracting the gauge and capillary tube from the dashboard (6).

7 Removing the fuel gauge is quite straight-forward, but here's a tip. If your fuel gauge does not seem to register fuel properly, it might be because the earth connection has come loose on the rear of gauge. Before dropping the petrol tank to look at the sender, check the earth for tightness.

8 Disconnect the choke cable from the carburetter and then, having undone the securing nut, withdraw it from the dashboard.

Removing the Dashboard

The dashboard is attached to the bulkhead via angle brackets (7) at the top of each A post with cross head screws visible beneath the crash roll.

To stop it vibrating the dashboard is also secured by two metal strips reaching forward to the front bulkhead.

9 The indicator lights are simple rubber ended tubes with green filters located by a pressed metal fabricated plate (8). The lenses are actually secured with clear sticky tape (9).

10 The MG or Sprite badge is held in position with two spring clips. These need to be prised off carefully to remove the badge.

Restoring the Dashboard

Restoration may consist simply of grit blasting and repainting the dashboard. Some holes may need to be filled since, over the years, many accessory switches, lamps and sundry fittings may have been installed. In this instance weld over the offending holes, grind smooth and fill as necessary prior to painting. A welder will be able to do this for you easily.

Wrinkle Finish Paint

Wrinkle finish paint is curious stuff that won't work well unless the environment is sufficiently warm. Either heat your garage in winter, use a powerful hair dryer, or wait until summer. The temperature needs to be at least 25 deg C.

Having primed the metal surface spray on two light coats of wrinkle finish paint within minutes of each other. Wait a few hours and then spray again with a thick coat of wrinkle finish paint.

Over a period of a few hours, the smooth paint will begin to wrinkle nicely.

Crash Roll

Replacement fabric comes with the trim kits. The crash roll is attached to the scuttle with studs, washers and nuts and can only be removed once the dashboard is out of the way.

Case Study: Hood & Frame
Removing the Folding Type Hood

Removing the hood should be a straightforward procedure. If the hood has been replaced it may be more difficult to do again. It is not uncommon to find that the rear studs and chrome retaining strip have been rivetted in position rather than being secured by screws.

If rivets have been used to secure the hood then there are two restoration possibilities:-

A. Use more rivets - as favoured by many hood specialists and trim fitters.

B. Refit the hood using screws and nuts, the cockpit finisher hides the nuts from view and allows easy removal in the future.

1. Remove screws or drill out rivets to release the chrome finisher at the rear of the hood (1).

2. Remove header rail screws (2) and lift the hood and header rail away from the frame.

3. Withdraw the header rail seal (3) and drill out the retainer rivets.

4. Realise that the header rail now rattles a lot - due to all those rivet heads.

The frame on my car may have come from an earlier model. Grey frames were superseded by black versions with the introduction of the "Leylandised" cars. I'm not ruling out that grey frames were still supplied on and off, especially since the tonneau sticks remained grey. It seems unlikely to me that a change was specified for one and not the other and, despite what people tell me to the contrary, I can easily believe that grey frames were supplied.

On the other hand, maybe my car had been rolled, and that my grey frame came from an earlier car.

5. If you want to get the rivet heads out, you'll need to drill a hole into the header rail. Your choice. I took forty five of them out, which allowed for three hoods having been fitted. I also broke a drill bit during the process of removing the retaining bar. Upon emptying the old heads out I discovered another broken bit in there as well(4).

6. The frame is secured with six bolts (5). Sandwiched between the frame and the body are some cardboard shims (6) - don't forget to replace them. Note also the position of the tonneau stick supports.

Restoration

The hood frame and the header rail can be grit blasted and repainted either in grey or gloss black. Otherwise no action is normally required.

If you are replacing the hood then by far the easiest way of doing it is to buy a hood and header rail together or, buy a good quality hood (by that I mean original equipment) and take it to a trim specialist. He will have the skills to make a perfect job of fitting it for just a few pounds. It will look good and be watertight.

Folding the Reclining Hood

My hood was tearing at the seams when I purchased the car and, as an impoverished student, it stayed like that until I went out to work and could afford a replacement. Torn seams are not uncommon and I know the reason why the seams give way - I've seen people damaging hoods on many occasions. The reason is that people don't take care when raising or lowering the hoods.

Imagine a hot day, you're in a stuffy queue of traffic and decide to put the hood down, bang bang go the safety catches, one quick push from inside the car and the hood is pushed back out of the way. The trouble is that this simple action has split the seams, torn the material away from the Dot Pegs and the scissor action of the frame has just cut a hole in the side window!

Here's how to do it properly.

1. Undo the studs at the windscreen corners (7).

2. Release the silver button clips which hold the hood to the frame behind the side windows.

3. Jump out and unclip the Tenax fasteners (8) around the rear of the cockpit (not forgetting the velcro or studs on the B posts).

4. Wind down the side windows.

5. Undo the header rail clamps and push up about 6in to separate the header rail from the windscreen.

6. Get out of the car again to lower the hood. As the frame folds, lift the hood away from the frame and lay it flat over the boot (9).

7. Fold the side window triangles over the main part of the hood (10) then carefully fold the hood back over the frame and into the parcel shelf area (11). Fit the tonneau cover.

With practice you can do it in 45 seconds!

Trim Details

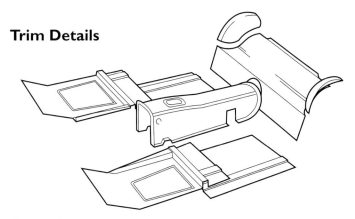

Sprite I

Body Colour	trim	Matting	Seats	Seat piping	Hood & Tonneau
Cherry Red	Cherry Red	Cherry Red	Cherry Red	White	Black or White[1]
Primrose Yellow	Black	Black	Black	Yellow	Black
Leaf Green	Green	Green	Green	Green	Black or White[1]
Dark Green	Green	Green	Green	Green	Black
Speedwell Blue	Blue	Blue	Blue	Light Blue	Black
Iris Blue	Blue	Blue	Blue	Blue	Black or White[1]
Whitehall (Nevada) Beige	Cherry Red	Cherry Red	Cherry Red	White	Black or White[1]
Old English White	Cherry Red[2]	Cherry Red or Black	Cherry Red	White	Black or White[1]
	Cherry Red[2]	Cherry Red or Black	Black	White	Black or White[1]

[1] White hood, tonneau & side screens offered from April 59
[2] Black seats & trim alternative offered from January 59 on

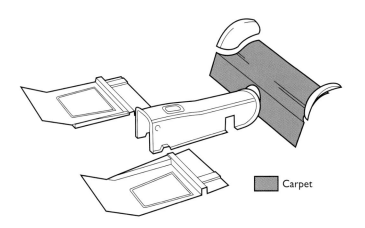

Carpet

Sprite II (HAN6)

Body Colour	trim	Carpet[3]	Matting[3]	Seats	Seat piping	Hood	Tonneau
Black	Cherry Red[4]	Red with Black Fleck	Cherry Red	Cherry Red[4]	Black	Grey	Red
Signal Red	Black	Black with Red Fleck[5]	Black	Black	Red	Black	Black
	Cherry Red[4]	Red with Black Fleck	Cherry Red	Cherry Red[4]	Black	Black	Red
Deep Pink	Black	Black with White Fleck	Black	Black	White	Black	Black
Highway Yellow	Black	Black with White Fleck	Black	Black	White	Black	Black
Iris Blue	Blue	Blue with Black Fleck	Blue	Blue	Blue	Blue	Blue
Speedwell Blue	Blue	Blue with Black Fleck	Blue	Blue	Blue	Blue	Blue
Old English White	Black	Black with White Fleck	Black	Black	White	Grey	Black
	Cherry Red[4]	Red with Black Fleck	Cherry Red	Cherry Red[4]	White	Grey	Red

[3] Carpet covered only the rear parcel shelf down to the floor and rear wheel arches.
    Rubber matting no longer fitted under under the seats!
[4] Cherry Red to February 62, then bright Red
[5] Red with Black fleck from March 62 on

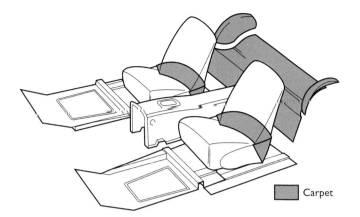

□ Carpet

Midget (GAN1)

Body Colour	Trim	Carpet[6]	Matting[6]	Seats	Seat piping	Hood	Tonneau
Black	Red	Black with Red Fleck[5]	As carpet	Red	Black	Grey	Red
Tartan Red	Black	Red with Black Fleck	As carpet	Red	Black	Red	Black
	Red	Black with Red Fleck[5]	As carpet	Black	Red	Red	Red
Almond Green	Green	Black with White Fleck	As carpet	Green	Green	Grey	Black
Clipper Blue	Blue	Blue with Black Fleck	As carpet	Blue	Blue	Blue	Blue
Ice Blue	Blue	Blue with Black Fleck	As carpet	Blue	Blue	Blue	Blue
Farina Grey	Red	Red with White Fleck	As carpet	Red	White	Grey	Red
Dove Grey	Red	Red with White Fleck	As carpet	Red	White	Grey	Red
Old English White	Black	Black with White Fleck	As carpet	Black	White	Grey	Black
	Red	Red with White Fleck	As carpet	Red	White	Grey	Red

[5] Red with Black fleck from March 62 on
[6] Fleck carpet covered the rear parcel shelf down to the floor, wheel arches and rear of the seat squabs. Elsewhere, matching textured fleck matting was used, including under the seats.

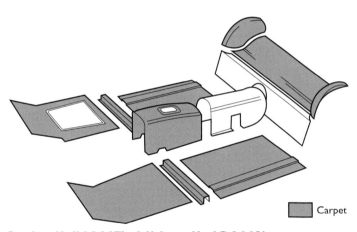

□ Carpet

Sprite II (HAN7); Midget II (GAN2)

Body Colour	Trim	Carpet	Seats	Seat piping	Hood	Tonneau	Notes
Black	Red	Red	Red	Grey	Black	As hood	Sprite / Midget
	Hazelnut	Hazelnut	Hazelnut	Grey	Hazelnut	As hood	Sprite only
Signal Red	Red	Red	Red	Grey	Red	As hood	Sprite only
	Black	Black	Black	Grey	Red	As hood	Sprite only
Tartan Red	Red	Red	Red	Grey	Red	Red	Midget only
	Black	Black	Black	Grey	Red	Red	Midget only
Fiesta Yellow	Black	Black	Black	Grey	Black	As hood	Sprite only
British Racing Green	Black	Black	Black	Grey	Black	As hood	Sprite / Midget
	Hazelnut	Hazelnut	Hazelnut	Grey	Hazelnut	Hazelnut	Midget only
Iris Blue	Blue	Blue	Blue	Grey	Blue	As hood	Sprite only
Ice Blue	Blue	Blue	Blue	Grey	Blue	Blue	Midget only
Dove Grey	Red	Red	Red	Grey	Grey	Grey	Sprite only
	Red	Red	Red	Grey	Grey	Red	Midget only
Old English White	Hazelnut	Hazelnut	Hazelnut	Grey	Hazelnut	As hood	Sprite / Midget
	Red	Red	Red	Grey	Grey	As hood	Sprite only
	Red	Red	Red	Grey	Grey	Red	Midget only
	Black	Black	Black	Grey	Black	As hood	Sprite / Midget

Trim Details

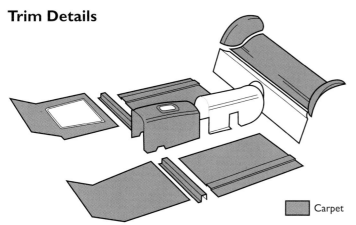

☐ Carpet

Sprite III (HAN8), Midget II (GAN3)

Body Colour	Trim/Carpet/Seats[7]	Seat piping	Hood	Tonneau	Notes
Black	Black	Grey	Black	Black	Midget II (GAN3) only
	Red	Grey	Black	Black	
Tartan Red	Red	Grey	Red	Red	
	Black	Grey	Black	Black	
Pale Primrose	Black	Grey	Black	Black	
Fiesta Yellow	Black	Grey	Black	Black	
British Racing Green	Black	Grey	Black	Black	
Riviera Blue	Blue	Grey	Blue	Blue	
Dove Grey	Red	Grey	Grey	Red	
Old English White	Black	Grey	Black	Black	
	Red	Grey	Grey	Red	

[7] Fascia panel and finishing trim (front and rear cockpit trim and door top) always finished in black.

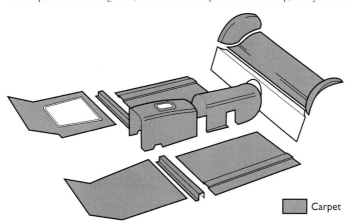

☐ Carpet

Sprite IV (HAN9), Midget III (GAN4)

Hood and tonneau always supplied in black.

Body Colour	Trim/Carpets/Seats	Seat piping	Notes
Black	Black	Grey	
	Black	Black	
	Red	Grey	
Tartan Red	Red	Grey	Midget III (GAN4)
	Black	Grey	
	Black	Black	
Pale Primrose	Black	Grey	
	Black	Black	
British Racing Green	Black	Grey	
	Black	Black	Sprite IV (HAN9)
Mineral Blue	Black	Black	
Basilica Blue	Black	Grey	
Old English White	Black	Grey	
	Red	Grey	
Snowberry White	Black	Grey	
	Black	Black	

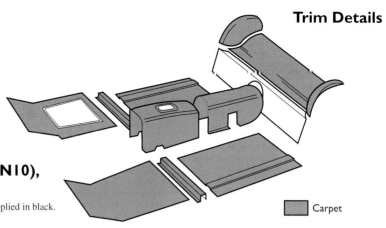

Carpet

Sprite IV (HAN10, AAN10), Midget III (GAN5)

Hood, tonneau and hood cover always supplied in black.

Body Colour	Trim/Carpets/Seats
Black	Black
Flame Red	Black
Blaze	Black
Bedouin	Black
	Autumn Leaf
Bronze Yellow	Black
Pale Primrose	Black
British Racing Green	Black
Racing Green	Autumn Leaf
Teal Blue	Black
Midnight Blue	Black
Blue Royale	Black
Glacier White	Black
	Autumn Leaf

Midget Mk III Round Wheel Arch (GAN5)

Hood, tonneau and hood cover always supplied in black.

Body Colour	Trim/Carpets/Seats	Notes
Black	Navy	
Flame Red	Navy	
Blaze	Navy	To July 73
	Black	August 73 on
Bracken	Autumn Leaf	
Bronze Yellow	Navy	
Harvest Gold	Navy	To July 73
	Black	August 73 on
Citron	Black	
Limeflower	Navy	
Green Mallard	Autumn Leaf	to August 73
	Ochre[8]	August 72 to August 73
Tundra	Autumn Leaf	
Teal Blue	Autumn Leaf	
	Ochre[8]	August 72 to August 73
Aqua	Navy	
Damask	Navy	To July 73
	Black	August 73 on
Aconite	Autumn Leaf	
Black Tulip	Navy	July 72 to July 73
	Black	August 73 on
	Autumn Leaf	
	Ochre[8]	August 72 to August 73
Mirage	Black	
Glacier White	Navy	To July 73
	Autumn Leaf	August 73 on

[8] Carpet colour was the same as Autumn Leaf, beige leathercloth was used to trim the carpet.

1500 Midget

Hood, tonneau and hood cover always supplied in black.

Body Colour	Trim/Seats	Carpet	Notes
Black	Black	Black	
	Autumn Leaf	Autumn Leaf	to September 77
	Beige	Chestnut	October 77 on
Russet Brown	Beige	Chestnut	
Sand Glow	Autumn Leaf	Autumn Leaf	
Vermillion	Black	Black	
Flamenco	Black	Black	
Harvest Gold	Black	Black	
Bracken	Black	Black	
	Autumn Leaf	Autumn Leaf	
Inca Yellow	Black	Black	
Chartreuse	Black	Black	
Citron	Black	Black	
Brooklands Green	Autumn Leaf	Autumn Leaf	February 76 on
	Beige	Chestnut	October 77 on
Tundra	Autumn Leaf	Autumn Leaf	
Tahiti Blue	Black	Black	
	Autumn Leaf	Autumn Leaf	
Pageant Blue	Beige	Chestnut	
Damask	Black	Black	
Carmine	Black	Black	February 77 on
	Beige	Chestnut	October 77 on
Glacier White	Black	Black	
	Autumn Leaf	Autumn Leaf	
Triumph White[9]	Black	Black	
Ermine[10]	Black	Black	

[9] Listed in Triumph books as White or New White
[10] Formally Leyland White

Paint Charts

Body colour	code	Sprite I	Sprite II (HAN6)	Sprite II (HAN7)	Midget (GAN1)	Midget (GAN2)	Sprite III (HAN8), Midget II (GAN3)	Sprite IV (HAN9), Midget III (GAN4)	Sprite IV (HAN10), AAN10, Midget III (GAN5)	Midget Mk III (GAN5 Round Wheel Arch)	1500 Midget	Period Notes
Cherry Red	RD4	●										
Primrose Yellow	YL3	●										to December 58
Dark Green	GN12	●										to December 58
Leaf Green	GN15	●										from January 59
Whitehall (Nevada) Beige	BG4	●										from January 59
Speedwell Blue	BU1	●	●									to December 58, Sprite II / Midget to August 61
Iris Blue	BU12	●	●	●								Sprite from January 59; Sprite II / Midget from September 61 on
Old English White	WT3	●	●	●	●	●	●	●				
Deep Pink	RD18		●									
Highway Yellow	YL9		●									
Signal Red	RD2		●	●								
Black	BK1		●	●	●	●	1	●	●	●		to July 72
Black	BLVC122										●	
Dove Grey	GR26			●	●	●	●					September 61 on
British Racing Green	GN25/GN29 2			●		●	●	●				to June 70
Fiesta Yellow	YL11			●			3					to late 65 only
Almond Green	GN37				●							
Clipper Blue	BU1				●							to August 61
Farina Grey	GR11				●							to August 61
Ice Blue	BU18				●	●						September 61 on
Tartan Red	RD9				●	●	●	●				
Riviera Blue	BU44						●					
Pale Primrose	YL12						4	●	●			late 65 to June 70
Mineral Blue	BU9							●				November 67 on
Basilica Blue	BU11							●				to October 67
Snowberry White	WT4							●				
Bedouin	BLVC4								●			June 70 on
Racing Green	BLVC25								●			June 70 on
Midnight Blue	BLVC1								●			June 70 on

Body colour	code	Sprite I	Sprite II (HAN6)	Sprite II (HAN7)	Midget (GAN1)	Midget (GAN2)	Sprite III (HAN8), Midget II (GAN3)	Sprite IV (HAN9), Midget III (GAN4)	Midget III (HAN10, AAN10), Midget III (GAN5) / Midget Mk III (GAN5 Round Wheel Arch)	1500 Midget	Period Notes
Blue Royale	BU38)							●			October 69 to June 70
Bronze Yellow	BLVC 1 5							●			October 69 to July 73
Teal Blue	BLVC18							●	●		June 70 on
Blaze	BLVC16							●	●		June 70 to August 73 on
Flame Red	BLVC61							●	●		October 69 to July 72
Glacier White	BLVC59							●	●	●	October 69 to August 77
Green Mallard	BLVC22							●			
Aqua	BLVC60							●			to July 72
Black Tulip	BLVC23							●			
Limeflower	BLVC20							●			July 72 to July 73
Mirage	BLVC11							●			August 73 on
Aconite	BLVC95							●			August 73 on
Bracken	BLVC93							●			August 73 to February 76
Harvest Gold	BLVC19								●	●	to February 76
Citron	BLVC73								●	●	August 73 on
Tundra	BLVC94								●	●	August 73 to February 76
Damask	BLVC99								●	●	to February 77
Flamenco	BLVC133									●	February 75 to August 77
Tahiti Blue	BLVC65									●	February 75 to August 77
Chartreuse Yellow	BLVC167									●	February 76 to August 77
Sand Glow	BLVC63									●	February 76 to August 77
Brooklands Green	BLVC169									●	
Carmine Red	BLVC209									●	
Triumph White [5]	BLVC206									●	August 77 to June 78
Inca Yellow	BLVC207									●	August 77 on
Vermillion	BLVC118									●	August 77 on
Pageant Blue	BLVC224									●	October 77 on
Russet Brown	BLVC205									●	October 77 on
Ermine [6]	BLVC 243									●	June 78 on

1 Midget II (GAN3) only
2 Same colour, different part no.
3 Sprite III (HAN8) only
4 Sprite III (HAN8) only
5 Listed in Triumph books as White or New White
6 Formally Leyland White

Cherry Red
Primrose Yellow
Dark Green
Leaf Green
Whitehall (Nevada) Beige
Speedwell Blue
Iris Blue
Old English White
Deep Pink
Highway Yellow
Signal Red
Black
Dove Grey
British Racing Green
Fiesta Yellow
Almond Green
Clipper Blue
Farina Grey
Ice Blue
Tartan Red
Riviera Blue
Pale Primrose
Mineral Blue
Basilica Blue
Snowberry White
Bedouin
Racing Green
Midnight Blue

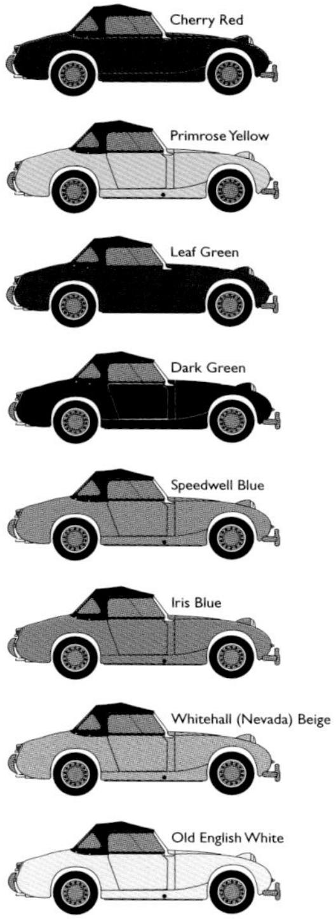

Sprite IV/Midget III (HAN9/GAN4)

Black
Tartan Red
Pale Primrose
British Racing Green
Mineral Blue
Basilica Blue
Old English White
Snowberry White

Sprite III/Midget II

Black
Tartan Red
Pale Primrose
Fiesta Yellow
British Racing Green
Riviera Blue
Dove Grey
Old English White

Sprite II/Midget I (1100)

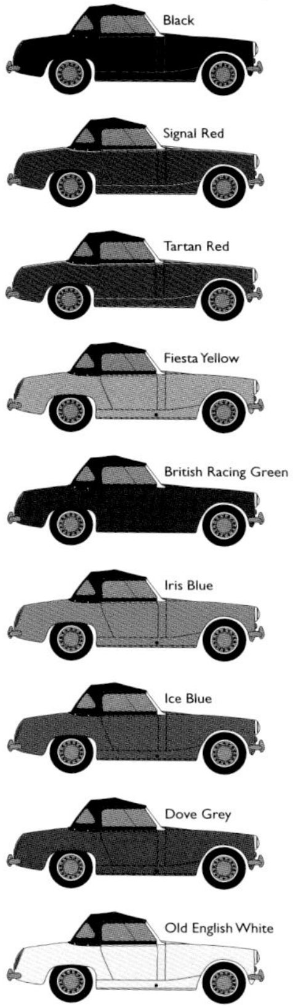

Black
Signal Red
Tartan Red
Fiesta Yellow
British Racing Green
Iris Blue
Ice Blue
Dove Grey
Old English White

Sprite II/Midget I

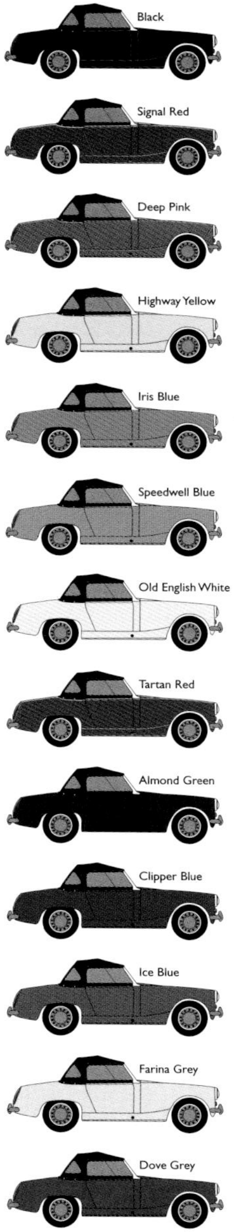

Black
Signal Red
Deep Pink
Highway Yellow
Iris Blue
Speedwell Blue
Old English White
Tartan Red
Almond Green
Clipper Blue
Ice Blue
Farina Grey
Dove Grey

Frogeye

Cherry Red
Primrose Yellow
Leaf Green
Dark Green
Speedwell Blue
Iris Blue
Whitehall (Nevada) Beige
Old English White

174

Blue Royale
Bronze Yellow
Teal Blue
Blaze
Flame Red
Glacier White
Green Mallard
Aqua
Black Tulip
Limeflower
Mirage
Aconite
Bracken
Harvest Gold
Citron
Tundra
Damask
Flamenco
Tahiti Blue
Chartreuse Yellow
Sand Glow
Brooklands Green
Carmine
Triumph White
Inca Yellow
Vermillion
Pageant Blue
Russet Brown
Ermine

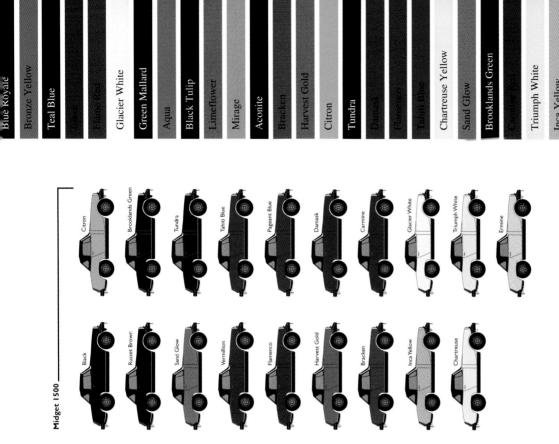

Midget 1500

Citron | Brooklands Green | Tundra | Tahiti Blue | Pageant Blue | Damask | Carmine | Glacier White | Triumph White | Ermine

Black | Russet Brown | Sand Glow | Vermillion | Flamenco | Harvest Gold | Bracken | Inca Yellow | Chartreuse

Midget III (Round Wheel Arch)

Tundra | Teal Blue | Aqua | Damask | Aconite | Black Tulip | Mirage | Glacier White

Black | Flame Red | Blaze | Bracken | Bronze Yellow | Harvest Gold | Citron | Limeflower | Green Mallard

Sprite IV/Midget III (HAN10/AAN10/GAN5)

Black | Flame Red | Blaze | Bedouin | Bronze Yellow | Pale Primrose | British Racing Green | Racing Green | Teal Blue | Midnight Blue | Blue Royale | Glacier White

Top: One hour's work with an angle grinder reduced the old bodyshell into enough small pieces to fit into the boot of a Volvo.

Middle: The Midget lay idle for years prior to restoration.

Right: The engine bay, original except for the addition of an electronic ignition unit and non-standard accelerator cable.

Top: Fully restored with the addition of badge bar, period spot lamps and racing style mirrors.
A single door mirror would have been original fitment. The number plate would not have been black and silver, but reflective white. This would have been seen as 'old fashioned' at the time. *photo: David Ward*

Right: The most useful Sprite or Midget accessory is a bolt-on boot rack.

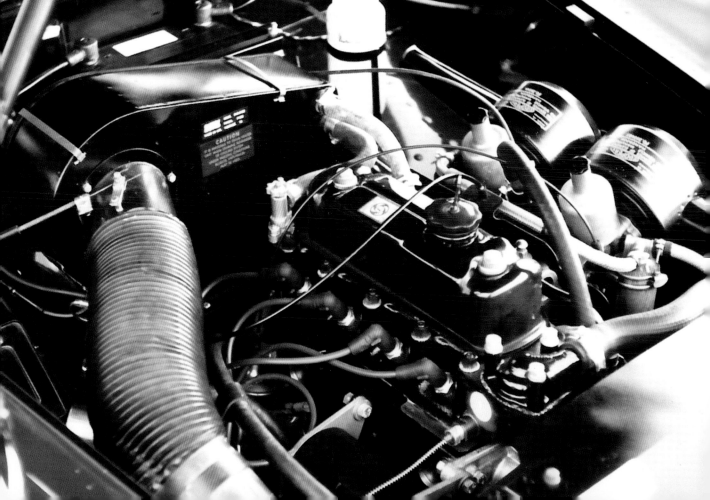

Left: Detail is everything. Finishing the engine bay means using the appropriate decals and avoiding the excessive use of metal polish. Ancillary components such as the carburetters were not polished during manufacture.

Below: Detail work such as the correct badging is the key to completing any restoration project - but it is also the hardest and most time consuming part of the job.

Clockwise from top: 1. Much of the interior can be purchased new, for later cars at least. *Photo: David Ward.* 2. The header rail should have a notice to avoid damage. 3. Door pulls have metal clamps colour matched to the trim. The door seal was bleached from black and dyed in the appropriate colour. 4. New carpets do not include the anti-scuff plastic strip. I stitched these in. 5. The door catch plates are zinc-passivated and are easily restored by electroplating.

Left and below: The original 'MG' badge, as seen on 'Old Number One' shown below, in the days when MG stood for Morris Garages.

Centre: Period driving lamps are a good way of adding extra night time visibility without resorting to Halogen conversions.

Bottom: Interior view of the finished car.

Rust never sleeps...

A German lady walked into our shop one day, wanting a sill plug for her Midget. I gave her a plug and off she went, only to come back a few moments later to tell me that it didn't fit. I was a bit surprised by this, the plugs only come in one size and I told her so but, no, she was adamant, the plug would not fit the hole. I thought that I should just have a look, perhaps we were talking at cross purposes.

I walked out of the shop with her, and, plug in hand, stepped across to her car. It was fitted with chrome oversills and when I bent down to fit the plug I discovered that the genuine sill, hidden behind, was completely rotten. I didn't know what to say, she had no idea what was wrong, or indeed how serious it was. She had simply bought a car that was a wreck and in two days time she intended to drive it home to Germany.

Building a Bodyshell

With hindsight, its easy to see problems, but problems and faults are only obvious when you have become aware of them or have had to deal with them in the past. My experience of buying a Midget was pretty much the same, though not so desperate. Rotten sills on my Midget had been carefully filled and painted and I had no idea that a problem existed until I removed some interior trim panels.

I have never learned to weld - even if I had, structural welding on a soft top car is fraught with danger - so I had to give this work to somebody else and was not happy with the result. Though I drove the repaired car for a number of years I could never get out of my mind that the job wasn't up to scratch. Not only that but there was more rust there, lurking in the dark recesses of the body, eating away at unseen parts of the car, waiting to appear one day. Re-shelling a car is not necessarily an easy option, but, once done, my car looked fantastic and every piece of metal was both new and electroplated against the elements. The best thing of all was cutting up the old shell into small pieces, stuffing them into the boot of the Volvo, and taking them to the dump. Very satisfying!

Many people can, and do, weld. Some with greater success than others. A friend from school bought an MGB and, experiencing the same horror as me when he discovered rotten sills, took matters into his own hands, hired a welding gun, bought some sills and, in the space of a few weeks, managed to turn his MGB banana shaped. If, like me, you have never welded before don't start with a sports car because the rigidity of the shell is all in the sills, gearbox tunnel and crossmembers. If the vehicle is not supported correctly, the chassis will twist and all sorts of problems follow. What is only millimetres out at one place will cause something else to be wildly out of true elsewhere. Having seen the vast array of jigs and fixtures used by British Motor Heritage to build a shell, I wouldn't even begin to look at doing my own welding work.

But, do what you will, it's your car!

Some History: Bodyshells

The Healey designed body was quite an innovation at the time. While many cars still had a chassis with a separate body bolted on, this type of welded mono-coque construction was shared by only a few more exotic and expensive cars. This is a point to remember when restoring your Sprite or Midget. These days, people expect everything to fit together as if it were a modern built Audi or BMW with fifty years of mono-coque body construction experience behind them. What people forget is that Sprites were designed in the 1950s and this type of construction had never been undertaken before, certainly not for large scale car production. They were working in the dark to a certain extent. Don't be surprised if, when re-shelling a car, some recourse to a hammer is necessary. Men with hammers were a common sight on the assembly lines of the 1960s and 1970s.

Rigidity and strength came from the gearbox tunnel, door sills and the crossmember (which runs in front of seats). The bonnet, incorporating the front wings, was a heavy one piece assembly hinged at the rear and opened with a grubby handle under the front valance. The underframe was built by John Thompson Motor Pressings with the body designed by Panel Craft and subsequently built in volume by Pressed Steel Company. The entire assembly, put together at Pressed Steel, was then painted at the Morris plant at Cowley and delivered to Abingdon for finishing and final assembly, so there were a few miles on the clock even before the the speedo had been fitted.

The Sprite II / Midget I had a new front end, designed by Healey, and a new rear end, designed by Syd Enever of MG. In redesigning the rear end Enever gave the car an opening boot and a larger cockpit area. Underneath the skin, however, the chassis was unchanged.

The Sprite III / Midget II saw the fitment of semi-elliptic rear springs necessitating a number of changes in and around the boot area. Fitting winding windows also necessitated changes to door construction, notably with the loss of the door pockets.

When the Sprite IV / Midget III was introduced the bumper height was raised to fit in with new legislation and, from 1971, round rear wheel arches were fitted.

The 1500 Midget saw changes to the body allowing an increase in ride height; also changes to the wings and valances to fit the impact resisting "black bumpers". The rear wings returned to their squared off shape to improve longitudinal strength, a problem shown up during crash testing of vehicles.

Over the years many minor changes took place due to the modification of components or to allow fitment of ancillary and auxiliary parts. These changes are too numerous to mention here. Sorry.

Notes on Bodyshells

This entire book is written around re-shelling an MG Midget or Austin Healey Sprite into a Heritage bodyshell. It does not include any instruction on how to repair damaged bodyshells for two reasons. Firstly, as I mentioned before, I can't weld and nor can many other aspiring DIY mechanics. Secondly, re-shelling a car has its own problems, not adequately addressed elsewhere.

I have worked for many years in the classic car industry, including time at British Motor Heritage, and have often felt that the great achievement of BMH in re-introducing these bodyshells has been belittled by those who do not appreciate the enormity of the task undertaken. It is rare indeed that any single company has managed to collect tooling and jigs, years after manufacturing has ceased, to produce a complete shell - let alone a whole range of shells.

Unfortunately, some purchasers of Heritage shells seem to expect a level of perfection that is simply not attainable, and which, even when produced first time round, was never possible. Anybody re-shelling a Sprite or Midget should necessarily expect some little trouble.

Mostly these traumas are not insurmountable and they are, as I mentioned elsewhere, the types of problems that would have been dealt with by panel beaters and assembly workers at the assembly stage. (Well I ask you, did you see your Sprite or Midget being built at the factory?)

Increasingly, people seem to expect a quality similar to that of a modern production car, well, forget it. If that is what you expect find a modern sportscar that's been written off in an accident, wipe the blood off the seats and restore that using an "off the shelf" bodyshell from the Far East.

Building a bodyshell takes effort, not the kind of effort involved in using angle grinders, chisels, lump hammers and welding torches, but effort all the same. If, building a bodyshell, you come across a problem don't whine about it and say that the shell is rubbish (it's not) instead, step back, have a rest and think about how to solve the problem. Inevitably, you will have to use some unpleasant tools, such as a rasp, drill, or even a club hammer, but your experience will be no different from that encountered daily on the shop floor in Abingdon and, let's face it, they built some great sports cars!

Case Study: Heritage Bodyshells

Unless you took a body shell apart, you would probably never realise the amount of work that goes into building one.

Sprite and Midget shells are made from a number of sub-assemblies, such as the main floor, boot floor, front 'H' frame assembly and so on. Even these are made up of a number of individual pressings and cut sections, all twisted, bent and formed to meet together for welding. Further back in the process still, you might find a piece of sheet steel that has a hole cut in a pre-arranged location, or a bracket with a nut welded into position which, when you build your car, will allow you to fit the demister vent or the fuel pump.

At British Motor Heritage Sprite and Midget bodyshells are still being built and I'd like to take the opportunity to give you a quick tour around the body building facility so that you can get an idea of what is involved in making a Sprite or Midget shell. I could go on endlessly about every weld, nut and every bracket but, rather than dull your senses and eyes with the minutest detail, I'll give you a brief sketch of what happens starting with the construction of one of the main sub-assemblies. From there we can see how a body takes shape.

Logistically speaking constructing a bodyshell is the biggest and most complex of jobs under-taken at the British Motor Heritage (BMH) facility in Witney, Oxfordshire. Before body building commences individual components have to be manufactured and then, about a week before the body build begins, the work force is busy manufacturing hundreds of sub-assemblies which litter the production area. Front wings, themselves complex assemblies, take shape in one area, while in another gearbox tunnels are being constructed. Everything from wheel arch assemblies to scuttle panels start appearing in neat rows around the facility.

I watched this process over a number of days, waiting for a chance to photograph the body building process. Gradually, come the end of the week, the facility became full of components and assemblies left in readiness to meet the needs of several weeks worth of body build.

Some jigs date back to the early 1960s. Due to space constraints in the facility, these were wheeled into position ready for build work when needed.

Production of the shells by BMH began in the early 1990s and I'm sure that for most of the staff this is old hat, but for me, the waiting got quite tense. After what seemed like weeks of waiting, I walked into the workshops to find the first shells of the week taking shape.

Rear Sub-Assembly

As a starting point I looked at how the rear sub assembly was constructed. The whole task takes one man about an hour and a half.

1 The boot floor is placed on a jig, where strengthening tubes are added to the main floor pressing (1 and 2) and tacked into position before being stitch welded (3).

2 The inner wheel arches are then fitted (4), followed by bump stop plates, boot floor extensions and finally the outer wheel arches.

3 Once completed the sub-assembly is ready to be fed into the main body assembly area.

Main Body Assembly

Before the body is built all of the components have been prepared with the exception of the rear outer skin - a fragile, easily damaged assembly. The skin consists of the rear valance and tonneau, outer rear wings and the outer sills.

1 A team, building the main body, will stitch these panels together first (5) and leave them close by as they begin work on the main framing jig.

2 The floor pan is locked into position on the main jig (using a number of guide pegs to aid alignment), along with the front sub assembly and crossmember - that long "top hat" section that gets in the way of your passenger's feet (6). Once locked into position the parts are all spot welded together (7).

3 The gearbox tunnel and rear bulkhead panels go in next (8 and 9). To cater for a number of welding requirements several different weld guns are used, so the jig, mounted on wheels, is pushed backwards and forwards throughout the operation to allow easy access for the guns.

4 The inner sills are then lined up and locked into position (10) using alignment grips attached to the main jig. The weld guns come back out again to spot them into position before the rear wing extensions and 'B' posts are placed in the jig and welded (11).

5 An extension is then added to the framing jig to allow accurate alignment of the tonneau panel (12). Once the panel is located, it is spot welded to the wheel arch and wing extensions.

185

6 The rear outer skin mentioned earlier, with its outer sills tacked into place, is then carefully lifted over the under body (13) and clamped at various points. Yet another jig extension is added to ensure accurate positioning of the assembly (14) and, once locked down, the entire outer skin is spot welded.

7 The boot is finished by the fitting of a boot lid stay bracket and courtesy lamp switch.

8 When the scuttle panel is fitted door gap jigs (15) are used to ensure correct spacing between the 'A' and 'B' posts.

9 Further jig extensions correctly align the 'A' post with the outer sill to avoid unsightly twists or steps between the panels.

10 Long arm spot weld guns reach down inside the footwells to complete the task of fitting the bulkhead, scuttle and 'A' post panels together (16).

11 Once this is completed, the whole assembly is wheeled to another location so that the gearbox tunnel can be welded in. At the same time the rear spring hanger strengthening plates are also fitted (to be later hidden by the seats).

At any time, quality inspection staff may come along to check the weld quality and, therefore, the structural integrity of each shell. Every shell is checked, sometimes two or three times, as are the various sub-assemblies used in the build process. Any problems found at this stage will need to be rectified before any further work can be carried out on the shells.

CO2 Welding

1 Once the shell has been "spotted" together, the assembly is lifted from its jig and placed onto a new platform which can be turned through 360 degrees (17). It is wheeled into a curtained chamber in which major load bearing sections of the shell are seam welded using CO2 weld guns.

2 Why is it wheeled into a curtained chamber? It's to protect people working nearby since the light from the process is so bright that eye damage can easily occur (18). The welder works on one side of the car and then rolls it over to work on the underside.

3   Once finished the body is now as strong as possible. Without this process the shell would be much more flimsy and suffer from a variety of handling problems. Not only that, but the shell would be inherently weaker.

Bodywork Finishing

Once the body has been fully welded there is still work to do. The assembly still needs front valance, front wings, a bonnet, doors and a boot lid. These items are added in the finishing booths. At the same time, some of the welded joints, such as those joining the rear valance to the tonneau sides, are filled with lead (19) and then rubbed down smooth.

If you think fitting body panels is a walk in the park, you couldn't be more wrong. Working in the classic car industry, I was often forced to endure complaints regarding panel fit, and yes, they are right, the panels never fit. The painful truth is that the panels never will fit properly and never have. What's needed are the skills and arts of a panel beater.

No two bodyshells are the same, each has its own individual peculiarity, caused by a million differences. Weld gun temperature, the fabric of the metal, even the humidity, all conspire to force changes in the way the sub assemblies go together. No matter how good the panel is, it still needs some tender blows from the hammer to make it fit (20).

I was amazed to watch a front wing being fitted into position. Getting a wing to line up with the 'A' post, bonnet and outer sill required considerable effort. The wing was fitted, examined, removed and modified three or four times before a close fit was possible. Even then, the final adjustment to get the line right along the 'A' post was made by pushing and adjusting the wing along its front edge where it meets the valance. Suddenly, it just fell into position. So it is, so it has always been.

Why is so much finishing work needed? Well just remember that the humble Sprite, designed in the late 1950s, was one of BMC's first ever monocoque bodyshells. When the car and jigs were designed Donald Healey and his crew were sailing into uncharted seas using techniques used on only a few hand-built cars. The build quality wasn't, and never would be, perfect, although it was excellent for the time. If you expect Y2K computer-aided build quality, you'd better get real.

Back in the good old days, the most sought after man at Abingdon was the one with the spoons and lump hammer. It can't be helped, but at some point you may need to do some of the work he would have done.

My new Midget bodyshell next to the last Midget ever to roll off the MG production line at Abingdon.

You couldn't write comedy like it...

At last most of the car components were restored and protected from dampness by being stuffed in plastic bags or sheeting and stored in my father's loft.

My new bodyshell had been painted and delivered, and I had fitted the axles so that I could roll it on a trailer and take it home. I took extra care on the long journey, so as to avoid any chance of damage while the shell was on the trailer. The journey completed, Kath and I removed the bodyshell from the trailer, shoe horned it inch by inch carefully along the narrow drive and through to the back garden on a brilliant crisp starry night. I parked the shell up, mounted it on axle stands and covered it with sheets and tarpaulins.

I went to bed for some well deserved sleep only to awaken the next morning to a gale which had ripped through the tarps and blown down my neighbours sheds, liberally sprinkling the new bodyshell with large pieces of rotten wood. It took forever to rub the scratches out.

A few months later, on a beautiful clear summer day, I was working on the shell fitting the carpets. It had been a hot day, with not a cloud in the sky. My eyes ached from the brightness of the light and, feeling a headache coming on, I went to snooze on the bed for half an hour. I lazily awoke to see the end of a terrific thunderstorm and looked out of the window to see my newly carpeted and water logged shell!

And it's not just the weather. Having fitted the bonnet on to the car my son took to walking up the bonnet and sitting on the windscreen frame causing me some undeserved apoplexy. Some weeks later, and about thirty seconds after I had fitted the battery, my boy found the horn button.

Final Assembly

Now what you should have is a large pile of restored components, a painted bodyshell safely supported on axle stands and a lot of spare time.

Professional restorers tell you to put the old shell next to the new and work between one and the other. Tell me who has space to do that; I'd really like to know. Restoration projects may run over years and items removed first will be the last to be refitted into the new shell. It is unlikely that side-by-side restoration will prove practical for most amateur restorers.

THE VERY FIRST JOB...

The very first job, before anything else, is to go around the shell with taps and dies to clean the threads and remove paint that may have got into them. Otherwise screws and bolts will be difficult to fit - and can even lead to cross-threading!

Sizes required	Taps	Dies
	3/16in	-
	1/4in	1/4in
	5/16in	5/16in
	3/8in	-
	7/16in	-

A 3/8in BSW tap is required for the windscreen frame bolts.

THE ASSEMBLY PROCEDURE

Through trial and error, I found that final assembly is most easily achieved by following the procedure in the ASSEMBLY ORDER GUIDE shown right.

I have grouped the final assembly into numbered sets. Most of the assembly procedure is straight-forward, but some sections may give some problems. Problem areas are listed on the subsequent pages. I hope they prove helpful to you as a first time restorer.

Assembly Order Guide - Build Your Shell Up Like This!

1 Pedal Box, with master cylinders and pedals
  Brake Pipes
    starting with the wheel arch union
  Clutch Pipe
  Control Box and Fuse Box
  Engine Bay Splash Plates
    to be fitted but left loose
  Wiring Harnesses
    front and rear harnesses
  Oil Capillary Tube

2 Crash Roll
  Wiper Wheelboxes, rack and motor
  Heater vent doors
    in footwell
  Demister nozzles and Tubes

3 Doors and Door Fittings
  Windscreen

4 Crash Roll and 'Lift-The-Dot' Pegs
    fitted in dash top
  Washer Jets and tubing

5 Dashboard (Fascia Panel)
  Speedo Cable

6 Heater Box and Motor

7 Stub Axle Assemblies
  Brake Hoses, front
  Steering Rack
  Front Wheels

8 Rear Axle
  Rear Springs
  Brake Hose, rear
  Handbrake Assembly and Cable
  Rear Wheels

9 Exterior Lamps
  Horns
  Oil Cooler Assembly
    if required

10 Fuel Tank
  Fuel Filler Pipe and Filler Neck
  Fuel Pump
  Fuel Pipe

11 Boot Fittings and Boot Trim
  Spare Wheel
  Tonneau Covers and Tools
  Bonnet Fittings and Bonnet Trim
    where applicable - including those on the
    landing panel - **but not the stay rod**

12 External Brightwork
    esp. sill, door, wing mouldings and badges

13 Grommets and Sill Drain Plugs
    cockpit area
  Under-Carpet Set
  Carpets
    glued carpet only
  Trim Panels
  Interior Trim Finishing Detail
    pegs, studs etc
  Hood

14 Bumpers
  Number Plates

15 Chassis Plate
  Engine (with ancillary components) and Gearbox
    inc. all engine and gearbox connections.
  Engine Earthing Strap
  Propshaft

  Clutch Bleeding
    easier prior to fitting the steering wheel.

  Fresh Air Tube for Heater
  Oil Cooler Hoses
    where required
  Steering Column
  Throttle and Choke Cables
  Exhaust System
  Radiator and Water Hoses
  Water Expansion Tank
  Air Filters

16 Gear Lever Gaiter
  Carpet Set
    stud secured items
  Seats
  Ash Tray
  Parcel Tray

17 Steering Wheel

18 Grille Surround and Grille

COMPLETE SERVICE
Follow the service guide as per the workshop manual.

BATTERY CAUTION!
Do not connect the battery until all connections have been made correctly.

ENGINE TIMING SET-UP
To be complete once the battery has been connected.

Notes: Assembly Section 1

BRAKE PIPE INSTALLATION

Original equipment brake and fuel pipe was always manufactured in zinc coated steel and pre-formed to the correct shape. This is a nightmare to stock so, you will need to bend it to shape yourself or you can try to buy it made up.

There are three grades of brake and fuel pipe available to classic car restorers (at the time of writing). Zinc coated steel, copper or kunifer.

Zinc coated steel pipe is difficult to bend to shape and tends to rust through after long periods of use, often internally since traditional brake fluids soak up water.

Copper brake pipe is the cheap, easy to bend alternative. It won't corrode like the O.E. steel tubing, but can break more easily during forming. Vibration can cause copper pipe to become brittle, so always ensure that copper pipes are properly secured.

Kunifer pipe is marginally more expensive than copper but closer in appearance to steel, is non-corroding and easy to bend. It is also more malleable and much less likely to become brittle. If you intend making your own pipes, this is the stuff to use.

Most of the pipe you purchase will be from a roll (1) which means that you need to cut the material to length, de-burr, fit the appropriate male or female pipe ends and produce the appropriate flares.

You will need a pipe cutting tool (2), flaring tool and a pipe bender. I made my own pipe bender with angle iron and repair washers (3).

Male joints used on the Midgets and Sprites are of the "double flared" type. Female joints are conveniently called "Female flares"
Practice first...

Having the old pipework will prove to be very useful when it comes to forming and fitting replacements. Try hard not to destroy them when removing the originals from the car. Note the position of any 'P' clips.

A pipe flaring tool includes a form (4) and cone (5), which together produces male (6) and female (7) flared pipe ends.

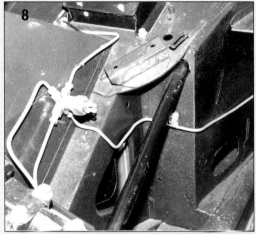

1. Install the pedal box, using new seals between the pedal box and footwell.

2. Fit the blanking plate to the opposite footwell.

3. Fit the four way union to the inner front wheel-arch.

4. Fit the new brake pipes (8), starting with the master cylinder to union pipe. Secure as necessary with pipe clips. The number of clips will vary depending upon the model year of the car and whether it is RHD or LHD, so take careful note of how the pipework originally fitted.

5. Ensure that the pipe in the propshaft tunnel is secured with pipe clips (9).

I know this may sound patronising, but if you make up your own pipes, don't forget to fit the pipe ends before flaring the ends or bending the pipes. It's really annoying to spend so much time forming the perfect pipe only to discover that you forgot to fit the nut on the end!

Finally, don't overtighten the pipes. It's better to check for leaks and tighten if necessary, rather than to strip the threads or damage the pipe ends.

6. Connect the pipes as necessary to the front and rear brake hoses (10) and (from there) to the brakes themselves. When you do this depends upon how you assemble the car. **Whatever way you do it, and before you go any further, you should bleed the brakes and test them to ensure that their are no leaks.** If there are, then rectification work can be carried out there and then.

Note: With regard to front hose fitting, 1275 models (and earlier) used an L shaped bracket into which the hose and pipe were joined and secured. 1500 models dispensed with this by connecting the pipe and hose through the wheel arch wall.

Heritage shells use the Midget 1500 method for hose fitment. If you want concours standard get out your MIG welder and grab some angle iron.

1275 owners will need to fit the longer 1500cc model brake hoses. The shorter ones will be stretched by the stub axles on full reach and may snap, or at the very least stop the stub axles from reaching the bump stops.

WIRING HARNESSES

Once the pipes have been installed the harness should be fitted. To install them properly you should first fit the splash panels into the wheel arches although at the time, replacements were being prepared for me by a local engineering company. Ensure that the appropriate 'P' clips are used throughout (11, 12 and 13), noting that the rear harness should be clipped to the rear lamp assembly studs.

Replacement harnesses no longer include the appropriate connector blocks for the control box or indicator switch gear. Also the length and break away points of some of the tails may prove to be a little short. There will be some pushing and pulling required to allow a comfortable fit of the harness.

Note: At no time should the cables be pulling against their connectors. Ensure that when a cable reaches any switch or electrical component that it is slack, preferably with a service loop. Without it the cable may pull off or snap.

SPLASH PLATES

The splash plates which attach to the radiator supports are fairly flimsy, being nothing more than light pressings. The 1500 versions have been re-fabricated and can be used for earlier models. The only problem being that the plates are about three inches too short for early cars due to the different steering rack fitted to the late 1275 and 1500 models.

Weld (or if necessary rivet) on extensions and cut to shape prior to fitment. Also note that the securing holes may not be accurately placed. When fitted the top of the plates should not sit too proud since they will interfere with the bonnet. I saw a case recently where a customer had fitted the splash plates, found that the bonnet then wouldn't close properly and to cure the problem simply folded them over.

The answer should have been to line them up to the bonnet, mark and drill new holes where required, not just bodge it!

Notes: Assembly Section 2

When fitting the crash roll, ensure that each stud is secured using a lock washer and nut. Once the dashboard has been refitted, you won't get to the nuts again. If they come undone, the studs will simply rattle for ever and the nuts have a knack of getting caught on a ledge and sliding noisily every time you go round a corner.

Notes: Assembly Section 3

CRASH ROLL

Fit the quarter lights into the doors and build them up, making sure that the windows wind up and down. Then fit the windscreen, followed by the dashboard.

DOORS

Dismantling process

The doors are best left until you are ready to build up the new bodyshell. Don't strip down both doors at one time, do one after the other - that way you can refer to the other door if you run into difficulties.

1 Begin by removing the inner door handles (14A), door pull (14B), winder handle (14C) and trim panel (14D).

2 Remove the door lock latch assembly and lock mechanism (15)

3 Remove outer and inner seals - these are likely to become damaged during removal but in all likelihood will need replacing anyway.

4 Undo the nuts and bolts that secure the regulator and quarter light (ventilator).

5 Once the regulator drops down you will be able to unclip the window glass from the regulator. This is achieved by sliding the regulator spring mounts along the window channel until they can be released.

6 The regulator can be withdrawn through the large aperture towards the rear of the door (in your dreams).

7 The window simply lifts out and can be pulled clear from the top of the door.

8 The ventilator can then be removed, having first been unbolted.

9 The rear channel should simply unbolt to allow removal.

Refitting the door components

Before starting, even if building a good original door it's worth fitting sound-deadening pads (16). The pads are bitumen sheets which mould to the contours of the doors and limit resonance caused by vibration. The immediate effect is that the door sounds more substantial and of better quality than the old tinny sound that your neighbours have grown to love (or hate).

The pads are sticky backed and often magnetic, easy to position and can be "cured" using nothing more exotic than a hair dryer (don't use a paint stripping gun - it's too hot).

If the doors are new or rebuilt then bitumen paint the lower parts of the inner shell, making sure that you don't block any water outlet holes. You can't stop water getting down inside the doors, but you can limit future damage.

Finally, in the bottom of the doors there should be a window glass stop, consisting of a metal plate attached by two screws, and a foam pad. This stops the glass from falling below the level of the window seals and allows a dignified end to the windows downward motion.

The foam pad fills with water, stays wet, rusts through the stop plate and eventually ends up on the bottom of the door keeping it wet and allowing rust to form. I dispensed with mine since many doors have been rendered useless by the damp sponge.

1. Fit the rubber seal (17) and new channel felt to the ventilator and push the glass carefully into the ventilator frame (18).

2. Refit the ventilator lower bracket (19) and then secure loosely to the door.

3. Fit the spacer stud into the door to correctly position the channel (20).

4. Adjust the position, carefully noting that the ventilator seal is located correctly, and secure the ventilator (21).

NOTE: The ventilator glass is easy to replace, simply requiring a push to get it into position. The weather seal is more tricky however and means that the hinge requires removal first. The rivets must be hammered into position (pop rivets are not suitable) - a job you may not be able to do easily.

5. Fit the exterior door lock and handle.

6. Fit the rear channel having first replaced the channel felt.

   Note: The rear channel seal must be glued into position, otherwise it will twist out of shape and simply fall out. The ventilator channel does not require gluing.

7. Fit glass to lower channel (22) if separated. Carefully push fit the glass into position. Then ensure that the glass sits squarely in the door channels by sliding it up and down.

   If the lower channel snags, then remove the glass and adjust the channel position. The glass should slide up and down easily.

8. Fit the regulator assembly (23 and 24) into the door, but do not secure it yet.

9. Reattach the regulator to glass channel.

10. Secure regulator and test the mechanism. Adjust positioning of the regulator if required until smooth operation is achieved.

    None of the above (from 7 onwards) is easy - especially refitting the regulator, have fun.

11. Fit the weather strips (25), using a special tool, which you can see from my photograph is dead easy to fabricate (26).

12. Install the door lock mechanism and latch unit.

13. Fit the door capping.

14. Fit the square inserts into the round holes in the doors (27). The 1500 Midget door pulls are not only a different shape from the earlier models, but also require different clips and different spacings between the holes. 1275 owners have to do a little re-working.

15. Fit the check straps.

16. Cover door apertures with draft excluder material (28).

REFITTING THE WINDSCREEN

The frame should only be fitted after the doors have been made up, so that the correct rake can be achieved in relation to the door ventilators.

When you look at the car from the side the windscreen should follow the line of the wing edge (29).

Fitting the windscreen into the new bodyshell proved very difficult and I think one should be prepared to spend considerable time and effort doing the job properly. A lot of cutting and filing took place before I could achieve a satisfactory result. Don't be surprised or put off by this.

Shell building is an art. Most production lines have areas where body shells are drawn off the line and reworked (often using the fabled large hammer), repainted and put back on the line for finishing. In a factory this is an everyday occurrence. For us, this reworking is a major problem and can unfairly give a bad name to the Heritage bodyshells on which we should be glad to have.

If you face this problem anywhere on a shell that you are rebuilding, grit your teeth, get the biggest hammer you can find and get on with it (unless, of course, you think its a bit more serious than a minor rectification problem).

Fitting the screen took me a day and a half.

The finished Stub Axle

Notes: Assembly Section 5
DASHBOARD

The captive nuts were not all correctly aligned on the new shell scuttle and so, in order to allow fitment of the dashboard, I needed to extend one of the slots. So I got my file out, you may need to do the same.

TIP: It's easier to fit the two angle brackets into the 'A' posts prior to hanging the dashboard from the scuttle. Ensure that lock washers are used throughout, as with the crash roll, you don't want any of the nuts coming loose.

Notes: Assembly Section 7

STUB AXLE AND WISHBONE

People build up the complete stub axle / wishbone assembly before realising that it is too heavy to handle. Fit the axle and wishbone to the car separately. Here are some other useful tips:-

BEFORE STARTING screw the fulcrum pin into the wishbone, to remove burrs clean the threads and make it easier to fit the wishbone and stub axle together onto the car.

SUSPEND the stub axle from the damper arm. It's easier than trying to manipulate the whole assembly.

Assembly

1 Mount the rubber bump stops.

2 Fit the dampers (30), remembering that they are handed left and right (right hand shown).

3 Fit wishbone arm.

   TIP: Fit the bushes into the arm, squeeze them lightly in a vice (31) and twist the arm up and down while slowly tightening the vice. The bushes will squash into place and make it easier to fit the wishbone (32).

4 Put a block of wood (about an inch square) under the damper arm to raise it slightly.

5 Fit the stub axle assembly into position by attaching the trunnion into the damper.

   The trunnion pin is held in place and stopped from twisting by the damper screw (33) and has a notch for this very purpose.

6 Attach the wishbone to the stub axle noting position of the cork seals.

   Use a jack to help support the assembly (34) while fitting the fulcrum pin. Align the cut out in the fulcrum pin with the hole in the king pin to allow fitment of the cotter pin (35).

   NOTE that the cork seals are different sizes.

7 Fit the springs using slave bolts (36).

8 Fit the correct bolts to secure the spring, jack up the suspension and remove the wood block.

FITTING THE ANTI-ROLL BAR

Refit the anti-roll bar assembly using new drop links and replacement bushes (37) as required.

If you are fitting the assembly for the first time (it was an optional extra for many years), there are no real tricks to it as the photographs will show. Note, however, the position of the end stops (38), not available for the larger diameter bars for some reason.

You may need to drill holes into the wishbone pan to fit the brackets (early pans were not drilled unless an anti-roll bar was fitted at the factory).

Where an ARB was fitted the wishbone pans were handed. Now all new wishbone pans are pre-drilled on both sides so that they can be fitted to the left or right hand side of the car.

STEERING RACK AND COLUMN

1 Fit the lower brackets, not forgetting the shim which fits under the passenger side bracket.

2 Drop the rack onto the brackets.

   Note: the earthing strap for the horn, which fits under one of the clamp bolts

3 Attach the steering column, fitting splines carefully onto the rack (39).

4 Secure column to footwell (40).

5 Tighten rack clamps.

6 Attach the track rod ends to steering arms.

TIP: If the track rod ends don't tighten up, this does not imply that they are damaged, simply that there is not enough weight on the track rod to hold the studs still. Wait until the car is on the ground and then tighten them up. While the steering is under tension the arm will lock solid allowing you to tighten the nut.

Notes: Assembly Section 8

REAR AXLE

TIP: Use some extra axle stands to hold the axle in position during fitting. This makes life much easier.

1 Fit the two rubber hanging straps to the axle before positioning the axle under the car.

2 Raise the axle into position and attach it to the shell so that it is suspended by the straps (41 and 42).

3 Attach the front spring shackles to the springs (43), align the assembly with the bodyshell and secure the shackles from below. Do not tighten.

4 Now fit the two shackle bolts that locate through the cockpit into the shackle from above.

5 Fit the rear shackles to the rear of the springs, join to the rear shackle plates and attach to the body (44).

Tip: The new shackle bushes don't squeeze into position easily making it difficult to fit the bolt through. Get some chunky water pump pliers and squeeze the two plates together. It'll give you enough thread to ensure a secure fit. As you tighten the nut and bolt the bushes will squeeze together.

6 Once the rear of the spring is in position, tighten down the front shackle plate bolts.

7 Secure the axle to the springs using new bushes (45 and 46), 'U' bolts and nyloc nuts.

Tip: Support the car on the springs. This will compress them enough to allow the axle to rest on the leaves. The 'U' bolts can then be attached

REAR DAMPERS

Fit new (not reconditioned) dampers. Lever arm units have an undeservedly bad reputation, by and large, due to a number of poor quality reconditioned units that are currently being sold throughout the marketplace.

I have only purchased reconditioned units once, two of the four leaked oil, a third had the arm spot welded into place but not for long. It broke after I hit the first pot hole.. They had been painted nicely though.

Notes: Assembly Section 9

LAMPS

Secure the headlamp bowls, using the appropriate method - be it rivet, screw or nut and bolt.

If you are fitting replica headlamp bowls, it will be wise to try assembling the headlamps before fitting the bowls to the wings. The outer chrome rim may not fit without extensive modification to the bowl lip, most annoying if you've just rivetted the bowls in.

The sidelamp/indicator assemblies can be confused. See notes in the lamps section to see which is which.

HORNS AND OIL COOLER

Prior to fitting, bitumen coat the inside area of the valance to protect against rust. Ensure that any drainage holes remain clear after painting.

Notes: Assembly Section 11

BONNET

All bonnet fittings, including the bonnet cable, can now be fitted with the exception of the bonnet stay.

The bonnet needs to be removed later to allow engine fitment. In the meantime, the stay will limit access into the engine bay. A prop may prove more practical.

BOOT

Fit the boot seal first and then mount the four buffers.

Notes: Assembly Section 13

UNDER CARPET

Where carpets have been fitted by the factory there are also under carpets. These are vital to the look and feel of the finished car and should not be ignored. Nobody sells under-carpet kits so visit a trim supplier and get some cut off a roll (47). Be warned though, it's a bit smelly.

Cut the material to shape, if possible using the original pieces as a template (48).

The under carpet, when glued into position fits under all the locations where the carpet is removable:-
>   gearbox tunnel (front) and front footwell carpets (49)
>   rear parcel shelf (50)

Glue into position using trim adhesive, you can't get much more ventilation than in a sports car with no hood fitted!

CARPETS AND TRIM

Buy a good quality carpet set from a specialist but note that even the carpet sets at the top of the range do not include shaped panels for the wheel arches (unlike the original item). These were formed by machine, the tooling for which has been destroyed. You'll need to do some careful scissor and gluing work.

Annoyingly the wheel arch pieces do not include the plastic strips which protect the carpet against damage from the folded hood frame. The strips probably cost pence and can be easily stitched in to position by a machinist, so not to include them smacks of unnecessary penny pinching. For originality I hand-stitched them in myself from the old carpets.

1   Shape and glue the footwell edge carpet and top hat section carpet (crossmember in front of the seat).

2   Carefully fit the wheel arch carpets starting at the edge nearest the wings, gradually working across the wheel arch cutting and gluing as necessary to achieve the best fit possible.

3   Glue the wheel arch corner sections into place.

4   Glue the rear axle carpet down, starting with the vinyl top lip and work downwards. Note and mark the position of the holes for the tonneau pins during fitting if necessary.

5   Fit the footwell trim panels, starting with the 'U' shaped section that glues into position at the front of the gearbox tunnel (51).

6   Glue the trim material to the 'B' posts, carefully folding the trim at the top (52).

7 Fit the door seals, followed by the door check straps. These door seals were bleached and then dyed the correct colour from black. Humbrol Enamel paint was used to finish the check strap plates (53).

8 Finish fitting the trim panels to the doors and rear wheel arch areas, followed by the rear parcel shelf panel, which should be rivetted into place.

9 Fit the studs fittings into the floors (54) and carpets before securing the loose carpets (55).

10 Fit the door seal cappings, followed by the rubber cockpit finisher. Note that the hood studs along the rear should be screwed and not rivetted.

11 Finally, fit the velcro hood strip where applicable. Note that it fits over the chrome trim finisher and not under it (56).

Notes: Assembly Section 14
BUMPERS

Try to ensure, if you need replacement bumper irons, that you get a matched set. In particular, ensure that the threaded portions are the same length and that they have been welded in the same positions. Otherwise the bumper may not be fitted correctly.

Shim out the bumpers as required, taking careful note in case the bumper spring bars are deformed (which is not unusual).

Notes: Assembly Section 15

The engine and gearbox should already be built up, as described in the previous section, ready to be lifted as one assembly into the engine bay.

1 Remove, with an assistant or two, the bonnet and store carefully.

2 Lift the engine and gearbox with a suitable crane. A tilting mechanism attached to the crane helps enormously because to fit the gearbox into the tunnel requires the assembly to be tilted at a breathtaking angle (57).

Final fit is a slow and careful process since there is little room to get the assembly past the 'H' frame crossmember.

3 Once all is in-situ, but before the crane is dispensed with, check that the engine mounts are in the correct position and attach the bolts noting that the fuel line is held under one of the left hand mounting bolts (58).

Check the gearbox mounting and ensure that it also is in the correct position to fit the securing bolts.

Once the engine and gearbox is resting on the mountings they won't move easily. Fitting the mounting bolts can be almost impossible without leverage or support.

4 Connect the speedo cable and the reverse switch connections if applicable.

5 Connect the fuel lines and clutch hose.

6 Secure the choke and throttle cable - refer to the workshop manual (59).

7 Fit the breather hoses (carburetter to crankcase) if not already attached.

8 Attach oil cooler hoses, following the correct route as shown (60 and 61)

9 Attach ether tube or temperature transmitter wire to the cylinder head.

10 Attach the oil capillary tube or sensor wire as applicable, noting the leather washer that fits in the connector at the gauge end (62).

11 Attach dynamo wires.

12 Attach coil HT lead.

EXHAUST

Heritage bodyshells use the 1500 boot floor. Note that the brackets used to fit the 1275 twin box system to the boot floor won't fit and you'll need to buy a pair of 1500 brackets instead.

No other alteration is required and I'm not sure why they even made the modification. The bolt holes for both brackets are simply closer together. Perhaps it was something to do with the 1500 rear bumper.

Always use new mountings. Many's the time I have seen nearly new exhausts being dragged inhumanely down high streets by tight fisted owners who won't spend a few pounds on doing the job properly. Shame on them.

1 Loosely attach the centre pipe near the rear axle (63) and at the gearbox (64).

2 Apply some exhaust paste to the pipe and manifold joints.

3 Supporting the pipe with a scissor jack (65) to hold it in position against the manifold you can join the two parts together (66). Again do it loosely and then fit the rear boxes using some exhaust paste and a lot of patience (67 and 68).

4 The system should hang without showing any signs of twisting or putting any stress on the rubber bushes. If there are signs of strain, then either you have put one of the brackets on back to front or you are fitting a stainless steel exhaust system. They are supposed to fit Midgets, but in my experience, they seem to fit Ford Escorts just as well.

5 Once the system is secured, straight and true, tighten up all of the fittings.

RADIATOR

1   Fit the radiator into the shroud.

New radiators are often fitted with metric threads. Replacement shrouds also have a weird collection of threads as well.

2   Fit the bottom pipe (69) - crossflow systems.

3   Get a slug of Barrs Stop Leak, crumble it up and put the powdered remains into the water pipe. Now smell your hands, yes, the stuff smells as bad as it looks!

Barrs Stop Leak (70) was standard fitment to all Sprites and Midgets during production. It was the most effective way of ensuring that the system suffered no leaks when the cars rolled off the production line.

4   Fit the lower hose and hose clamps.

5   Fit screws and washers into the lower edge of the shroud (71). Drop the assembly into place ensuring the screws fit into the valance slots.

7   Somehow you need to fit the four bolts through the valance, spearing the shroud, splash plates and the angle brackets and screw the bolts into the captive nuts on the 'H' frame uprights. Oh, and just to make it more interesting, you need to poke the screws through the valance into a deep dark hole.

If by any chance you manage to locate a screw you should not tighten it up too much. In fact, don't tighten up anything yet - otherwise you may not be able to get any other screw holes to align correctly.

8   Once all screws are in-situ tighten them up.

9   Fit and secure the radiator hose (bottom pipe to water pump and heater pipe). Fit the top hose and heater hoses.

12 Install the expansion tank, gluing the rubber strip behind it (72).

DECALS

Any decals that need fitting into the engine bay should be fitted now (ie 73 and 74).

A warning label was used to identify silicon brake fluid (75).

AIR FILTERS

Secure the air filters.

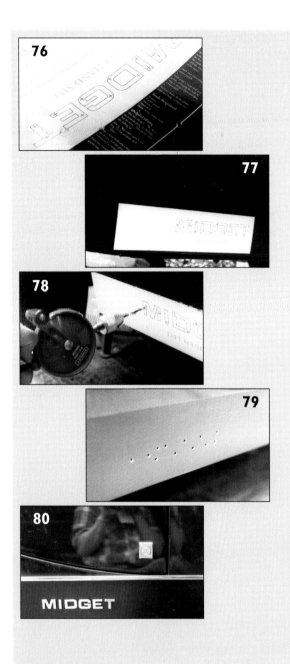

Notes: Assembly Section 18
GRILLE

Unless you plan to fit any auxiliary lights, it's now time to fit the grille. **See the appendix on page 207 for auxiliary lamp fitting.**

Remember that the process used to build the front valance is not that accurate, you'll find that this most important area of restoration is also an area prone to giving a good deal of trouble.

Almost certainly, fitting the grille mouldings, especially the side mouldings will take a great deal of twisting, pulling, pushing and unpleasant bending. Once bent into an acceptable shape the mouldings should be secured using rivets, not screws. Screws are very bad, very, very bad and anybody caught suggesting that you might want to finish your car with such a ham fisted approach should be incarcerated at her Majesty's pleasure.

Rivets...not screws.

Thankyou

That Fiddly Midget Badge

Sprite owners are lucky. The Leylandised Sprite badge is held on with only two clips. Midget owners have to drill twelve holes into each sill to fit the Midget badge.

While at Heritage I produced a self-adhesive label with guide lines and cut marks to help make sill badge fitting easier.

1 The label is a single sheet with cut-lines to produce a left and right hand template (76).

2 Simply line up the template, peel off the backing and stick it in position on the sill (77).

3 Use a punch to mark the holes and then drill carefully (78).

4 Peel off the template to leave some neat holes (79).

5 Paint over the bare metal (to guard against rust), leave to dry and fit the letters (80).

Finishing The Job

So, at long last, the restoration is complete. Now is the time, before turning the key, to make sure that everything has been done so that nothing goes wrong when the car is finally started up.

Give the car a complete service.
- Are the engine, gearbox, rear axle and steering rack full of oil?
- Is there fluid in the brake/clutch master cylinders?
- Is the oil filter (and cooler if fitted) topped up?
- Are all the pipes and hoses fitted?
- Have all grease points have been greased?
- Is there water in the radiator?
- Are all fuel lines connected?

Before connecting the battery
- Are all switches off?
- Check the resistance across the battery cables.

  There should be some resistance in the circuit. If there is an open circuit somewhere, then you may want to check it out before connecting the battery.

  Tip: Use a good multi tester - one that has different scales of resistance. Some circuits, (e.g. the courtesy lamp) offer only a few ohms of resistance. Cheap meters may show this as an open circuit causing you needless frustration. A good tester will be worth its weight in gold.

- Do a final check of the electrical fittings to ensure that they are connected correctly.

  There shouldn't be any loose wires with the exception perhaps of the auxiliary cigar lighter/radio wire under the dashboard, and even that should have a connector attached to avoid possible short circuit.

- Set the ignition timing, spark plugs and contact breakers.
- Check the carburetter settings.

Connecting the Battery
WARNING WARNING! Due to stricter legislation, many small auto-parts stores do not store battery acid. The batteries arrive only partly charged and should be topped up in the store at the point of sale. Unfortunately many batteries get topped up with distilled water and will not operate correctly. Buy batteries from a proven good supplier (such as a battery specialist).

Test the circuits before starting the engine. Do the lights, horns, wipers work? What about the heater, reversing lamps, brake lamps, etc? Does the ignition light come on?

Starting Up

Take out the spark plugs and turn over the engine for a few seconds, which should allow some fuel to work its way through to the carburetters.

Refit the spark plugs, have one last check for leaks and pray that you've got it right.

Turn the key and...

If it started, hooray! Well done...

Check the oil pressure. Have you got any. It may take a few seconds before the system loads up with oil, but if there is no pressure after a few seconds you may want to switch off the engine and try to rectify the problem.

Fault Finding

Experiences will vary with every restoration, but the most worrying aspect will waiting for the oil gauge to flicker into life.

During the start up and initial running of my car I suffered these faults:-

Fuel Pump - points had corroded over in storage and needed cleaning.

Battery - though brand new, it wasn't strong enough to turn the engine over that first time and needed serious recharging.

Ignition Light permanently on - the dynamo armature had corroded during storage and the brushes were unable to make good contact. The armature needed cleaning.

Courtesy Light Circuit - the door switches failed to operate (quite normal really).

Wiper Motor Switch incorrectly wired (but correct to factory diagram).

Brake Light Switch failed!

Heater Blower Switch connection caused problems. Connectors proved faulty and required cleaning.

Following a four year restoration, all of these faults proved to be very minor and easily fixed, though annoying. More importantly is the government test. In this case, the vehicle passed with flying colours and I guess that, at the end of the day, the MOT certificate is proof enough of the job you've done.

Appendix:
Fitting Fog or Driving Lamps

Though driving lamp kits (including wiring and those useless locking connectors) are easily available, many owners prefer period style driving or fog lamps. These lamps look the part but don't always come with the wiring, fuses and relays needed to install them.

Electrical accessories must be protected against short circuit. The diagram shows how lamps should be connected and protected.

Cables not protected by the fuses (ie between the power supply and the fuse), should be of a fire proof material. Unfortunately, your local parts stockist won't know what that means, so you may experience some difficulty there.

Fuse sizes vary depending upon what lights and relay are fitted. You'll need to calculate this.

Fitting a pair of 60W driving lamps

$$\frac{2 \times 60W}{12V} = \frac{120}{12} = 10 \text{ amp fuse rating}$$

To allow for different tolerances of bulbs, cabling and so on some "head room" must be built into the equation. 20% is sufficient. In this example 10 amps plus 20% needs a 12A fuse.

Some relays are supplied with their own fuse. If you buy a relay without one you need to make a calculation based on the coil resistance of the relay. This is often marked on casing, but if not, measure the coil with a meter.

Selecting a fuse for a 500 ohm relay coil

$$\frac{12 \text{ volts}}{500 \text{ ohms}} = 0.025 \text{ amp fuse rating}$$

Again add 20% "head room" to get 0.03A (30mA).

Now, there's a problem with this, well, a couple actually. Manufacturers make fuses to "preferred sizes". The nearest fuse you'd get would be a 40mA fuse (in a 20mm fuse body). In a 30mm fuse body, a 100mA fuse is available. Both of these will be not available from your local parts stockist. You'll need to try an electrical store instead. Stick with it and make sure the relay is protected. After all, they cost a lot more than a fuse!

If using an illuminated switch, or warning light, you need to take it into account when doing your calculation. In fairness, the value will probably be so small as to make little difference when selecting the nearest equivalent fuse.

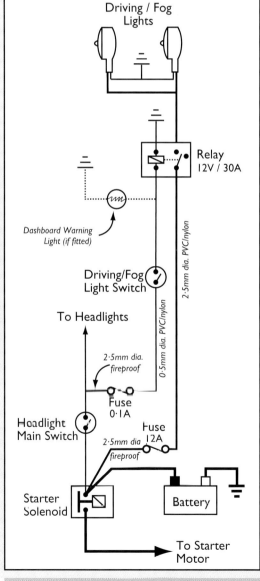

Driving / Fog Lights

Relay 12V / 30A

Dashboard Warning Light (if fitted)

Driving/Fog Light Switch

To Headlights

2·5mm dia. PVC/nylon

0·5mm dia. PVC/nylon

2·5mm dia. fireproof

Fuse 0·1A

Headlight Main Switch

Fuse 12A

2·5mm dia fireproof

Starter Solenoid

Battery

To Starter Motor

Index

Index

Acknowledgements

There are so many people that have helped me in writing this book that it is difficult to know where to begin. Throughout the rebuild process **Jim Kassim** was "the man" by helping get me all of the right parts for my car and sending them just in time to get each job done. **Browse Engineering** of Malvern did all of the grit blasting for me and various engineering jobs that I hadn't got the skill to do myself, well done lads. **McCruddons** Bodyshop at Brize Norton painted my bodyshell brilliantly and, along with **Graham Payne** and **Mark Greer**, helped me out by lending me old colour charts with which I was able to produce the paint section of this book. **John Bevan** loaned me a very useful tarpaulin which I promised to return within six months - sorry, I actually had it for four years, please accept my sincere apologies.

I have gleaned tons of information, histories and annectodes over the years from many people in the classic car industry, the most helpful and knowledgeable of whom are **Peter Taylor** and **Peter Wigglesworth** who both deserve a mention. The **Bay 3 workforce of British Motor Heritage** deserve special thanks for allowing me an opportunity to photograph the building of bodyshells.

When all hope was gone, **Cheshire Classic Car Spares** found all sorts of rare bits and pieces, proving themselves to be real stars. **Doreen Fulmer** was a star for sorting out my wheels and getting them electro plated. Also, **Gordon Horne**, of Mayflower Vehicle Systems, is to be thanked for his help and kindness with this, and other projects!

Much of the photography was taken by me. The best shots in here though are by **David Ward**, brilliant photographer and friend, to whom I owe a great deal. Many thanks.

On to big brother **William**, who, despite being very busy, took great pains to help me with the electrical section and some subsequent problem solving on the vehicle electrics. My uncle, **Rene Sauterau**, involved in the car parts business of Botswana (a very different world to mine), furnished me with the story about bearings. Then of course there are my **poor, long-suffering parents** who not only endured having to clear up behind me but ended up with a bodyshell stuck in their garage for three years along with a loft full of restored car parts. Sorry!

Publishers are often thanked for their patience, now I know why. All credit goes to **John Dowdeswell**, who must be the most patient, helpful and understanding of publishers for waiting so long for this book. I hope it was worth the wait, or perhaps, the weight - there do seem to be more pages than he asked for!

Illustrations, Sketches and Photographs

Illustrations, line art and photography found within these pages were produced by the author, except where stated otherwise. Many of the pencil sketches were based on drawings found in various BL/BM~ ~ ~o redrawn and corrected where necessary or from the author's own photographs.

Bibliography

Title	Author	Publisher
Austin Healey Sprite 1958-1971	various	Brooklands Books
Back From The Brink	Michael Edwards	
BMC/BL Competitions Department	Bill Price	Haynes
Classic & Sportscar Magazine (various issues)	various	Haymarket Press
Drivers Handbooks (various)	Technical Dept	BL
MG by McComb	F Wilson McComb	Osprey
MG Midget 1961-1980	various	Brooklands Books
Original Sprite & Midget	Terry Horler	Bayview Books
Parts Book: Sprite I/II, Midget I, body (AKD 3567)	Technical Dept	BMC
Parts Book: Sprite I/II, Midget I, mechanical (AKD 3566)	Technical Dept	BMC
Parts Book: Sprite III/IV, Midget II/III, body (AKD3514)	Technical Dept	BMC
Parts Book: Sprite III/IV, Midget II/III, mechanical (AKD3513)	Technical Dept	BMC
Parts Book: Sprite III/IV, Midget II/III (AKM0036)	Technical Dept	BL
Parts Fiche: Midget 1500 (AKM1 153 FL)	Technical Dept	BL
Parts Book: Sprite IV/Midget III, 1500	Taylor, Wigglesworth et al	BMH
Repair Operation Manual: MG Midget, 1978	Technical Dept	BL
Workshop Manual: Sprite Midget (AKD4021)	Technical Dept	BL
Workshop Manual: Midget 1500, 1975-79	Technical Dept	BL
Sideglances, articles by Peter Egan (Road & Track)	Peter Egan	Brooklands Books
Sprite & Midget 1958-1980	various	Brooklands Books
Sprites and Midgets	Eric Dymock	MRP
Use & Effects of Modern Technology in the Automotive Industry	Grahame Bristow	SDUC, Lampeter